SHORT COURSE SERIES

WORLD TRADE PRESS®

Professional Books for International Trade

THE SHORT COURSE IN INTERNATIONAL TRADE SERIES

A Short Course in International Business Culture

A Short Course in International Business Ethics

A Short Course in International Business Plans

A Short Course in International Contracts

A Short Course in International Economics

A Short Course in International Intellectual Property Rights

A Short Course in International Joint Ventures

A Short Course in International Marketing

A Short Course in International Marketing Blunders

A Short Course in International Negotiating

A Short Course in International Payments

A Short Course in International Trade Documentation

A SHORT COURSE IN

International Economics

3rd Edition

Understanding the dynamics of the international marketplace

Jeffrey Edmund Curry, MBA, Ph.D.

Published in arrangement with World Trade Press by

ATLANTIC
PUBLISHERS & DISTRIBUTORS (P) LTD

7/22, Ansari Road, Darya Ganj, New Delhi-110 002
Tel: 40775252, 23273880, 23275880, 23280451; Fax: +91-11-23285873
E-mail: orders@atlanticbooks.com; Web: www.atlanticbooks.com

World Trade Press
800 Lindberg Lane, Suite 190
Petaluma, California 94952 USA
Tel: +1 (707) 778-1124
Fax: +1 (707) 778-1329
USA Order Line: +1 (800) 833-8586
E-mail: sales@worldtradepress.com
www.WorldTradePress.com
www.WorldTradeREF.com (international trade and logistics)
www.BestCountryReports.com (business travel, communications and culture)
www.GiantMapArt.com (Giant maps for building lobbies, conference rooms and education)

A Short Course in International Economics, 3rd Edition
By: Jeffrey Edmund Curry, MBA, Ph.D.
Short Course Series Concept: Edward G. Hinkelman
Cover Design: Ronald A. Blodgett
Text Design: Seventeenth Street Studios, Oakland, California, USA
Desktop Publishing: Edward G. Hinkelman

ISBN 978-81-269-1247-6
First Indian Reprint 2009

Disclaimer
This publication is designed to provide general information concerning aspects of international trade. It is sold with the understanding that the publisher is not engaged in rendering legal or any other professional services. If legal advice or other expert assistance is required, the services of a competent professional person or organization should be sought.

This book is dedicated to my siblings. "animus et astutia"

Library of Congress Cataloging-in-Publication Data
Curry, Jeffrey E., 1953–
A Short Course in International Economics : Understand the
Dynamics of the International Marketplace / Jeffrey Edmund Curry -- 3rd ed.
p. cm. — (Short course in international trade series)
Includes bibliographical references.
1. International economic relations. 2. International trade.
I. Title. II Series.
HF1359.C87 2009
337--dc21 09–16123
CIP

Printed in India at Chaman Enterprises, 1603, Pataudi House,
Darya Ganj, New Delhi-110 002

INTRODUCTION

ECONOMICS IS HAUNTED BY MORE FALLACIES THAN ANY OTHER STUDY KNOWN TO MAN. — HENRY HAZLITT

THE EXPANSIVE TRADE OF NATIONS

The most dramatic feature of late twentieth-century commerce has been the rise of international business. Never before has there been such an exchange of products, currency, culture and people among the nations of the earth. While trade between countries is far from new, the sheer size and consequence of present-day commercial activity has prompted even the tiniest economy to look outward for both products and profits. Even when not consciously looking, the effect of foreign economies can be felt in domestic markets. The intent of this book is to show the reader the interdependency of the world's economies and how the effects can be monitored if not completely controlled. The text is aimed at active business people currently considering moving into the international arena as well as readers wishing to gain practical insights into the complex world of global business.

THE ROLE OF SELF-INTEREST AND PERSPECTIVE

One of the recognized leaders in economic thought is Henry Hazlitt whose 1946 work, *Economics in One Lesson*, demystified in many updated editions the arcane principles of economics and exposed the fallacies of many governmental policy decisions. His words are as true today as they were then, but his work put a focus on domestic issues and treated international economics as a cause, not an effect. The role of the book you are reading is to take the main insights put forth in Hazlitt and apply them to global economics. The first of these precepts is Hazlitt's belief that self-interest is at the heart of most economic decisions at both the public and private levels. The second precept that drives this discussion of international economics is that of maintaining perspective when looking at both the causes and effects of any economic policy or decision. Short- and long-term ramifications of decisions must be understood in the context of their total effect on all peoples and economies. Prior to discussing common fallacies and problems, basic concepts will be explained along with historical background material. The book is designed to take the basic principles of economics and place them in a contemporary, global context.

WHY NATIONS TRADE

While many countries may be able to claim self-sufficiency from the standpoint of foodstuffs, very few, if any, are able to provide all of the goods necessary for a "modern" standard of living. Foreign-supplied goods, services and raw materials have become a necessity, not an option. Rather than produce everything needed in an economy, countries have, over time, become specialists in certain goods and services. Agrarian, industrial, technological and the new service-based economies all coexist and coalesce in today's world of commerce. Countries vary greatly in their export-to-import ratios but there is not a nation on the planet that does not actively seek out opportunities to sell or purchase goods and services from its neighbors.

World trade in 1950 totalled little over US$50 billion but had exceeded US$4 trillion just four decades later. This remarkable growth was triggered by advances in transport and communication as well as the opening of world markets brought about by the Bretton Woods Conference of 1944. In many ways the flow of goods and services between nations became as facile as trade among the provinces of a domestic market. Nations now began to view each other as trading partners and as sources of materials that were unavailable at home. As market interdependencies replaced political rivalries among the major economies, former enemies and current allies began to work out balance of payments and trade deficits over conference tables rather than take to the battlefield.

AN OVERVIEW OF FREE MARKETS

While all countries have markets, there are varying degrees of "openness" when dealing with investment. Some are quite welcoming while others are openly hostile. China, for instance, is notorious for its tight control of foreign investment even going so far as to make land ownership essentially illegal for foreigners.

Japan and France both have heavy-handed central government control of many industries and investment segments although to a lesser degree than the Chinese. Many of the Arab countries, though rich in oil reserves, have a singular take on profit making that is dictated by the Islamic doctrine against usury. And finally, in an extreme turnabout of economic philosophies, Russia is even now undergoing the pangs brought on by its aggressive attempt at decentralizing its economic planning.

Arguably, the most free of the major national economies is the United States. Much to the dismay of its domestic firms, foreign companies are given access to all business sectors with the exception of a few industries considered to be strategic. Foreigners can also own property. The United States has been the leading proponent of dropping trade barriers via GATT (now the WTO) with the belief that absolute and comparative advantage will protect the markets that the United States was "naturally" determined to maintain. This service-technology giant's formation of NAFTA with Canada acting as the industrialized second tier economy to Mexico's emerging market status was seen as a prototype of global "borderless trade." But for all of its talk of free trade, the United States still has considerable protectionist legislation on the books to coddle favored industries.

Readers with global business aspirations must understand how the various nations of the world approach markets, the transparency and effectiveness of domestic laws regarding ownership of property, and the necessity of international companies to access the free flow of information. Failure to comprehend the various approaches to what is loosely termed "market economics" will be a serious deterrent to a successful outcome. This new commercialism where each nation interprets the principles of markets for itself is at the heart of international mega-economics.

Jeffrey Edmund Curry
San Francisco, California

TABLE OF CONTENTS

CHAPTER 1

The Science of Economics

NO LESS THAN WAR OR STATECRAFT, THE HISTORY OF ECONOMICS HAS ITS HEROIC AGES. — ALDOUS HUXLEY

The Meaning of Economics

One of the unfortunate misnomers in business literature is the constant referral to economics as "the dismal science." It is unfortunate, because it prevents many people from attempting to understand a set of principles which drive commerce, and by implication much of human life in general. In its general form economics is often defined as "the study of the allocation of resources" or "the science of production and distribution of wealth." Beneath that umbrella are some further major divisions: normative economics attempts to determine how economies ought to run, while positive economics seeks to discover how economies actually operate. This book will assess both the normative and positive approaches, as well as look at macroeconomic and microeconomic principles (see Chapters 3 and 4).

The word "economics" has anything but a dismal derivation. Its etymology is from the Greek *economos* meaning "one who manages a household" or what we commonly call a "steward." This sense of stewardship is what has guided the economic policy of nations and individuals since before recorded history. Managing the household evolved into managing the village, which in turn became managing the town and so on up to the nation-state. As we will see throughout this text, stewardship is practiced on a global basis in contemporary society. Before we leap into the vastness of global economic applications, we must preface it with a look at how this science came to be an academic discipline, and how its practitioners became valued specialists for both commercial and political interests.

The Commerce of Nations

Western academics designate the beginning of economics as a discipline around 1500 A.D. The sixteenth century saw the dawn of what is considered by most to be the first "school" of economics: mercantilism. In this book we will also take a look at feudalism, which pre-dates mercantilism. The feudal system characterized economies for centuries before the rise of merchant-capitalism. This was as equally true in the Far East as it was in the West. In fact, feudal societies remained the dominant mode of economic organization for a much longer period in Asia.

The ancient Greeks, Egyptians, Chinese and Romans all traded within their respective territories and, to a much lesser degree, with the peoples that touched their borders. If the neighbors were wealthy, every attempt was made to annex their wealth to the empire, usually by conquest. Each newly conquered area received, in the form of a governor, a "steward" whose job it was to maintain order and secure the resources now under the empire's control. Money was issued—minted and printed—but not used as widely as bartering goods in exchange for other goods. Credit was extended but either only at the micro/neighborhood level or on a grandiose royal scale, with little lending available for the majority of people. Goods and the few services available were produced and consumed in the community. These empires only sought to gather more communities under their aegis in order to tax, not unite, them. Interaction among the communities was generally discouraged as a form of illegal assembly.

Of course, the world grew more populous and more complex. Simple stewardship was no longer adequate to control internal commerce; external forces came into play as empires expanded to the point where they began to butt up against one another. Trade, not conquest, became the more accepted means of acquiring resources (though force is still an option even at the beginning of the 21st century). As empires stabilized, nationalism brought about the rise of singular states and the consequent call for resource protection. The most efficient of these states acquired great wealth, especially but not exclusively in Europe; their leaders in turn needed more refined methods of controlling its distribution. The Roman praefectus, the Chinese mandarin, and the Gallic thesaur all evolved into some form of the Minister of the Treasury or Exchequer. Beneath these grandees were the thousands of administrators that saw to the day-to-day distribution of resources throughout the nation, feifdom or kingdom.

The Dawn of the Economist

Much of what governments did up until the 16th century was to react as best they could to changes in their financial situation. Proactivity was impossible since no one understood the forces at work and an organized system of accounting was still in its infancy. The invention of double-entry accounting in 14th century Italy resulted in accurate bookkeeping records. Over the next few centuries, the monks and scribes of Europe began to see patterns in these records. Advances in mathematic theory, imported from Arab culture, began to allow compilers not to just see patterns but also to predict future events. Suddenly, the steward, like the farmer planting crops or the fisherman putting to sea, could foretell when and where the nation's fortunes were headed and react accordingly. By the 16th century economics as we know it today had arrived, and the Age of the Economist had dawned.

Emperors, kings, chieftains and mayors could, with the aid of their economic administrators, begin to manage their fortunes, not just retain them. Nations, if properly managed, could regularly feed, clothe, educate and employ the vast majority of their people and thus quell much of what was at the root of internal conflicts. Trade with neighboring countries could be conducted on a more efficient basis as each nation knew which resources it needed to obtain to maintain growth, and which would not contribute to overall development. The Roman "res publica" (public things) and the English "common weal" (general wealth) were the sum total of what a nation held in trust for its population. These terms soon became synonymous with the central function of the state and today are seen in the standard political nomenclature of "republic" and "commonwealth." The combination of general well-being and statehood could only have been accomplished through the stewardship and calculations of the economist.

As the role of economists grew, so did their knowledge and ability to forecast. Like forecasters everywhere, some were better than others. Those that were accurate often reached their conclusions through decidedly different means. Some looked at the exact same set of records and came to diametrically opposed opinions. Still others refined previously used techniques or sought out new types of data to derive even more divergent predictions. Methods that attracted large numbers of followers became known as "schools." A few of these schools developed into full-fledged political entities (e.g., socialism), while most simply provided a diversity of thought within the larger category of economic thought, to be discussed in Chapter 2.

Influential International Economists

The history described above, though considerably compressed, was lived and formed by many nameless economists whose influence on international economic theory will never be fully credited. Other economists have achieved considerable fame, and sometimes blame, for the theories and principles they developed. These economists have shaped the world we live in and will continue to influence the globe for generations to come. They will also appear throughout this book and in any discussion of international economics. Though mostly Western, they are a diverse and often cantankerous group. What follows is a brief listing of these notables along with a summary of their work:

THOMAS MUN (1571-1641)

Employed as a Director of the East India Company, Mun is credited with formulating the mercantilist doctrine in 1630. In *A Discourse of Trade from England Unto the East Indies* (1621), and the posthumously published *England's Treasure by Foreign Trade* (1664), he argued that as long as total exports exceeded total imports for a nation, the outflow of cash from any single business was not consequential.

JEAN-BAPTISTE COLBERT (1619-1683)

As the French Minister of Finance from 1661 until his death, Colbert promoted mercantilist principles at the highest political levels. His "bullionist" outlook led to the expansion of French exports, the reduction of imports, and the passage of laws to prevent the outflow of bullion (gold in bulk form) as payment. His strict approach to national productivity, including mandatory work for peasant children beginning at age six, and the categorizing of priests, nuns and monks as "dead" for taxation purposes, is known as Colbertism in France.

A. ROBERT JACQUES TURGOT (1727-1781)

As a successor to Colbert one hundred years later, Turgot used his position as Minister of Finance to revamp France's feudalist and mercantilist framework. His promotion of internal trade and dismantling of the guild structure were part of the Physiocratic movement's belief in natural order and laissez faire ("let it be") approach to economics.

RICHARD CANTILLON (1680-1734)

Born in Ireland, Cantillon was a wealthy banker and speculator whose main contributions to economics were published after his death. His *Essay on the Nature of General Commerce* (1755) developed the early theories of price and value as well as supply and demand. Cantillon is credited with laying the groundwork for the Classical school of economics. His text is the first known to use the term entrepreneur to describe the innovative, risk-taking businessperson.

DAVID HUME (1711-1776)

Another contributor to the Classical school, this Scottish-born academic gained fame in economic circles as the author of *Political Discourses* (1752). He is the originator of the "price specie-flow mechanism," which promoted the idea (and its reverse) that as national wealth increases so does the price of goods and labor, thereby making a nation's exports less affordable to foreign importers. Although the theory relied heavily on the fact that all trading nations worked on a gold standard at the time, Hume's concept of "international equilibrium" was enormously influential on the next generation of economists.

ADAM SMITH (1723-1790)

Smith, a fellow Scot and academic colleague of Hume, is the most famous of all 18th-century economists and the acknowledged founder of the Classical school. Though originally a professor of logic, Smith resigned to become a tutor for the stepson of Britain's Chancellor of the Exchequer. His duties sent him to France for several years where he was befriended by the Physiocrats Turgot and Quesnay. It was through discussions with these staunch anti-mercantilists that Smith first formulated his doctrine of the productivity of labor, and the circular process of production and distribution. These and other important Classical school principles coalesced in his monumental work, *The Wealth of Nations* (1776). The work remains a standard text for all serious students of economics worldwide.

DAVID RICARDO (1772-1823)

Smith may have founded the Classical school, but it was the Dutch-born David Ricardo who developed those ideas and first applied them to the real world of international commerce. His work, *On the Principles of Political Economy and Taxation*, was the first to focus on the needs of the three classes (landowners, capitalists and labor), and emphasize the necessity for distributing income properly rather than through simple economic growth. Largely self-educated, Ricardo is best known for his groundbreaking work on price/value relationships, the theory of "comparative cost" (modern day "comparative advantage"), and for almost single-handedly forcing the Bank of England to go back onto the gold standard in 1819.

THOMAS MALTHUS (1766-1834)

This English academic is best remembered for the "Malthusian Theories" of population and market gluts. His work, *An Essay on the Principle of Population* (1798), claimed that most of humanity's economic ills were caused not by institutions or custom but by overpopulation. With the publication of *Principles of Political Economy* (1820), Malthus attempted to show how the over-production of goods (gluts) can drive profits from the marketplace and how full employment can only be assured when all surplus materials are removed. This latter theory is counted as the first true explanation of unemployment.

JOHN STUART MILL (1806-1873)

When Mill, considered the last of the great Classical economists, published his own *Principles of Political Economy* in 1848, he hardly could have realized that it would become the standard text on economics well into the 20th century. His clear delineation of the interaction of supply and demand along with his theories on elasticity have become the cornerstone of modern (neo-classic) thought. It is his work which fueled the capitalistic fires of the Industrial Revolution and later became the target of numerous counter-theories of economic development.

CHARLES FOURIER (1772-1837)

Pre-dating Mill's work, other (non-classical) theories were being formulated in France, in the wake of its own revolution. Fourier, a self-educated clerk, railed against capitalism, as the classical principles were called. For him, commerce was the problem, not the solution. Competition was inefficient and the only answer was communal living, which he based on his own system of "phalanxes." His theories, along with those of Saint-Simon and the Swiss economist Sismondi, helped lay the groundwork for the later theories of state socialism.

LOUIS BLANC (1811-1882)

Blanc, a French journalist and historian, is considered to be the father of state socialism. In his two works, *Organization of Work* (1839), and *A Catechism of Socialism* (1849), Blanc looked to the government to become the "banker of the poor" to finance new enterprise, guarantee full employment and control the profits of capitalists. His work was instrumental in developing the notion of "class struggle" and in understanding the effects of competition on labor as well as on the "bourgeoisie." With contemporaries Charles Kingsley (1819-1875) in Britain and Pierre-Joseph Proudhon (1809-1865) in France, Blanc led the new revolt against capitalism.

KARL MARX (1818-1883)

This Prussian-born academic turned journalist was exiled from several European countries for "radicalism," before finally landing in London where he was to spend the bulk of his life. His theories on exploitation, the state and capital were indeed radical. They formed the theoretical basis for a number of societies that changed the face of the planet under the banner "scientific socialism," or what is more commonly known as communism. With his partner Friedrich Engels (1820-1895), Marx wrote the *Manifesto of the Communist Party* (1848) and later his most influential work, *Capital* (1867). His theories, which predicted the fall of capitalism due to under-consumption and revolution, will be discussed in detail in Chapter 2.

MAO TSE-TUNG (1893-1976)

There were several attempts to mold Marxism to the needs of individual societies. The Fabians in Britain and Eduard Bernstein in Germany all disposed of those elements of Marxism they found problematic. The most famous of these revisionists, however, was China's Mao Tse-tung. Having achieved greater military strength than any "economist," Mao renounced the peaceful seizure of power proposed by Marx and Engels as well as their belief that the proletariat would lead the revolution. Mao's was an economic state led by peasants with none of the elite bureaucracies that plagued, in his mind, the Soviet Union. His hold on the economic structure of China resulted in his sobriquet of "the Great Oarsman," and the death of millions by starvation.

MAX WEBER (1864-1920)

Berlin lawyer Max Weber was a proponent of the evolutionary and nationalistic approach to economics, which was referred to in the late 1800s as the German historical school. Derived from the writings of Friedrich List (1789-1846), the Historical School viewed economics as part of the whole history of a nation, not just specific regimes or periods. Weber is most famous for his proposals on the influence of religion on economic development, which he put forth in his book, *The Protestant Ethic and the Spirit of Capitalism.*

CARL MENGER (1840-1921)

This Austrian professor was a leading exponent of the Marginalist school, which proposed that the role of the individual is supreme and demand is the primary force in the setting of prices. The school's opposition to labor unions and theories of unemployment caused by inflexible wages led to its being branded a "conservative" set of doctrines. Menger's *Principles of Economics* (1871)—the title is rather common in the field—laid out his theory of "marginal utility" that predicted a decrease in satisfaction will occur as more of a product is consumed. This introduction of psychological motivation to economic forecasting, though generally accepted today, was revolutionary for its time.

ALFRED MARSHALL (1842-1924)

This British academic is the most famous proponent of marginalist principles. His most famous work (yes, you guessed it!), *Principles of Economics*, continued the school's refinement of the theory of marginal utility along with detailed expositions of supply, demand, pricing, distribution, and industrial costs. The wide dispersal of his work, and his extensive academic following (by 1888, half of the British university economic "chairs" were held by Marshall's former students), has resulted in his inclusion alongside the greatest names in the field. Marshall's interest in teaching led to his becoming the founder of "diagrammatic economics" where charts, rather than mathematical formulas, are used to explain fundamentals.

EDWARD HASTINGS CHAMBERLIN (1899-1967)

This Harvard professor's doctoral-thesis-turned-book, *The Theory of Monopolistic Competition* (1933), fused the previously exclusive theories of monopoly and competition. He is also credited with the refinement of the theories of "marginal revenue" and "marginal cost," which state that as long as the additional revenue brought in by producing another unit of goods exceeds the additional cost involved in producing that unit, then expansion is profitable and desirable. His demonstration that monopolies create lower production and higher prices for consumers has seen almost as many editions and revisions as his book.

JOHN MAYNARD KEYNES (1883-1946)

Probably the most famous of Marshall's students at Cambridge, Keynes is as well-known in academic circles as in the world's boardrooms. While his personal fortune came from commodity and currency speculation, he also served as a member of the Bank of England and as a British representative to the Paris peace negotiations after WWI. Keynes' other international influence included acting as his nation's chief negotiator for the founding of the International Monetary Fund, where he proposed a global monetary unit, "the bancor," for use in rebuilding post-WWII economies. His influential works include *The Economic Consequences of the Peace* (1919), *The End of Laissez-Faire* (1926), *Treatise on Money* (1931), *The General Theory of Employment, Interest, and Money* (1936), and *How to Pay for the War* (1940). His theories on capitalism and governments will be discussed in the next chapter, but it is worth noting here that his influence is so great that a leading modern-day economist, Milton Friedman, stated in 1965, "We are all Keynesians now."

JOSEPH ALOIS SCHUMPETER (1883-1950)

This Moravian-born, Vienna-educated economist rose to the office of Austrian Finance Minister before emigrating to the United States to teach at Harvard. Like Marx, Schumpeter foretold the downfall of capitalism, but for different reasons and with no sense of delight. Schumpeter's work centered on the study of business cycles and innovative development. Central to his theories of innovation was the entrepreneur. For him, capitalism owed its success to the existence of entrepreneurs, although the system would eventually kill off innovation by depersonalizing and automating the process. His theories remain influential, even if his predictions were premature. His greatest works are *The Theory of Economic Development* (1911) and *Capitalism, Socialism, and Democracy* (1947).

JOHN KENNETH GALBRAITH (1908-2006)

Born in Canada, this American economist was, among a host of other titles, the U.S. ambassador to India during the Kennedy Administration and a professor at Harvard University. One of the more widely read economists, Galbraith was an "institutionalist" who posited that economic development was affected most by the laws and institutions of the society itself. His most popular works were *The Affluent Society* (1958), and *The New Industrial State* (1967). These widely read, non-academic books, along with frequent television appearances and magazine articles, resulted in Galbraith's being labeled the first "pop" economist.

PAUL SAMUELSON (1915-)

This student, though not follower, of Schumpeter was the first American to win the Nobel Prize for economics. His "neo-Keynesian" views made his academic home, The Massachusetts Institute of Technology (MIT), the center of the universe for economic thought for many decades. Samuelson's *Economics* (1948) quickly became the standard college textbook for introductory economics. Its fifteen editions have sold 4 million copies, and have been translated into an astounding 41 languages.

This review of famous economists was offered not to give credence to any one theory or set of doctrines over another. Instead, it was submitted to show that modern-day international economics did not spring from a single society. It is the result of a combination of many cultures. Each system's principles have been refined over a long period of time through many trying circumstances. Let us now take a look, not at the individuals who promulgated economic systems, but at the systems themselves and the societies that implemented them.

CHAPTER 2

Economic Systems

Feudal Lords to Technocrats

Economics is a subject that does not greatly respect one's wishes. — Nikita Khrushchev

THE CURRENT state of global economics is the result of a combination of numerous economic principles that were developed in many cultures and over a long period of time. In this chapter we will look at these principles as functions of the societies in which they were the basis of the political system. Although it was mentioned earlier that economics as an academic discipline first began in the 16th century, our study will start somewhat earlier and look at the medieval European period. The reason for this is that many aspects of that period remained functional centuries after the "Middle Ages" (400-1500 A.D.) ended. As we will see, no economic system is permanent, nor will any have a clear-cut beginning or end. Economics is a discipline of overlaps, both temporal and philosophical.

Feudalism

The term feudalism refers to an economic, social and political system that was strictly bound by a class structure, with nobility at the top and peasantry at the bottom. In between were various strata that acted as go-betweens for the two extremities. A simple explanation would be that the peasantry belonged to the soil, and the nobility owned that soil. The tradesmen and artisans in between were freemen, but organized by mandate into guilds which in turn were overseen by magistrates appointed by, and answerable to, the nobility.

The word "feudal" derives from the Latin *feodum,* meaning "fee," not just in the sense of a payment, but in the legal sense of inherited land. Feudal systems are also referred to as "fiefdoms," wherein the "fief" is the legal inheritance or land grant issued by the nobility and only to males. Each parcel of land came with the people who lived and worked on it, all of whom would give over a portion, usually the majority, of their produce to the member of the nobility appointed as their "lord." In return, the lord would be responsible for the safety and well-being of all those associated with the fiefdom over which he was master. This class distinction can still be found in common forms of address such as the German "herr," meaning "lord," and the English "sir," derived from "sire" which was the medieval form for addressing male nobility.

ONE SYSTEM, THREE FATHERS

Feudalism was a very enduring economic structure that frowned on private possessions or ownership—except among the elite classes. Almost all major societies experienced it, although for differing periods of time. It remained in effect in France until well into the 18th century and in Russia into the latter parts of the 19th. In Japan, feudal samurai were roaming the lands in the late 19th century until the nobility realized the futility of resisting modern-day external forces. For China, feudalism was still going strong during the first few decades of the 20th century. In Arabic lands, the sheikh feudal system is still widely practiced today and royal families retain much more than perfunctory status. Land and its ownership were of particular importance in all feudal systems, for this is where "lords and masters" derived their power over the masses. There were three types of feudal system: the European, the Asian and the Arabic. Each developed separately and from different traditions, though the end-products were surprisingly similar.

European

In Europe, feudal structures derived from the Scholastics of ancient Rome and Greece, as interpreted by medieval philosopher-priests. The most famous of these interpreters was the 13th-century scholar Thomas Aquinas, who sought to reconcile Aristotelian principles with those of the dominant force in Europe at the time: the Catholic Church. Because of his preeminence in written thought on this topic, medieval European feudalism is often referred to as Thomistic economics.

Thomas' greatest contribution to European feudalism was his interpretation of the concept of private property. Building on the principles of human rights versus heavenly rights laid down by Augustine of Hippo (354-430 A.D.), Thomas reasoned that while goods may be owned by individuals, land was the common property of the community. This concept of "eminent domain" allowed nobles (as a divinely appointed government) and the Church to control land in a form of stewardship (economos). Land and its produce were owned by everyone, but managed by an elite for the betterment of all. The nobility and the Church were, by design, the greatest beneficiaries of this process.

VALUE AND MONEY

Thomas also spoke to other key economic issues. The feudal Christian world needed to resolve the concept of value and money: an inanimate pearl drew a high price while a rat, one of God's creatures, was considered of little or negative value. Aquinas resolved the value question by declaring, like Augustine, that value was purely a human issue and the result of man being able to make choices. Money posed a greater problem, because the nobility had accorded itself the exclusive right to mint coins and change the metallic content at will. The nobility also retained the right to establish prices for goods or services within their fiefdom. The standard formula for the price of goods was determined by *bonitas intrinseca* (internal good), which equalled the cost of labor and expenses, both determined by the lord. Each fiefdom may have had its own pricing and money, but exchanges between and among fiefdoms became a microcosm of modern-day international trade disputes.

The Thomistic resolution was to recognize the interplay of supply and demand. Value and a "just price" could not be set with mathematical precision for extended periods, but must work for a fiefdom, both internally and externally, within a range of estimates. Transactions would be worked out on the "spot" (a term in use today), with prices being a compromise between the buyer's need to buy and the seller's need to sell. However, this first formal recognition of market forces, like many feudal economic principles, had to be fitted to religious doctrine.

ETHICAL ECONOMIES

Certain practices common in today's marketplace were determined to be both sinful and illegal. Forestalling (buying up goods before they reached the market), regrating (buying goods at market for resell later) and engrossing (price manipulation) were all medieval economic sins of the first order with severe corporal and spiritual consequences. Another of these "sins" that hamstrung medieval European economic development was the prohibition against usury. For Thomas and his fellow contemporary philosopher Duns Scotus, usury meant the gaining of interest—any interest—by lending money. The biblical position was definitive and prohibitive, yet the Thomistic school recognized the commonality of lending (usually by non-Christians) and its beneficial effect on commerce. The problem was that no "just price" for interest could be set because medieval economists did not consider money (even gold specie) to be a commodity but merely a means of measuring value.

The problem was resolved with a clever etymological proof by Duns Scotus. By pointing out that the legal Latin term for "loan," *mutuum*, was derived from *meum* (mine) and *tuum* (yours), he bolstered Thomas's argument that lending was actually an exchange that brought value to both parties, not just the lender. Money was value, not just a measurement of it. This bit of philosophical interpretation revolutionized commerce in Europe and removed lending from a specialized class (the much-berated Jews) and brought it into general use. It set the stage for the development of modern banking, and even the concept of paper money. As we will see later, usury is still the subject of controversy in the Islamic and Arab world.

Asian

The feudal economics of Asia and their endurance into the modern era are directly related to the popular teachings of K'ung fu Tzu, known more commonly as Confucius (552-479 B.C.). Confucian philosophy, found primarily in the *Analects*, directs its followers to adhere to a strict social hierarchy, respect the ruling class, accept responsibility for the common good, perform all things with a sense of duty, avoid individual merit, observe the rule of law, and live by a code of behavior that relies on everyone knowing their place. It is an economic system that Europe's medieval nobility would have found familiar.

Asia's emperors and kings started much earlier to organize their fiefdoms and the racial homogeneity of their individual cultures gave the systems a solid start.

These circumstances, coupled with self-imposed isolation from the West, as well as from each other, allowed Asia's feudalism to endure over many centuries undisturbed and unchallenged.

HEAVENLY MANDATES

The concept of an emperor was essential to the successful functioning of the feudal Asian economy. The Confucian belief in the "mandate of heaven" makes the assumption that the emperor and his noblemen are a natural part of the universe. Judgement can only be passed on whether they rule well or poorly. However, their right to rule, and to distribute wealth, power and land was deified and could never be called into question. Japan maintained this attitude towards its emperor through the end of WWII. In reality, it is not dissimilar to the long-held belief in the "divine right of kings" seen in Europe.

Confucian economies of the feudal period were built along strict class lines with, of course, the peasantry at the bottom. Farmers could work land they did not own; tradesmen, the next rung up in the hierarchy, worked at the behest of the local nobleman (sometimes "warlord"). An educated class (the mandarins in China) kept records and interpreted the wishes of the emperor. Over time this last group evolved into the Asian bureaucracies. With the rare exception of the few who were plucked from the lower classes for training as bureaucrats, mobility outside of one's class was virtually impossible.

THE CHINESE MODEL

These Confucian fiefdoms were most prominent in China, the Korean peninsula and Japan. For the purposes of reviewing feudalism in Asia, this triumvirate will be the focus of discussion. As in Europe, the period that could be termed "feudal" was of differing lengths and starting points in these three culturally related societies. China, the most ancient and culturally influential of the three, can be said to have entered into a fief-based economy as early as 221 B.C., when the powerful king of the Ch'in region conquered neighboring provinces. Declaring himself Shih Huang-ti (first emperor), he divided China into thirty-six provinces, with further subdivisions into prefectures. Each province had a *shou* (governor), a *chun-wei* (military commander), and a *chien-yu-shih* (emperor's representative). This emperor's attention to economic controls set the benchmark against which all other Asian lords would measure their competence.

Coinage, weights and measures, and even the axle lengths of wagons were standardized. Exercising absolute control over the peasantry, the First Emperor put them to work erecting 1400 miles of the Great Wall to protect his feudal holdings from the northern barbarians of Mongolia, thus fulfilling his responsibility to his "vassal" subjects. The Ch'in empire was followed by the two Han dynasties (206 B.C.-220 A.D.), which eventually suffered economic and administrative disintegration as rich, far-flung lords became unmanageable, and foreign forces made inroads. The rise and decline of feudal dynasties, coupled with periodic foreign invasions, would be the underlying historical pattern in China well into the 20th century until the communists came to power in the 1940s, bringing in an entirely different system of economic organization.

THE KOREAN MODEL

The Korean peninsula has a somewhat similar economic history to that of China, though of a much younger vintage. Korea was first consolidated politically in 668 A.D. with the expulsion of the Chinese. The first appearance of a fief-based system came during the Koryo dynasty of 918-1392, which gave the region its present-day name. The Korean feudal economy was based on the Chinese model, although it took class structure a bit further by making the bureaucracy an aristocratic institution accessible only through inheritance. The Koreans also concentrated economic power and wealth in the capital of Kaesong, where the nobles, regardless of the location of their fiefs, were headquartered. The consequences of losing tight control of the nobility by the emperor had been another lesson learned from their Chinese cousins.

THE JAPANESE MODEL

As a consolidated nation, Japan is much older than Korea (660 B.C.), though its present-day boundaries are considerably younger. Originally organized in a series of semi-autonomous units called *uji*, they were comprised of people claiming common descent, not unlike a Scottish clan. All land and produce were shared communally with chiefs at the top and slaves at the bottom of the economic heap. The uji were further divided into *tomo* along similar, but smaller, hereditary lines. In the 5th century A.D., after centuries of inter-uji rivalry, the first phase of a Japanese imperial state came into being and was structured along the lines of Chinese fief-systems. The second phase of Japanese feudalism (1100-1500 A.D.) was characterized by a move away from the early Chinese economic model.

Wealth and culture had been greatly increased and extended in Japan during this latter period. Provincial leaders sought more autonomy, with the result being the establishment of the *shoen* (estate) system. Unlike the European or Chinese system of large, consolidated fiefs, the shoen system scattered a landholder's fields over a wide area. Family groups held lands dispersed over the entire country. A class structure pervaded this scattered system, with the *honjo* acting as legal interpreters for the *ryoshu*, the owner-aristocrats. Beneath this layer, a series of managers oversaw the actual field cultivators. Japanese feudalism is unique in Asia for its early introduction of a written legal code called the *shiki*, which clearly spelled out each group's economic entitlement to the produce of the estate.

The final phase of Japanese feudalism runs from the 16th century through the latter part of the 19th century, and is referred to as the Tokugawa period. It was during this phase that the arrival of foreigners caused Japan to retreat into isolation under the 17th-century *shogun* (supreme general). Japan was to emerge two centuries later into a world that had left it behind both economically and technologically. Unlike China and Korea, 19th-century Japan wasted no time in throwing off the feudal yoke and modernizing on a massive scale.

VESTIGIAL FEUDALISM

Many remnants of feudal order have endured throughout this century in Asia's three biggest economies. In South Korea, the bureaucracy of government (those inheritors of the decision-making nobility) is a strongly sought after career path, attracting the best and the brightest. By comparison, in the West such positions are often considered "dead end" jobs with little remuneration or status. And in

China, though its system is ostensibly communist, land still belongs to the central government which, while holding it in trust for "the people," doles out prosperity in a time-honored fashion. Finally, in Japan, the same imperial bloodline that came to power in the 5th century still sits on the throne in Tokyo, thus making it the oldest royal line in the world.

Arabic

If European feudalism relied on the church for its tenets, and Asia sought the wisdom of Confucius, then it can be surely said that the Arab countries found their early economic model in the book of Islam, the Qu'ran (Koran). When the Koran's prophet, Muhammad, died in 632 A.D., his followers struggled to structure the region and its economy along the precepts of their religion. Arab tribes were widely scattered across North Africa and the Middle East with no central political power to control them. Muhammad's father-in-law, Abu Bakr, was chosen as the *khalifa* or successor to the great prophet. The caliphate system was at first a means of religious succession and unification, though it soon gave way to the development of economic and political consolidation.

The rule of the first four caliphs (632-661 A.D.) is referred to as the reign of the *rashidun* (rightly guided). With the caliphate of Mu'awiya (661-680 A.D.), the position began to change and the title became hereditary. The center of power was moved to Damascus from Medina, and the language of the administrative classes shifted from Greek and Pahlavi to Arabic. Wars of conquest had expanded the range of Islam from Morocco to northwest India. No longer just tribal leaders, the rulers in Damascus began to structure their government along the lines of the Byzantine emperors.

RISE OF THE NOBILITY

Various caliphs sent their new noble class to oversee the conquered lands with the establishment of palaces to control the local economies. As early as 690 A.D., caliph 'Abd al-malik introduced a uniform coinage to the realm that featured, not figures of human leaders, but words alone (in Arabic) which proclaimed the truth of Islam. This period also saw the first wide-scale erection of grand *masjid* (mosques) not just as places of prayer but as forums in which to transact public business. The new "landlords" in the conquered areas (held in aggregate by the caliph) entered into a sharecropping agreement with the conquered cultivators. Taxes, like fiefs, were paid to the lord and the produce apportioned in the familiar feudal arrangement.

Arab territory was vast, so extensive lines of trade, by sea and land, were established. Traders and their routes were authorized by the caliph. Soon the Abbasid gold dinar became the standard coin of exchange. Large merchants and the *mawali* (clients) of powerful men could make loans and accept deposits for safekeeping, though usury was expressly forbidden. Commerce flourished and united the realm. Laws were codified according to Islamic interpretation, enforcement was strict and punishment usually corporal. Hierarchies were clearly delineated with everyone made decidedly aware of what degree of servitude was required of them (Islam actually means "to submit"). Islamic territory had become a feudal society nonpareil.

ARABIC EXPANSIONISM

Beginning in the third Islamic century (Europe's 9th century A.D.), the Arabs began to make major inroads in Europe, Spain and Italy, in particular. While much of this conquest represented the fulfillment of religious zeal, its economic nature cannot be ignored. All lands under Moslem domination were introduced to the Arabic form of feudal control, and a fierce control it was. So dominant was the economic power of the Arabs (and so weakened were the finances of medieval European states), that by the 12th century the majority of the gold coinage circulating in Europe came from Arab mints.

Unfortunately, another product of this three-century period was the disintegration of the caliphate system and its power over the far-flung Arab empire. This period also saw the rise of the image of Arabs as plunderers and pirates, with the word "Saracen" (eastern) becoming a code word for treachery. Rogue Arab *djichs* (armed bands) went as far north as the upper Rhine in search of riches and slaves to be sent back to the expanded feudal landholdings. A new form of taxation was imposed on the conquered locals in the form of ransoms for kidnapped officials and churchmen. Eventually, Europe had enough of this economic "death by a thousand cuts" and its medieval kings successfully began a centuries-long campaign to expel the Arabs that ended in 1492.

EASTERN SKIES

Having lost their holdings in Spain and Italy, the Arabs pushed into Anatolia (Asiatic Turkey) and India. Along with them came the extensive technological, mathematical and cultural achievements that Islam had developed over the previous nine centuries. Most importantly for the new territories was the introduction of the feudal economic system that was to be the dominant force for the next 300 years. Even after the rise of the Turkish Ottoman empire in the late fifteenth century, Arab feudalism would remain as the cornerstone of most of the Middle East's economic structure. Some say that Islamic countries are to this day locked into the feudal production system and fief-based class structure that arose with the first caliph.

Mercantilism

Each of these regions may have emerged from its feudal economy at different times, but most took the same next step: mercantilism. In its most basic sense, mercantilism can be defined as the policy of building a strong national economy through the constraint of imports and the encouragement of exports. It has risen, died and risen again many times since its birth in 16th-century Europe. It was at this time that the regional powers of the declining feudal era began to form powerful nation-states. The word "nation" derives from the Latin *nasci* meaning "to be born" and when states are born they have an inherent need to protect themselves. A mercantilist system became part of the economic protection that all nations have practiced at one time or another.

MONEY AND THE MILITARY

The European mercantilistic period (roughly 1500-1860) is, as this book cites early on, the traditional starting point for viewing economics as a discipline. The reason for this is that for the first time outright economic policies were discussed, modified, negotiated and codified. Basic mercantilist policy stipulated that the merchant class, and to some degree the agricultural class, agreed to pay taxes, not in tribute or fief, but in exchange for having the government protect their right to do business inside and outside of the state's national borders. This was also the first time that governments formally recognized the close interplay between economic power and military might. This resulted in the establishment of colonies as economic resources on a much broader scale than had been seen before. The explorations of North and South America in the early part of this period were the primary examples of this development.

The policies that governments made to protect business came in many forms and in varying degrees. As the reader will see, many of these policies are still alive and well at the beginning of the 21st century. States could use their power to finance new business, permit or disband monopolies, impose tariffs, prohibit a wide range of contraband, control labor, and if necessary blockade competing nations. The Europeans, the Asians and the Arabs all recognized the importance of shipping as a means to promote and protect exports, though none took it to such an extreme as the European powers.

SEA POWER

Spain, the Netherlands and Portugal, through early advances in navigation, were the first nations to exploit the riches of the "New World" across the Atlantic with the establishment of both military and commercial fleets. Not to be outdone, the French, under the guiding hand of Colbert, began in the 1660s to subsidize domestic shipbuilders and levy massive duties on any foreign vessel that might visit their ports. No country during the mercantile period, however, managed to gain the comprehensive grip on protecting domestic business that Britain did.

Beginning with the Navigation Laws of 1650, England prohibited foreign vessels from all trade on its coasts, insisting that all imports be carried on British ships and that all trade with her growing colonies be handled by English captains or their colonial counterparts. This was tightened further in 1663 with the passage of the Staples Act, which required all exports from British colonies to be sent to England prior to being forwarded to European buyers. All of these restrictions had to be vigilantly enforced by an expanding and expensive military. Merchants were willing to pay and the government was willing to act.

EXPORT POWER

Many mercantilist policies were based on the notion that if a nation could expand its imports of gold by exporting goods, it would thereby deprive its rival nations of the gold needed to finance armies and navies. Since strong militaries were needed to protect a nation's commerce, gold (and silver) simply bought more protection. Gold was used by these nations to measure their relative strength. If one country could produce the majority of goods and sell them to everyone else for gold, then that country would be the most powerful. This meant that a strong nation would have to produce everything from agricultural goods to finished products to protect its gold from being "exported" to a potentially dangerous competitor. This line of thought persisted in Europe well into the 18th century until the convincing arguments of Adam Smith and David Ricardo demonstrated the value of specialization and comparative economic advantage. But thoughtful argument did not work alone.

Several factors led to the end of the first great period of mercantilism. By the end of the Napoleonic Wars (1803-15), Europe was exhausted from the drain that this form of hyperbolic competition placed on its manpower. The earlier appearance of the United States as a sovereign nation, after a war fought primarily over import/export taxation, gave many hope that there was another, less conflict-based, way to approach commerce. Finally, the Industrial Revolution (1750-1850) simply overwhelmed the international marketplace and its attendant governments with useful, desirable, low-priced goods produced on a massive scale.

MERCANTILE DECLINE

By 1860, England had dismantled its mercantilist legal structure and risen to power as the undisputed ruler of both the newly industrialized world and its seas. Having lost the American colonies, it kept a tight grip on its other colonies. Germany, Russia and France would pursue a similar approach to international economics. Much colonial expansion took place in the still feudalistic Arab and Asian societies; industrial economies still needed raw materials and new markets for their goods. One feudal Asian economy was visited in 1853 by an American naval fleet. Led by Matthew Perry, the Americans were seeking new markets and negotiated a one-sided trade agreement with an isolated, astonished and technologically backward Japan. Within a matter of decades Japan would be following a mercantile system unlike anything else seen in Asia in an accelerated move towards industrialization. The world was on the verge of new approaches to economic trade that would alter the balance of power forever.

Mercantilism may have died out as the driving force in international economics by the late 19th century, but its policies made brief appearances for another century. After WWI, which many believe was caused by a return to protectionism in Europe, the gold standard was in ruins internationally. This brought about the widespread manipulation of currency exchange rates (see Chapter 4) by governments during the Great Depression (1930s); currency arbitrage was added as a new tool for protectionists. The stability so strongly advocated by David Ricardo was pushed aside. After WWII, which was fought primarily to stop the economic expansion of Germany and Japan, European and Asian economies found their shattered trade markets propped up once again by government, albeit the United States government.

PROTECTIONISM LIVES

In the modern age, the mercantilist spirit has re-emerged in the form of numerous non-tariff barriers that the "free market" nations employ to protect very specific industries. The import/export licensing, quarantines, and trading blocs that will be discussed later in Chapter 8 are all really just manifestations of mercantile protectionism. In many of the closed or semi-closed economies of the world (e.g., Cuba, China), protection of domestic producers is still very strong.

FALLACIES OF MERCANTILISM

Mercantile behavior, past and present, has been underpinned by some rather notable fallacies regarding protectionism. The first of these false arguments is usually proffered by politicians bent on curing "deficit" problems. Current account deficits, where a country borrows money from foreign lenders to purchase more products than it will sell, is often hurled about in speeches as being "bad for the country." It can indeed be bad, but only if the borrowing does not result in a profitable return on the capital that was borrowed. The problem is not in borrowing but in what is done with the loan over the long-term. While borrowing from foreigners goes against the mercantilist's ideal of seizing a competitor's gold permanently, the reality is that you can use the loan to defeat the competition if you invest wisely.

The other fallacy inherent in protectionism is the notion that imports reduce the number of jobs in the domestic market, and that foreign goods extract cash that could have been used locally. This theory is a holdover from the days when importers and exporters exchanged gold for goods, and imports resulted in an outflow of assets in the form of specie. Paper money, the lack of a gold standard and floating exchange rates have eliminated this fear—at least for those who understand economics. For example, domestic consumers in country "A" pay for foreign products from country "B" with "A's" currency. The exporter from "B" must either use that money in "A's" market to buy products, or "sell" (through bank exchanging) the money to another foreign firm "C" who wishes to buy goods in "A's" market. This example removes a number of go-betweens but the reality of the transaction is intact. Imports don't decrease overall domestic employment—they actually encourage it. In fact, under a free system of currency exchange, a country cannot have exports without imports since there is no way to pay for products, in reality, except with other products—the money just keeps score. This topic will be taken up again in detail when trade is discussed in Chapters 8 and 9. For now it is enough to say that on the battlefield of global economics, mercantilism has become a useful, if occasionally wrong-headed, foot soldier in the army of capitalism.

Capitalism

In its most basic sense, capitalism consists of a set of economic principles based on the concepts of private property and entrepreneurship. Business in a capitalist society is carried on for the most part by profit-making private companies; the means of production (land, machines, buildings) are privately owned. Commerce is not completely incompatible with government regulation. Such regulations are for the most part confined to minimal restrictions upon business and only in rare circumstances do they actually direct business in any way. Government is seen as a brake upon, rather than a spur to, business.

A CAPITAL IDEA

The term "capitalism" was originally one of deprecation that was coined and circulated by 19th-century socialists. Adam Smith described capitalist societies a century earlier, but had given them the title of "economic individualists." Self-interest and private ownership of property were, for Smith, not only morally defensible but desirable and efficient. Essential to this line of thought was the idea that the state existed solely to protect the rights of individuals. These capitalists and their customers could produce, price, sell and buy whatever they deemed suitable without limit to size, scope or location.

As we draw closer to the 21st century, this all seems quite reasonable in light of the recent moves towards capitalism in most national economies. However, much of the 19th and most of the 20th century were characterized by a great deal of conflict over the merits of capitalism and the effects of individualism. The socialists were the first to decry the disparities that capitalism wrought, with the Marxists and communists soon to follow with their attacks on economic individualists. These groups will be discussed in detail later, but for now we should look at the heyday of capitalism and determine if it still exists in its purest form.

INDUSTRIAL CAPITALISM

Nineteenth-century Britain and the early 20th-century United States operated under capitalist tenets. Companies were permitted to erect enormous textile factories, expansive railroads, massive oil fields, huge mining operations and belching steel furnaces without much government restriction and often with political complicity. The formation of business monopolies and cartels was considered a symbol of success, not greed. Workers were hired and fired as easily as tools and machines were bought and discarded. Women and children, long confined to home or agricultural duties, were now working 12 hours a day, 6 days a week in factories and mills. The disparity in living standards between the workers and those of the owners (capitalists) was gigantic. America's "robber barons," like Carnegie and Rockefeller, became quasi-governments unto themselves. They could dictate terms to their national or local assemblies and even use the nation's military to suppress labor uprisings.

This conventional view of early capitalism, though accurate, overlooks the overall increase in living standards that their endeavors created. These entrepreneurs created highly efficient companies that could provide more work, more money and more goods to society than the pre-industrial, agriculturally based economy ever could. Women and children did work in factories but prior to this they had worked all day, every day on the farm for essentially a subsistence living. Nineteenth and early 20th-century capitalism was far from ideal, but certainly a significant cut above the economic life that most pre-industrials had led. While the living standards between owners and workers was significant, real wages (the ability to buy goods) actually increased for industrial-society workers after 1820 (midway through the Industrial Revolution).

SOCIAL PROBLEMS AND CAPITALISM

While the rise of capitalism did have its positive aspects, there was certainly a downside. Urban overcrowding, pollution and disease took an enormous social toll, causing people to disregard the economic advances and focus on the abuses. Monopolies were dismantled by governments, legal regulation grew, workers' rights became codified and unions gained footholds. By the time the "Great Depression" paralyzed the world's economies in the 1930s, people worldwide were demanding that their governments control, not facilitate, commerce. Capitalists were blamed for the problem and could not be trusted to fix it. Economic individualism was dead in its pure form. But had it really ever existed?

LAISSEZ-FAIRE VERSUS LAISSEZ-ALLER

Early capitalism is often confused with the laissez-faire ("let the people do as they see fit") economics that was proposed for domestic trade by the 18th-century French economist Gournay. For Gournay, private interests would coincide with public interests if individual competition was allowed to dictate what was made, how it was priced, how much was produced and who produced it. Government should stay completely out of the picture. In fact, no such economy has ever existed on a national scale.

A more realistic approach was what Adam Smith had actually proposed: a laissez-aller ("let the people grow") style economy. In this format, entrepreneurs would be able to grow businesses using the capital and management skills necessary up to the point where there was a serious conflict with the public good. Monopolies, if they did occur, would be natural ones (e.g., those created by being the strongest competitor), rather than mandated monopolies created by governments (e.g., power utilities) where competition is regulated out of existence.

DOES CAPITALISM STILL EXIST?

Americans like Rockefeller, Carnegie, J.P. Morgan and their ilk did create natural monopolies albeit with some government complicity. However, their day is long gone. Nowadays, with the exception of Microsoft, few individuals or companies can be called "monopolists." Corporations, with a revolving door of CEOs and board members, sell shares to faceless millions 24 hours a day. Rarely does a single private individual own the majority of a large company. When they do, they are still subject to government regulation at local, national and international levels. Yet capitalism and private ownership persist worldwide, even flourish, within this tight framework.

A major strength of capitalism and the reason for its persistence is the ability of entrepreneurs to control the level of government regulation to their greatest benefit. As we saw in the section on mercantilism, capitalists regularly influence governments to protect profits in the short- and the long-term. Some economists see this use of government as a sign that capitalism does not exist in a true sense. Only "mixed economies," they say, using socialist (see below) and capitalist principles, can function in reality. This view stems from a lack of recognition that many successful capitalists view government regulation as a useful resource for advancing a company's interest. Regulation, like the forces of nature, is to be manipulated—through resistance, if necessary—to achieve profit and expansion. As we will see in the section on government (Chapter 5), capitalists have been most successful at this task when working on an international scale.

Socialism

The term "socialism" refers to an economic system that requires central planning in which the government has direct and complete control over the means of production. Production is done in the interests of the entire citizenry without regard to pricing or individual product demand. Private ownership is discouraged or even outlawed. This format can be used to varying degrees by different societal groups, thus resulting in the following types of socialist economies:

STATE SOCIALISM

In this form, a government that exists within a basically capitalist society takes upon itself the ownership and operation of certain sectors of the economy for the purposes of pursuing a social objective rather than profit. State-run health care systems ("socialized medicine"), hydroelectric dams and municipal transport systems are common examples of state socialism.

UTOPIAN SOCIALISM

Roughly midway through the Industrial Revolution (1800), socialists such as Saint-Simon, Fourier and Owen proposed an economic structure based on the slogan "From each according to his ability, to each according to his work" (see contrasting communist slogan below). Rather than a struggle between different economic classes, utopians avowed a society where each person works for the benefit of the group with no concern for personal gain. Loosely based on Thomas More's 16th-century work *Utopia* (aptly titled from the Greek word meaning "not a place"), utopian thought has never been put into practice on a national, and it has even failed on a smaller, scale.

ANARCHISM

This form of central planning took the idea of "central" down to the grassroots level. Russia's Mikhail Bakunin (1814-1876) coined the slogan of this movement with "The state is the root of all evil." He and other anarchists recommended not social disorder, as is commonly believed, but that small self-governing groups come together freely by association. Private property would give way to collective ownership, with associations of producers determining production levels and associations of consumers coordinating price. Anarchism is utopianism without a formalized central government.

MARXIAN SOCIALISM

Many economists hold that this form of central planning should actually be called Leninism, as Karl Marx actually wrote very little about socialism. It is based in a continual "class struggle" that requires that each successive economy be "revolutionized" by the classes that it oppresses. Slavery gave way to feudalism, which became mercantilism, which evolved into capitalism. For the Marxian socialist, capitalism will be overthrown by the "proletariat" (non-agrarian working classes) who will establish socialism. Private ownership will be permitted solely for consumer goods, as only the state will possess the means of production and its planning. Rates of investment, competition and profit motive will have no effect on a socialist economy.

SYNDICALISM

In this system, centralized planning is not performed by a government, but rather by a federation of individual, autonomous industrial unions. This form of socialism, promoted by Georges Sorel (1847-1922), relied exclusively on general strikes and "direct action" to overthrow capitalism. Like anarchism, and unlike the Marxian variant, syndicalism also favored the complete abolition of private property.

GUILD SOCIALISM

This primarily British form of socialism was devised by an Oxford professor, G.D.H. Cole (1889-1959). It saw the state as a necessary institution that organized economic policy to be carried out by the various trade guilds. Such a government would be divided equally between the producer and consumer associations, and each would share members.

UNEQUAL EQUALITY

Socialism as a movement received extensive international consideration and even the most capitalistic nations practice some components of state socialism. As we will see below, countries that have been deemed to be "communist" were, in reality, socialist, with the former U.S.S.R. and the People's Republic of China being the largest practitioners. The failure of these socialist experiments to implement their own tenets (or even to feed their own people) without capitalist economic assistance dramatically points up the problems with socialist theory.

Socialist theory fails to recognize that individuals do not have equal ambition, intelligence or motivation. The talented see little value in performing if the talent is not compensated. The incompetent have little motivation to improve themselves if there is no reward. Socialism punishes rather than rewards human nature.

CENTRAL PLANNING PROBLEMS

Even if equality could be mandated, central planning creates another set of problems, mostly bureaucratic ones. Socialist governments stressed production rates and not quality since consumers were never asked for input ("soap is soap, cars are cars, bread is bread"). Management, released from the need to secure profits or increase sales, simply concentrated on making government-assigned quotas. As the government also dictated universal employment, factories had to be kept operating regardless of need. This resulted in a great misallocation of resources, material and human. Goods were produced but not the ones people wanted, or even needed, to buy. Unable to consume, socialist workers saw little relation between going to work and making a living, resulting in major worker morale problems ("we pretend to work, and they pretend to pay us").

Socialism as a major economic political entity saw its demise in the late 1980s when then-Soviet president Mikhail Gorbachev implemented a policy known as *perestroika* (restructuring). Private ownership of capital and competitive markets were introduced, along with free exchange with the capitalist nations. The breakup of the Soviet Union soon followed, with socialism eschewed by all of the newly independent republics. China and Vietnam, fellow "communist" states, were moving in a similar direction. It is worth noting that the deconstruction of institutional socialism has not been universally successful nor have socialist components disappeared from capitalist economies. As will be seen throughout this book, virtually all nations represent a mix of economic ideas rather than a pure form of any single model.

Marxism

The central doctrine of Marxist economics is the labor theory of value. In simple terms, it stated that the value of any product can be directly measured by the amount of labor needed to make the product. Though originally posited by David Ricardo, Marx (in *Capital*) extended the theory to demonstrate how, under capitalism, workers were exploited. Management, rather than labor, determined the value of a product regardless of how much "work" was actually done. A gold ring and a cut nail may take the same amount of time to produce, but the ring was valued more highly. The material, not the labor, was the determining factor. For Marx, this was wrong.

Marx also developed the concept of "labor power," which stated that work was actually a commodity unto itself. Employees in a capitalist economy "sold" this labor power to capitalists, at a rate unfair to the worker. For Marx, capitalism was doomed because it made its profits from cheating labor out of its proper value. He was certainly no fan of management and was unwilling to see, as subsequent economists have, that profits are actually derived from organizing production, controlling investment and proper risk management.

Marx was equally hard on utopian socialists and preferred to link his own theories to science rather than to moral yearnings. For Marxists, the world was divided into two classes: the bourgeoisie and the proletariat. Their struggle was historical and ancient with the outcome being inevitable; capitalism would cause its own demise by succeeding to the point where only monopolies existed. These few remaining capitalists would exploit labor well past the breaking point and revolution would ensue. Private property, money, market exchange, investment, competition and even profit/loss accounting procedures would disappear as useless relics of an exploitive past.

WHITHER THE PROLETARIAT?

Marxian revolutions have occurred throughout the 20th century, but never in the major capitalistic nations as Marx had predicted. Most economic revolutions (Poland, CIS) nowadays are movements to install capitalism. Hard-core followers of Marx can console themselves with the fact that capitalism may not have reached its monopolistic zenith as yet so true revolution may still be in the offing.

Monetarism

Followers of this school of economics believe that the amount of money in circulation in an economy determines growth and wealth. Governments must maintain a money supply equal to the actual growth of the economy. If money supply exceeds growth, inflation (a persistent increase in prices) results. Too little money and the trend is reversed to deflation (persistently decreasing prices). Monetarism also supposes that when inflation is high, interest rates will be high, causing the foreign exchange value of a state's domestic currency to drop (soften) relative to the world's more stable currencies (hard currencies). The first effects, positive or negative, of changes in the money supply will be felt in a nation's output, as the ability to buy raw materials is affected. This will ripple through an economy to affect, up or down, the inflation rate. As money supply decreases, output drops, and recession ensues (a drop in demand with a rise in unemployment).

STANDARD OPERATING PROCEDURE

Monetarism is in fact a part of every modern nation's economic policy, though some are occasionally loath to implement needed adjustments. Almost all governments have come to see price stability as an important, even necessary, goal. More and more governments are attempting to "peg" their currency to those of more stable nations (e.g., the U.S. dollar, German mark) in order to "borrow" stability from nations with tight monetary controls. Monetarism will be discussed later in the section on currency, but it should be noted now that many recent monetarist policies were failures (e.g. U.S. Federal Reserve policy in the early 1980s) but it can be attributed mostly to poor information. As economic forecasts become more accurate, monetarist policy shows greater success and acceptance (e.g. U.S. Federal Reserve policy in the 1990s).

Communism

The slogan of this economic form is "From each according to his means, to each according to his needs" (for contrast, see utopian socialist slogan above). Communist economies presuppose an abundance of products, a selfless devotion to other members of the society, and the elimination of money. Work is not required (or paid for) but will be given freely to the society. The state will be non-existent because it will not be needed to control these selfless citizens. People will come together to administrate production, not rule governments.

Communism, for all the political speeches delivered against it, has never been implemented on a national scale. Only small, private "communes" have existed around the world and their success is generally short-lived as human nature comes into play as it does with socialism. Communist countries, or those that go by that title, are actually socialist economies preparing for the day when communism can be installed. Only Cuba, North Korea, and Laos are attempting to hold onto the economic policies needed for a communal future. The U.S.S.R. gave up its political and economic communist structures during the 1980s, while China and Vietnam maintain a communist party hold on politics as their economic planning becomes progressively decentralized.

Fascism

Fascism, also known as corporatism or statism, is a political and economic system first formulated in the 1920s, and still active in today's global economics. Fascism exists squarely in between the extremes of communism and laissez-faire capitalism. Unlike socialists or communists, who foresee a gradual diminution of the state, or capitalists, who see a subservient economic function for government, fascists believe that the state is central to true economic health. Not satisfied with just planning the economy, fascist governments actually operate commercially at all levels. Unlike socialism, where the state operates a few key industries, the "corporate state" performs the role of "parent company," and private businesses act as "subsidiaries." Fascists recognize the value of private property and profit, but only if they do not conflict with national goals.

The doctrines of fascism were formalized by Italy's leader, Mussolini, as a combination of syndicalism and nationalism—sort of a "workers of the world, unite to serve the state." In the 1920s and 1930s, Mussolini organized enormous public works, instituted wage and price controls, took firm control of banking and made the government the arbiter of labor disputes. All of these ideas were openly copied by many nations during the Great Depression, including the United States under Franklin Roosevelt (a bundle of wooden shafts encircling an axe-blade known as a *fasces* appeared on U.S. coins of the period). Of course, fascism suffers from its political association with Hitler and the Nazi movement (the term "nazism" is short for national socialism). The Nazis, however, were significantly more anti-capitalist and anti-communist. Hitler claimed to have "nationalized" the German people rather than the economy.

CURRENT MANIFESTATIONS

Fascism, despite its unfortunate political associations, is still widely practiced by many states around the world as economic policy. Any nation where there is a tendency towards greater intervention by government in commerce, rather than less, there is a movement in the direction of fascism. Many emerging markets are especially characterized by almost total government dominance in the affairs of business. In some nations, like Indonesia or Kenya, any sizable private project must receive the direct approval of the nation's top leadership. At a lower level, the licensing and inspections carried out by the globe's municipal and provincial governments, all done in the name of the "public good," are manifestations of fascist economics.

FASCIST FAILURE

As with state socialism, fascism is practiced successfully to some degree by all nations and the distinction between the two can become blurry. When fascism is the central economic policy, however, it shortcomings heave into view quite readily. Because fascism places all power in the state, the government and its members cannot resist the opportunity to direct their decisions towards serving the state apparatus rather than its people: the consumers. (Even before the start of WWII, Italy's fascist ideal showed its weaknesses: private consumption dropped below 1929 levels, overall production between 1929 and 1939 was lower than other Western European nations, and the industrial base was non-competitive.) Ultimately, as with socialism, fascism removes the allocation of resources away from the entrepreneurial sector and into the hands of government bureaucracy. Even when corruption or political repression are not an issue, bureaucracies are extremely inefficient when operating businesses. Indonesia and Kenya are today coming to that conclusion reluctantly.

Socialist-Market Economics

The Chinese government has of late been referring to its economic system, where communist political doctrine is wedded to a limited form of capitalism, as "socialist markets." In this system, the opposite of state socialism occurs: selected parts of a centrally planned economy are permitted to pursue capitalist goals. Private ownership is permitted, along with profit-taking. New private firms are even permitted to sell stock and to compete with state-owned industries. Results have been dramatic, if non-uniform.

Utilizing a major influx of foreign capital (who could resist 1.3 billion consumers?), much of coastal China has seen double-digit rates of economic growth in recent years. Manufacturing in many industries has moved quickly from backward, almost 19th-century levels to high-tech in a matter of years. Per capita income has skyrocketed in these cities, and roads built for bicycles must now contend with automobiles and trucks. No one doubts the entrepreneurial determination of the Chinese people. But all is not well.

PROBLEM WITH HALF-MEASURES

Just as the socialist/communist economies could not compete with the capitalists on a global scale, the same has happened in microcosm in China. By keeping some large industries under state control and subsidy, the government has allowed some very inefficient behemoths, especially banks, to become drags on the overall growth of the economy. Efficient private businesses are taxed to pay for the non-competitive, over-staffed state-owned companies. Resources better used elsewhere flow down a black hole of bureaucratic inefficiency. Added to this is the fact that China does not have a currency that is convertible on international markets, although it is pegged to the U.S. dollar. Beijing resists "floating" its currency in the open market for fear of finding its true value. The government protects itself by declaring all economic statistics to be "state secrets" and, thus, not open to corroboration by external analysts. Everyone agrees that China is doing better, but few believe it is doing as well as it says.

THE FUTURE OF SEMI-FREE MARKETS

Currently, "socialist markets" as a compromise to full-blown socialism have had varying degrees of success, due mainly to the poor allocation of resources. Vietnam has tried to imitate China's model of reform, with a much less successful outcome. Some of this failure is due to competition from China for FDI (foreign direct investment) and the difference in market size. Most economic observers find greater potential in the former communist nations such as the Czech Republic, Poland and (to some degree) Russia, which have made dramatic, though painful, transitions to capitalism. By dismantling the state commercial bureaucracy in one fell swoop, Czech and Polish entrepreneurs along with their respective governments were forced to operate decisively and without a safety net. Consequently, their companies, no matter how large, could not be bailed out by the government and only the best, most competitive survived. This absence of "moral hazard," as such bailouts are called, is fast becoming the difference among successful, mediocre, and failing transition economies.

The Primacy of Mixed Economies

Now that the world has declared communism to be dead and socialism marginalized, the primacy of capitalistic markets may seem undisputed. But that is hardly the case. The reader may have already perceived the fact that there are no pure "-isms" when defining a national economic structure. All of the economies that could be deemed successful in the international community are really a mixture of all or some of the doctrines delineated in this chapter. But so, too, are the failures. Let's look at a few different countries and take an encapsulated look at how the mosaic of their economies is composed:

JAPAN

The undisputed leader of the Asian economies is Japan. From a long-running feudalistic base, Japan entered the 20th century as a formidable military power with a strong nationalist set of politics and a decidedly mercantilist economy. Mercantilism gave way to fascism in the 1930s as the economic leadership, via the military, went in search of raw materials throughout the rest of Asia. After WWII, Japan faced submission to the Allied powers and found itself being molded in the economic image of the United States. The *zaibatsu* (financial cliques) that had overseen the pre-war Japanese economy were dismantled, land redistributed and markets were made less subject to government control. The Korean War, along with the threat of Soviet and Chinese power in the 1950s, forced the United States to rethink its policies toward Japan. Political circumstances demanded that Japan be allowed to build a strong economy fast as a "bulwark of democracy" in Asia. The United States encouraged a rebuilding of the zaibatsu—now dubbed *keiretsu*—and unions were allowed to function along a syndicalist pattern. Powerful ministries in the government directed financial resources to those sectors of the economy deemed to have greatest potential. The Ministry of International Trade and Industry (MITI) became the de facto overseer of the nation's business. Government and business were deeply linked, and a multi-party democratic political atmosphere (including nationalists and communists) prevailed.

■ SPECIAL MIX

Japan, to this day, has maintained this mixture. For all of its economic sluggishness and political/commercial scandals of the 1990s, Japan remains the second largest economy in the world. The Japanese do not see themselves as being built on a Western economic pattern, although the corporatist Friedrich List and management specialist Charles Demming are counted heavily among their influences. Japan's "Asian model" applies Confucian principles mixed liberally with fascist economics, and it has developed a commercial sector that is almost indistinguishable from the state. The government, through MITI, directly controls, rather than protects, the capitalist sectors of the economy. Private property and enterprise are respected but only in so far as they contribute to the good of the nation. Japan also incorporates some socialist ideals in its economy, including lifetime employment (usually for men only), and a cradle-to-grave system of benefits.

Although economic reality has seen these last two components wane, such caretaker business practices and the existence of an interventionist state have led many commentators to mistakenly refer to Japan's economy as a "socialist-free market" economy. However, as any foreign company will attest, Japan's markets are far from free. The reader should also note that the intrusive role of government is seen by the Japanese as a permanent, desirable factor and is therefore decidedly non-socialist. Since the term "fascist" is so unpalatable, perhaps we can best describe Japan as a "corporatist-market" economy for the purposes of discussion.

UNITED KINGDOM

The United Kingdom has instituted every major economic policy at some time during its existence. It can be readily stated that most of the world's important economic thought, from Adam Smith to Karl Marx to John Maynard Keynes, was developed in this island nation. From its feudalistic roots (still remnant in the British House of Lords) the United Kingdom became the greatest mercantile nation ever and set the standard by which others measured their success. As a major colonial power, its navy ruled the seas primarily to protect its merchants and then, after the Industrial Revolution, to protect its capitalists.

As in Japan, WWII brought many changes to the United Kingdom, even though it was on the winning side. The London government took steps after 1945 to dissolve its own empire, and within a few years had even divested itself of its jewel in the crown, India, with minimal bloodshed. The post-war government switched hands from the pro-capitalist Tories to the pro-socialist Labor party who swept to power with a motto of "Let us face the future!" The state would take responsibility for education, health, jobs and welfare. More and more industry was taken over by government bureaucracy, and private enterprise was pushed into the background—although it was definitely not eradicated.

■ DUAL BRITANNIA

Britain maintained this socialist-dominated market system through a variety of governmental changes until the early 1980s when the Tory leader Margaret Thatcher began to "privatize" everything from mines to municipal railways. The move from socialism towards free enterprise was on, but not without considerable hardship and resentment. Even today, though the United Kingdom is one of the healthiest economies in Europe, Thatcher's anti-socialist agenda draws arguments. Britain is by no means free of socialist aspects, as can be seen in its state-sponsored health and education system. Even with Labor back in power, the United Kingdom is still reluctant to back away from free enterprise towards a full-blown socialist agenda. Much of its deferment from joining the European Union in complete economic consolidation stems from a distaste for the EU's decidedly socialist social agenda. For the United Kingdom, experience has been a dutiful teacher—if there must be a mixture, socialism will be but a small percentage.

ARGENTINA

Until 1810, Argentina (from the Latin for "silver") was a colony of Spain. Its economy was primarily a resource to be tapped by its rulers in Madrid. The decade-long revolution that started in that year resulted in the ejection of Spain, the fissure of the territory into Peruvian and Argentinean sectors, and civil war. This last phase resulted in the extinction of a central government, and the rise of the provincial *caudillos* (leaders) into what became a feudal society. For the next 30-plus years, the fiefdoms warred against each other; each sought support from foreign powers to replace the economic, if not political, ties that had been shattered with mercantile Spain. By 1852, the *saldero*s (salted meat eaters) of Buenos Aires began to consolidate economic and military power into a single nation-state. The control of most of the foreign trade in the region was the main factor in their primacy. By the 1880s, Argentina had become a true nation-state poised on the brink of an economic revolution.

PAX ARGENTINA

Peace and unity brought an agricultural boom as soldiers returned to their land. Wheat exports multiplied six-fold, and sheep raising (much of it by Irish immigrants) expanded by fifty percent over the previous decade. By 1914, Argentinean per capita income rivalled that of Germany and exceeded that of its former colonizer, Spain. Much of the urban middle and working classes were immigrants bent on establishing a popular democracy. Among these immigrants were anarchists from Italy, and less radical socialists from Spain. By 1916 the first national elections were won by a unionist party, which stayed in power until 1930 when it was displaced by a military coup d'etat.

JUNTA ECONOMICS

This new military junta had remarkable economic success, raising the nation's 1939 GDP by 33% over the 1932 level—all during the Great Depression! By 1943, however, another military coup brought new generals to power, which set into motion the circumstances that would result in the free election of Juan Perón in 1946. Perón was swept into power in the wake of WWII by trade unionists and urban workers with a mandate for social reform and industrialization. Staunchly anti-communist and highly nationalistic, the former political prisoner Perón added pension schemes, lay-off protection, statutory work weeks, accident compensation, mandatory arbitration and legal status for trade unions to the government's duties during his early socialist period.

AUSTERE FUTURE

Beginning in the 1950s, Perón also created nationalized oil refineries, merchant fleets, airlines and hydroelectric plants, all the while making overtures to the Soviet Union and promoting private manufacturing. By 1955 this brew of economic doctrines created stagnation, and Perón was ousted by yet another military coup. For the next 27 years, a series of plodding juntas ruled the country with increasingly autocratic (fascist) economic and political policies. In 1982, the disastrous Falklands War against Britain signalled a move towards a more open economy and political system. The democratically elected government introduced a convertibility law that pegged the currency to the U.S. dollar and other "austerity measures" to rectify past economic problems. Results were painful but good. Have all the vestiges of colonialism, feudalism, fascism and socialism been eradicated? By no means, but those that remain are being subjected to the rigors of free markets.

UNITED STATES

The United States is a nation that just over 200 years ago was a relatively small colony in the ever growing British Empire. It is now the largest economy the world has ever seen, and it is nearly twice the size of its nearest competitor. Of its approximately $12 trillion-per-year economy, over 75% is in the production of services. This gargantuan economy rose to the top as much by its own doing as by the undoing of others.

ECONOMIC REVOLT

The thirteen original colonies that had won independence from Britain in 1783 spent the next decade organizing themselves into a functioning nation-state. The war itself had been based almost entirely on Britain's economic treatment (especially taxation) of its colony. (It is worth noting that the American Declaration of Independence and Smith's *Wealth of Nations* were both published in 1776.) Even after nationhood was achieved, the individual "states" saw to their own economies, collected their own taxes and issued their own currencies for many more decades to come. Many of the Southern states actually developed economic models that pre-dated feudalism, using slavery as the major source of labor in their primarily agricultural society. The North, following the advice of Alexander Hamilton in his *Report on the Subject of Manufactures*, pursued an industrial, mercantile model with a dependence on protectionism.

In 1860 another conflict was to rewrite the economic history of the United States, as the Southern states seceded from the nation in order to protect their slave-based economy. The industrially superior North spent five years suppressing the rebellion, using economic blockade as one of their most effective weapons. This was also the dawn of "total war," as the North physically destroyed the South's economy and therefore its ability to wage war. The North's strategy proved that starving, homeless citizens cannot produce arms for a military, no matter how motivated they might be. Never before had such a dramatic linkage between economics and military power been offered for public view. The European powers took notice.

■ EXPANSION AND INDUSTRIALIZATION

After the Civil War, the United States concentrated on further industrialization, the rebuilding of the Southern states, and the exploitation of the western half of its continent. The western part of the country, as if to underline the economic nature of nation-building, had been bought from a literally cash-hungry Napoleon in 1803. The native peoples living in this territory were systematically moved into small reservations or decimated by disease, as the United States continued its economic policy of "manifest destiny" laid out in the 1840s. In 1867, the United States expanded once again by purchasing its largest territory and future state, Alaska, from Russia. Its annexation of the Hawaiian Islands in 1898 was the last of its business deals to acquire territory. What western territory that could not be bought was taken over time from Spain and Mexico by force.

At the beginning of the 20th century, the United States was physically large, though not an especially economically imposing nation. All that would change as the "war to end all wars" began in Europe in 1914. Like all modern wars, WWI was primarily a conflict over economic interests fought by nations that brought the latest and deadliest technologies to the battlefield. In 1914, the United States was still a largely protectionist, isolationist country that viewed Europe with suspicion, both financially and politically. By shipping supplies to its allies (Britain and France), the United States found its merchant fleet the target of Germany's effective version of "total war" via torpedoes. Entering the war late (in 1917), America arrived just in time to assist with an allied victory and to oversee the rebuilding of a devastated continent. The European participants on both sides were near destitute, and Russia had taken the opportunity to slide into full-scale revolution. Within a few years the second-rate U.S. economy had become the most powerful on the planet.

A GIANT AWAKES

The boom years of the 1920s followed as America rebuilt Europe. It all went bust in the 1930s with the worldwide depression although the interim had made the United States a great trading and industrial power. When WWII started in 1939, once again primarily about global economics, the United States tried to remain out of the conflict. The United States was willing to sell supplies (to all sides for a while), though it wanted to keep its men in the factories and off the battlefields. Japan, deterred in its war efforts by having its oil and scrap metal cut off by U.S. mandate, attacked Pearl Harbor in 1941 and the "sleeping giant" awoke. While its young men were sent to battle, America's older men and women worked at home to build an industrial juggernaut the likes of which had never been seen before. The "arsenal of democracy" simply overwhelmed its enemies in Europe and Asia with war materials, while destroying the opposition's ability to manufacture.

The post-war period saw the opportunity for the United States to make its economic mark worldwide. In Europe, the United States and its allies instituted the Marshall Plan, which provided low-interest loans to European nations, allies and enemies alike, in order to rebuild their economies. It also allowed these countries to buy the U.S. agricultural and manufactured goods that came flooding across the Atlantic on the sea lanes protected by, not the British, but the American, navy. In Japan, the American economic influence was even more direct, as alluded to earlier. The formerly isolated United States was now the undisputed leader in the world economy. In addition to becoming the "world's policeman," it had taken on the role of Chief Financial Officer, and capitalism was the order of the day for those nations outside of the socialist bloc.

SOCIALIST INFLUENCE

Domestically, many socialist-style programs had been put into operation by the charismatic leader Franklin Delano Roosevelt, both prior to and during the war. The National Labor Relations Board, legalized unions, public education, social security and farm subsidies were now part of the national fabric; the immediate post-war boom era was hardly the time to dismantle them. As the Soviet Union gained in power, the United States was loath to give the appearance of being socialist, and the late 1940s and early 1950s saw a major anti-socialist (anti-communist) agenda nationwide. Citizens were "blacklisted" and virtually put out of work for advocating socio-economic programs that had been considered tame ideas in the 1930s. Free-enterprise became equated with freedom, capitalism with patriotism. Large corporations began to exert power in Washington and sayings like "What's good for General Motors is good for America!" were pronounced without irony.

Links between industry and government grew to the point where outgoing President Dwight Eisenhower warned the nation in 1961 about the dangers of a too powerful "military-industrial complex." Private companies supplied the military with materials under lucrative contracts, and the government had become the largest employer in the nation. The Korean War (1950-53) and the Vietnam War (1955-75) were "capitalist versus communist" conflicts resulting in less than stellar outcomes for either side. The early 1970s saw the United States float its currency internationally and drop any connection to the gold standard. During the presidency of Ronald Reagan, the nation began an active campaign to further globalize its trade as it worked to reduce international tariffs in the 1980s, just as Japan came into its own as a pre-eminent financial power. As protectionist Asian countries expanded their economies, America demanded to be let in to compete head-to-head. Trade deficits grew and were exploited by politicians beating the drum of "free trade" while demanding protection for their own constituents.

In the 1990s, the doldrums that plagued the U.S. economy in the 1980s moved to Japan, while the rest of Asia (with the exception of China) cooled off their overheated economies. At the beginning of the 21st century, America found itself still on the top of the economic heap with no contenders in sight. Its ability to quickly reverse economic downturns has made "big problems" (currency fluctuations, banking closures) into brief worries. Today, its politicians whittle away at long-standing social programs (welfare, public education, farm subsidies), while income disparities between top and bottom widen but overall standards of living improve. The rise of the BRIC economies (Brazil, Russia, India, and China) are more of a concern for the EU than the US as the American economy keeps well ahead of its closest competitors. Other nations line up to join the World Trade Organization (WTO) that will end the trade tariffs the United States has long disparaged. The United States is moving itself and the world towards a more standardized form of capitalism. Whether this standardization can be achieved (or if it is even desirable) remains to be seen.

CHAPTER 3

Basic Principles: Microeconomics

EVERYONE IS ALWAYS IN FAVOR OF A GENERAL ECONOMY AND PARTICULAR EXPENDITURE.
— ANTHONY EDEN, 1959

PRIOR TO THE DOMINANCE of Keynesian principles in post-war economic thought, economics was divided into pricing theory and monetary theory. Today, those divisions have been given the titles microeconomics and macroeconomics. As the names indicate, the former looks at the smaller picture of day-to-day economic decisions while the latter takes a larger view of the world. However, these are not exclusionary branches. One cannot look at the behavior of individual consumers without contrasting it to all consumers, nor can one understand the economic policy of a nation without analyzing how its individual firms function. Nor, and most importantly for this chapter's discussion, can we understand how international economics functions until we comprehend the actions of smaller units.

Microeconomics

Microeconomics is the study of individual economic units. These include workers, consumers, landowners, businesses, investors, shareholders and service providers. The main goal of microeconomics is to explain how and why these units review choices and make decisions. Microeconomics also studies how individual units interact to form (or not form) larger units. Consumers form into market segments, which are part of general product markets, which are subgroups of local markets, which are in turn part of national markets, all of which form the international market. There is certainly a case to be made that every nation-state fulfills a microeconomic function in the larger (macro) global marketplace.

POSITIVE VS. NORMATIVE

Microeconomics (as well as macroeconomics) deals with both positive and normative concepts. Positive concepts focus on the realities of economic life, while the normative questions look at how things ought to be under ideal circumstances. The theories that will be presented are open to interpretation (hence, the chapter's opening quote) and we will look at things from several perspectives. Our concern will be with both competitive and non-competitive markets: a competitive market is not dominated by any single buyer or seller who can seriously impact prices, while non-competitive markets are controlled by a single player or a cartel. (A monopoly occurs when there is a single seller, and a monopsony occurs when there is a single buyer.)

Pricing

Within each individual market (the globe in aggregate is a market economy) the indicator of relative economic health is the price of goods and services. Prices can be measured in *nominal* terms, which is the amount of currency required to make a purchase at a specific point of time, or as *real*, which is the purchase price relative to other goods and services in the marketplace as measured over time. For instance, in 2012 the nominal price of gasoline in Germany may be 1.80 euros per liter, while in 2002 it may have been 1.20 euros per liter. Nominally, this represents a 50% rise in the price of fuel [(1.80 -1.20) / 1.20] over ten years. However, in real terms fuel may have remained stable or decreased relative the price of other goods and services in Germany.

Most national governments use some form of consumer price indexing (CPI) to track the price of goods (if they don't, foreign investment houses most surely will). These indices track the value of a set number ("basket") of goods (e.g., bread, rice) and services (e.g., college education, telephone rates), considered to be necessities. Against this basket, the price of all other products can be measured. With this idea in mind, the mathematical formula for determining the real price of German fuel in 2012 is as follows:

$$\text{Real Price 1999} = \frac{\text{CPI 2002}}{\text{CPI 2012}} \times \text{Nominal Price 2012}$$

While the reader may not have the opportunity to put this formula to use on an everyday basis, it is presented as a reminder that when people begin to bemoan a rise in prices, they are often only looking at the nominal, rather than real, structure. Many of the problems that the average citizen has when tackling the subject of international economics, or for that matter domestic economics, stem from not having the essential and, most times, simple information needed to make decisions.

Supply and Demand

All variants of capitalist economies have at their heart the market mechanism. Unlike socialist economies, where the state determines what, how much and the price of products, market economies allow several factors to come into play:

- SUPPLY The quantity of goods or services that a producer makes available at a particular price.
- DEMAND The quantity of goods or services that consumers are willing and able to purchase at a particular price.
- PRICE The amount of money or money equivalent used to purchase goods or services.
- MARKET MECHANISM The tendency for the price of goods and services to adjust until the quantity supplied is equal to the quantity demanded (a.k.a. market clearing or equilibrium).

The relationship of these factors is most often and most easily represented graphically by utilizing a "supply and demand curve."

SUPPLY / DEMAND CURVE

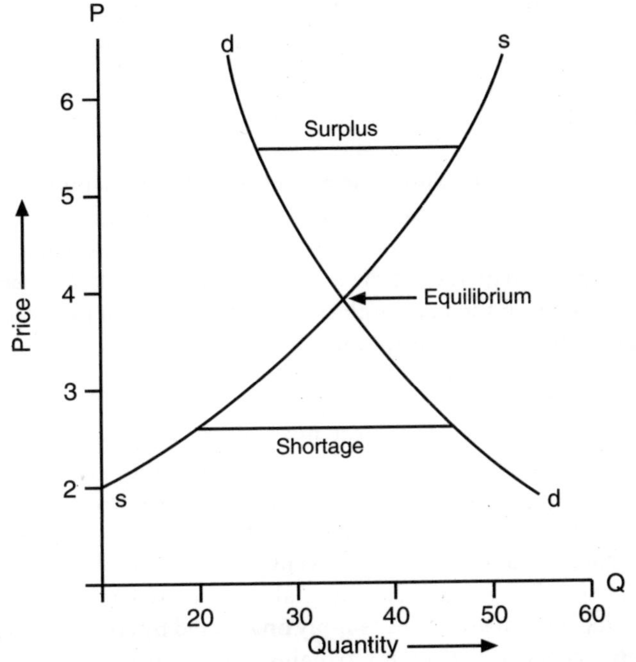

The supply curve (S) shows how much producers can sell (axis Q) at each different possible price (axis P). Higher prices increase a producer's desire and ability to increase production. Price increases may also attract new producers to a market formerly thought to be unprofitable. Under either scenario, production expands. As prices decrease, producers cut production or leave the marketplace altogether in search of more profitable areas. As price increases, supply increases, with the result that the supply curve slopes upward.

The demand curve demonstrates how much (axis Q) the consumers in a market are willing to buy relative to the stated prices (axis P). As the price decreases, consumers buy more and new consumers are encouraged to make purchases as well. Higher prices drive consumers from the market in search of lower-priced alternatives. As prices decrease, demand increases, so the demand curve slopes downward.

EQUILIBRIUM

A state of equilibrium occurs where the supply curve and demand curve intersect. This is the point where the supply produced equals the quantity demanded, at a price suitable to both consumers and producers. There is a natural tendency towards price equilibrium, if the market is free of outside interference. For instance, products put into the market at too high a price will go unsold, creating a surplus. Producers will lower the price to alleviate the surplus and decrease production. Conversely, if products are priced too low, consumers would demand additional quantity, thereby creating shortages. This in turn drives prices up as consumers compete for products now in short supply while encouraging suppliers to increase their production. In either case, as consumers and suppliers interpret the market information, and everyone from steel magnates to housewives does, the market will "clear" (equalize) for a period until new circumstances arise.

Market Shifts

Virtually every adult understands supply and demand intuitively, yet we rarely see their effect in pure form. This is due to the constant changes in market circumstances, some natural, some artificial. These changes are referred to as shifts in supply or demand. In the modern world these shifts occur more often and their effect is felt in the marketplace more quickly than in generations past, due to the increasing pace of information flow.

SUPPLY SHIFT

Every producer is subject not only to the desires of consumers, but to the companies that supply it with materials or labor. Those "primary" suppliers are in turn subject to the forces of nature and to governmental oversight. Costs of production may rise or fall suddenly due to causes beyond the control of the producer. Interest rates set by central banks, employee wages set by government edict, or changes in raw material costs caused by the weather can all cause a producer to raise or lower supply unaffected by consumer demand. When a supply shift occurs and demand remains stable, pricing will be impacted. A supply increase (a shift in the supply curve to the right), due to dropping costs that encourage production, brings about a drop in price. Supply decreases caused by rising production costs (the supply curve shifts to the left) meet the same level of demand with an increase in price.

DEMAND SHIFT

Demand, of course, is subject to the same types of shifts. In fact, a company's marketing efforts are designed to spur an increase in demand. But demand can move up or down for reasons beyond marketing. Periods of political strife, natural disasters and seasonal needs can all supersede a producer's marketing efforts. When there is a demand shift and supply remains stable, there will be an immediate impact on pricing. Demand can expand due to a change in income, currency value or cultural influences, for instance, and consumers will compete among themselves for an increasingly scarce supply by offering to pay more. World Cup Final or Super Bowl tickets are good examples of a limited supply meeting a demand shift. As game time approaches, prices soar. A drop in demand caused by a reversal of any of the factors above results in a decrease in the equilibrium purchase price. Any tickets left over after the World Cup Final has ended are still in limited supply but not in high demand.

SUPPLY AND DEMAND CONTROLS

This last example pre-supposes a fixed supply of sports tickets, which is a perfect example of an artificial control on supply. Sports facilities can be of any size, as can be seen in the wide variety of seating capacities available worldwide. A Brazilian soccer stadium may seat 100,000 while a new U.S. baseball stadium is designed for 40,000. Multi-use stadiums actually shift the number of seats depending on the event. The supplier in this case is attempting to keep the supply at the point that generates the most profit while satisfying just some of consumer demand. Suppliers match pricing to the level of demand in such a way as to maximize their profits over a chosen period of time. This relationship between demand and pricing is called *elasticity*.

Elasticity of Demand

The ratio of the proportional change in demand created by the proportional change in price is referred to as the *price elasticity of demand*. Not all products react the same way to price changes, and there are four main categories of this price-demand relationship:

ELASTIC DEMAND

In cases of elastic demand, when price is changed by a certain percentage, demand changes by a greater percentage. Normally, demand will drop dramatically as price increases, and rise sharply as price decreases. However, consumers sometimes use price as an indicator of quality causing demand to actually rise with price increases or drop with price decreases without any pressure from the supply area. Artwork, wine, and classic automobile pricing all can be a function of this "quality effect" where value and prestige are linked to price.

INELASTIC DEMAND

In cases of inelastic demand, when price is changed by a percentage, demand changes by a lesser percentage. Prices of goods or services considered to be necessities (medical treatment), or near necessities (flour), can absorb very large price increases without affecting demand. Similarly, some goods can have a sharp price decrease, and demand will change only slightly, as there is a limit to the amount that people are willing to consume (e.g., milk).

UNITARY DEMAND

When price is changed by a percentage, demand changes by an equal percentage. As with elastic and inelastic demand, the two percentages usually (price up, demand down, etc.) run in opposite directions but it may not always be so for some luxury goods or those subject to short supply and high demand.

CROSS DEMAND

When goods are used in conjunction with other products, their price will fluctuate proportionally with that of the other product. For example, as the price of videotape players (VCRs) began to decrease and their consumption increase, the demand for and production of VHS cassette-tapes increased. Prices of both devices declined as widescale production lowered per-unit costs. If consumers switch to CD-players for video, the VHS producers will meet the same fate as that of the VCR suppliers unless they change their product lines.

QUESTION: Another product experiencing cross-demand in this example is the movie itself. Many films make more money in video-release than in theaters. Consumers can now cheaply rent movies for convenient home viewing while avoiding high ticket and refreshment prices at local movie theatres. As VCRs and DVD players became cheaper, rental prices dropped and consumption of movies—a service—soared. How will the move towards downloadable videos affect movie rentals?

ELASTICITY FORMULA

The various forms of elasticity can be calculated. The formula for determining elasticity is as follows: (E = the coefficient of elasticity)

$$E = \frac{\text{Percentage Change in Quantity Sold}}{\text{Percentage Change in Unit Price}}$$

(If E >1, demand is elastic. If E < 1, demand is inelastic.
Unitary demand exists when E=1.)

It is important to understand the principle of elasticity because it is an easy measure of how consumers make decisions. It must be stressed that a wide variety of factors affect consumer behavior, some of which may be disagreeable to an outside observer (e.g., the consumption of snake meat or the cosmetic use of plastic surgery). One need not agree with consumer behavior to understand its effect on pricing.

Utility Theory

The way in which consumers determine how to spend their income is described as consumer behavior. Adam Smith described consumption as the "sole purpose of production," where consumers vote for goods and services with their money. This is the basis for "the customer is always right" axiom. Consumers make their choices depending on how much satisfaction they derive from the product under consideration. This level of satisfaction is call "utility." Utility is measurable but very subjective, and it is worth stating that satisfaction does not necessarily mean that the product has a practical use.

The study of utility theory makes some assumptions. The first is that consumers are rational and capable of making informed decisions. The second is that consumers actually have preferences for one product over another. Thirdly, consumers must have a limited income, which necessitates the making of a choice between two similar products (brand choice) or among a range of differing products (World Cup tickets or food). Lastly, utility theory assumes that a set of price differences exist due to limited resources and an expanding demand.

MEASURING UTILITY

Utility may be measured cardinally (absolute measurement—as in Product A is three times as good as Product B) or ordinally (relative measurement—as in Product A is first, Product B is second, and Product X is third). The rate at which total utility changes is called *marginal utility.* Marginal utility decreases as consumption (total utility) increases, since consumers tend to derive less and less satisfaction from each additional purchase (e.g., business suits). At some point for each product, prices may have to be reduced to get consumers to purchase in the same quantity. New "satisfaction" will be had from obtaining the product at a lower price. Another alternative is for suppliers to be able to predict when consumers will be "satiated," and thereby start to limit production to maintain price levels.

Product Substitution

Producers compete not only against other producers that make similar products, but against all products in the marketplace as well. Under a variety of circumstances, consumers will decrease their consumption of one product to increase their consumption of another. The *marginal rate of substitution* (MRS) is a function of the marginal utility (MU) a consumer derives from each product. The formula for calculating this rate (MRS) for two products (a & b) is as follows:

$$\text{MRS} = \frac{\text{MUa}}{\text{MUb}}$$

Because the MRS is a representation of how much of one product a consumer is willing to give up in order to purchase another, it can also be represented as:

$$\text{MRS} = -\frac{\text{a}}{\text{b}}$$

(a minus sign is used since the change in "a" will always be negative)

Additionally, this substitution rate is also a function of the price (P) which gives us:

$$\text{MRS} = \frac{\text{Pa}}{\text{Pb}} \quad \text{and therefore} \quad \frac{\text{Pa}}{\text{Pb}} = \frac{\text{MUa}}{\text{MUb}}$$

Maximum utility (the point at which consumers derive the greatest satisfaction from their purchases) occurs when the marginal utility per currency-unit-spent is the same for each product or:

$$\frac{\text{MUa}}{\text{Pa}} = \frac{\text{MUb}}{\text{Pb}}$$

Profit Maximization

Just as consumers must be able to derive a level of satisfaction from transacting a purchase, so must a producer from making a sale. Producers measure their satisfaction in terms of profit. When the goal of a business organization is to make as much profit as possible, economists refer to this as *profit maximization* (PM). Economists assume PM when discussing microeconomic concerns as it allows them to predict business activity more accurately. PM theory avoids concerns about the private motivations, short- and long-term, of individual managers by focusing on the owners of a business.

Profit is the difference between the cost of production and the revenue that the production generates when sold. The following formulas apply to calculating revenue:

$$\text{Total Revenue} = \text{Sales Price per Unit} \times \text{Quantity Sold}$$

$$\text{Average Revenue} = \frac{\text{Total Revenue}}{\text{Quantity Sold}}$$

$$\text{Marginal Revenue} = \frac{\text{Change in Total Revenue}}{\text{Change in Quantity Sold}}$$

COST-PROFIT RELATIONSHIP

The cost of producing something represents the lowest possible price that can be charged for a product without incurring a loss. There are several types of production costs to be considered. *Fixed costs* are those expenditures that do not change regardless of how much is produced. These include such items as rent, salaries, depreciation and property taxes. Because these costs remain static for extended periods of time, the fixed-cost-per-unit will decline as production increases and the operation spreads them out over a greater number of units. *Variable costs* are those expenditures that change, depending upon the quantity of product produced. These might include employee wages, materials, transportation and packaging. The variable-cost-per-unit may actually decrease when production expands as efficiency increases and the savings that come with mass raw material purchasing become evident. *Total costs* are the sum of all fixed costs and variable costs. *Marginal cost* is the added cost that occurs when a single unit of production is added to current levels. It only affects variable cost, and is used to determine the effectiveness of expanding production and its ultimate effect on pricing and, therefore, profits.

Pricing Schemes

A producer must design a pricing scheme that maximizes profit in any given market. Pricing, however, is not an exact science and several different approaches can be taken.

- COMPONENT COST PRICING A very simplistic price-setting measure used by small firms is *component cost.* This strategy takes a single component of cost—usually a major variable cost such as labor or materials—and expands it by a standard percentage to arrive at a market price. (e.g., unit material cost x 300% = sale price) While common, this method disregards consumer demand and does not take into account total-cost-per-unit or competitor pricing.
- COST PLUS PRICING In a *cost plus strategy*, a producer adds a profit percentage to the total-cost- per-unit. This is more efficient than the component cost method, as now all costs are considered, though there is still no accounting for changes in demand. The strategy also relies on production costs remaining relatively stable and, when large fluctuations occur, they are difficult to absorb.
- AVERAGE RETURN PRICING Some companies use *average return pricing*, which adds a fixed amount of profit (rather than a percentage) to the total cost

of a projected quantity of production. This amount is then divided by the total number of units to be produced in order to derive the price. This scheme relies on the selling of an entire production run in order to realize profits.

- BREAKEVEN POINT PRICING Larger companies use *breakeven point pricing* by figuring the level of unit sales at which revenue equals total costs. Beyond this point, all sales will represent profit; below this point all sales will incur a loss. The breakeven point will vary for different prices and projected sales volumes. This method assumes that whatever quantity will be produced will also be sold and that variable costs will remain stable during the production period. This very useful formula is helpful in determining a product's potential:

$$\text{Breakeven Point} = \frac{\text{Total Fixed Costs}}{\text{Sales Price per Unit} - \text{Variable Cost per Unit}}$$

PRICING ON MARGIN

Another type of pricing is used by a company seeking to gain access to more consumers with the hopes of maximizing profit over the long term. Called *margin pricing*, products are sold below total cost to gain dominance, and thereby take advantage of long-term efficiencies and gradual price increases over time to make up for early losses. The greatest advantages that come with expanding production are the characteristic increases in the efficiency and the decrease in variable costs and fixed costs per unit. These economies of scale are brought about by the discounts of volume material purchases and increased worker experience. For manufacturing processes, this can amount to a 15% decrease in per-unit costs for every 100% increase in production levels.

Competitive Pricing

In a market economy, a firm working in a perfectly competitive (see monopoly and monopsony below) arena will be unable to affect the market price of a product, since that firm only sells a fraction of the total product-type available. Products will be sold at a price determined by the market (all consumers and all producers), not a single producer. Therefore each firm is a "price taker" not a "price maker" in competitive markets.

In the short term, a firm must operate with a fixed level of capital and make choices about its variable costs (labor, materials) in order to maximize its profits, since fixed costs are not subject to control. The basic formula for calculating profit is:

$$\text{Profit} = \text{Total Revenue} - (\text{Fixed Costs} + \text{Variable Costs})$$

DIMINISHING RETURNS

At low levels of production, there may be negative profit (loss) as revenue cannot cover total costs. After the breakeven point is reached where all costs have been recouped, additional sales begin to generate a profit. *Marginal revenue* (revenue generated by selling one more unit) is always equal to the price-per-unit-sold because it is independent of profit. Marginal cost (the cost of producing one more unit) decreases (thus increasing profits) as production expands due to efficiencies. This occurs only down to the level where additional inputs (such as labor) cease to add efficiency, and begin to cause cost increases. The Law of Diminishing Returns (also called Diminishing Marginal Product) states that efficiencies gained during expanded production in the area of variable costs eventually maximize and begin to decline. (Example: Labor and fertilizer may make an acre of land more productive, but not infinitely so. Continual increases of those two factors will eventually drive the cost of that acre's production beyond the revenue derived.)

MAXIMIZING PROFIT

When marginal costs begin to equal marginal revenue, a proper relation among price, production and costs has been made, thus maximizing profits. On either side of this equilibrium, profits decline. Determining where profits will be maximized for a given price helps a company determine its production levels. Since prices are set by the marketplace, companies must strive to bring marginal costs in line with those prices by responding to consumer demand. As can be seen in the number of employee layoffs (downsizing) in competitive markets like the United States, labor is often the first target of companies seeking to control marginal costs. As we will see in Chapter 7, this particular microeconomic principle can often be overridden by unions and governments, thereby limiting a company's (and oftentimes an entire nation's) competitiveness.

Efficiency and Competition

In an unregulated, fully competitive market (an ideal not found in contemporary society) producers sell and consumers buy at prices set by all of the factors mentioned earlier. For all of Adam Smith's reliance on the "invisible hand" of free markets, such economies do have inefficiencies at the micro level. Understanding these efficiency problems will assist the reader in analyzing the overall impact of economic policy in the marketplace.

Some consumers purchase products that, for them, have a far greater value than the price paid, and they would be willing to pay higher prices should they become prevalent. This phenomenon is very common in fine art and other collectibles. However, because they pay the lower market price, these consumers receive a benefit in what is called *consumer surplus*. This surplus represents revenue that producers forego, but it should be noted that consumer surplus represents consumers as a group, not individually. Three people with identical financial means may purchase the same product at the same price yet derive three different degrees of value; some derive a surplus, some do not. For consumers receiving surplus, the market is beneficially inefficient.

SELLERS AND BUYERS BEWARE

Producer surplus occurs when sellers price their products at levels above their minimum profit level. Just as consumers can "get more than they paid for," so, too, can the producer obtain a surplus revenue for products that could have stayed in the marketplace at lower prices. This surplus covers all areas of real profit up to where the market reaches equilibrium. When governments institute price controls—usually at the request of consumers—there is the potential for both consumer and producer groups to lose surplus.

Under normal (elastic) circumstances, price controls depress production and thereby create excess demand. While some consumers may be left out of the marketplace ("rationed out") by decreased supply, those that can make purchases receive an increase in surplus at the controlled lower price. All producers lose surplus, which is exacerbated by decreased production. Since some consumers, and all producers, lose surplus, this is referred to as a *deadweight loss of total surplus*. When demand is inelastic, the number of consumers rationed out of the market greatly exceeds those that can stay in and retain a surplus. This results in a net loss of consumer surplus along with concomitant losses to producers. Gasoline price controls and rationing during the late 1970s in the United States caused this type of net loss to consumers; government policy actually made consumers worse off while attempting to protect them.

Monopolies, Oligopolies, Monopsonies and Competition

Competition can oftentimes be a long way from the "perfect" version that market societies idealize. Markets do not always have many producers, zero price regulation, completely informed consumers and unchecked forms of exchange. The imperfection in the marketplace can take several forms.

STANDARD

We can deem this variety "standard" because it is the level of imperfection that most capital markets are most acquainted with and most willing to tolerate. Here we find many producers for any one product, with the differences among them sometimes being real ("contains 15% more active ingredient") and sometimes fanciful ("new and improved"). Consumers are not always well informed and depend on the producer's marketing efforts to make decisions. Prices are heavily administered by the producers who often dictate the sales price to retailers, thus avoiding the possibility of consumer bargaining at the point of purchase. This take-it-or-leave-it pricing is very common in the West where no one would consider haggling with their local drugstore about the price of toothpaste. In most of Asia and the Middle East, however, such bargaining for everyday purchases is still the norm. Even with the existence of producer-administered prices, no single producer can control all pricing.

MONOPOLY

- REGULATED MONOPOLIES - Governments will often decide that certain industries should be operated by a single producer, with all others made illegal. These created monopolies (from the Greek *mono* meaning "one" and *polist* meaning "seller") are ostensibly formed for the public good (e.g., power utilities), or for the purposes of control (e.g., nationalized postal, television or telephone systems). Prices are usually set by the regulators to lock in profits for the producer, so consumers have no influence other than to not consume the product at all. Some regulated monopolies, like the three communications systems mentioned, are coming under increased competition from international companies (e.g., FedEx, Sky-TV, the Internet).

- NATURAL MONOPOLIES - These companies gain market dominance (and total price control) not by government regulation but through their own methods—some seemly, some not. In some instances, a company may have a product so superior that competition is driven from the market. Such monopolies are short-lived for the most part, as unfettered competition usually finds its way into the marketplace. Somewhat more common is the monopolist, who uses its superior financial resources to prevent any competitor from entering a market it wishes to keep as its own. AT&T did this for many decades in the U.S. telephone market, and Microsoft is accused regularly of doing the same internationally with its computer operating systems. Natural monopolies usually fall to government rulings, spurred on by companies that want a slice of the marketplace.

OLIGOPOLY

This is a market dominated by just a few companies; they are created because the huge amount of investment needed to enter the particular marketplace prevents widescale competition. There are two distinct types:

- IDENTICAL PRODUCT COMPANIES

  Here, the few firms involved have products of a very similar nature. The steel industry, chemical manufacturers and freight carriers are good examples. Since the products are virtually interchangeable, each firm is very sensitive to any price changes instigated by its limited competition. Buyers see no difference among the products (an I-beam is an I-beam, ammonia is ammonia), and base their choices on price and convenience. No single firm is a monopolist, but each can affect the pricing for the entire market.

- DIFFERENTIATED PRODUCT COMPANIES

  These firms tend to gain dominance at the retail level where similar products can be differentiated in the consumer's mind, even though these differences may be small. The automobile industry is a prime example of this type of dominance by the few capital-intensive firms selling very distinct products (at least to the consumer) that do essentially the same thing. Consumers believe they are making choices (the auto's color, interior, CD player), whereas the bulk of what they pay for (a transport vehicle) differs little from one manufacturer to the next. So deep is the power of these differentiated oligopolies that consumers become upset if the firms show signs of financial trouble (e.g., Chrysler, Jaguar). When national pride or massive layoffs are at stake, consumers sometimes demand that the government intervene.

MONOPSONY

This form of competitive imperfection comes about when there is a single customer for a product. A monopsonist can literally set the price. This situation can be thought of as a monopoly on the demand side of equilibrium. In a national market, governments often act with monopsonistic power when they purchase weapons for defense systems. In the private sector, a monopsony is most common when it comes to "buying" labor in a marketplace dominated by a single company, where labor has little mobility. In these so-called "company towns," the monopsonist can keep the price of labor low simply because workers have few or no choices when it comes to employment. Mining and large-scale agriculture in areas without union representation are regular practitioners of monopsonistic labor practices. In international markets, companies regularly move manufacturing to regions where labor prices are low and labor has nowhere to go. More of this will be discussed in the section on government regulation.

OLIGOPSONY

Somewhat more common and generally tolerated is an oligopsony, where a few buyers control pricing. A good example of this can be found in the automotive markets, where the few sellers that make up the oligopoly are also acting as oligopsonists when they purchase parts and materials for making their specialized products. The recent trend in manufacturing towards "outsourcing" (buying rather than making parts in-house) has vastly increased the number of parts manufacturers who sell to the big automakers, thereby increasing competition. The automakers are consolidating and becoming fewer in number, which increases their oligopoly. Companies attempting to enter the marketplace (such as Indonesia's "national car") often find that the oligopsonists have convinced some of their suppliers not to sell to these start-ups, thus raising the barriers to market entry. Like monopolies and monopsonies, oligopsonies often attract the attention of local, national and international government agencies when their power becomes abusive or they step on the toes of government cronies.

General Equilibrium

Even at the smallest level of microeconomics, a single market does not operate in a vacuum. Regardless of the degree of imperfection, each market impacts, and is impacted by, other markets at both the domestic and global levels. Every impact delivered or absorbed will influence decision-making. Each market will tend towards a state of equilibrium (the point where supply and demand converge to the satisfaction of consumers and producers alike) if left free from outside interference. Partial equilibrium occurs as markets of particular products are analyzed. For instance, the rice market can be viewed independently from other seed and grain products like corn or wheat. The supply of rice can be seen to meet demand for rice without factoring in other products.

GENERAL EQUILIBRIUM

However, as was mentioned before, a consumer's ability to substitute one product for another (such as wheat for rice) will have an effect on pricing and equilibrium (see marginal rate of substitution). Economists must also analyze the general equilibrium that must occur among all products that compete directly with each other (wheat and rice), as well as indirectly (clothing and rice). This type of equilibrium makes all products subject to changes in all other products sought in the marketplace. Price and quantity adjustments in one market caused by price and quantity adjustments in a related market are called *feedback effects*. These effects can take place at the local level, the national level, and, as is increasingly evident in the world's business journals, at the international level. Let's look at some examples from these three arenas to get a better picture of how equilibrium works.

LOCAL EQUILIBRIUM

If a petrol station operator in Dublin decides unilaterally to lower his prices, the effect of such a move can ripple through the local markets in a variety of ways. As customers flood to his station to take advantage of the lower price, these same consumers may also choose to curtail their use of public transport, now that gasoline is so cheap. Or they may use the money saved at the petrol pump to make purchases of other products that previously were left out of the home budget. In the first case, municipal transport will have to adjust to the new drop in demand, while parking facilities may see a sudden increase in activity. In the second scenario, other local businesses, such as theaters, pubs, electronics stores or clothiers will need to respond to the sudden rise in demand created by this freeing up of income that can now be spent on non-essentials (referred to as *disposable income*). All of this takes place outside of the partial equilibrium that must be adjusted among local petrol dealers.

NATIONAL EQUILIBRIUM

Using the gas-hungry U.S. market as an example, what would occur if California, the nation's most populous and mobile state, decided to institute a new 15% tax on all gas sold within its borders? As this tax was passed along to consumers in the form of higher prices, inside the state we would see feedback effects similar to the local ones already listed, but in reverse. As disposable income declines, tourist attractions like Disneyland (accessed mostly by automobile) would see a sudden drop in attendance, and non-essential producers would find themselves with a choice between overstocked warehouses or reduced sale prices. At the national level, other states with their own tourist attractions would become instantly more attractive (or at least bearable) to local residents as expensive auto travel to California dropped. Airlines and trains might see an increase in passengers and freight as their modes of travel would remain unaffected by the gas tax. California would most likely see a drop in its seaport activity as importers moved shipments to Oregon, Washington or even East Coast cities in search of cheaper ground transport costs. Lastly, the cost of California's large agricultural output, mostly shipped out by truck, would rise causing consumers nationwide to make adjustments to their buying patterns and levels of consumption. Demand and supply across the country would have to find new equilibrium both partially and generally.

INTERNATIONAL EQUILIBRIUM

When OPEC (Organization of Petroleum Exporting Countries) decides to limit production in order to increase the price of oil, how does this affect equilibrium? The petrol station owner mentioned above will find it difficult to maintain the discounts that threw his local market into imbalance, although he may still offer a lower price relative to his competitors. California's state treasurer, in turn, may find that she has to administer a tax that is now much more of a burden than originally thought. Internationally, the stakes are much higher. Japan, which is completely dependent on oil imports, will see the price of just about all of its products rise along with its imports. Its exports may lose their competitive edge against those of the United States, a nation with substantial oil reserves and production of its own. California shrimp might replace those of the Hokkaido fishing fleets in Tokyo supermarket displays. Russia, a nation with large oil deposits but not an OPEC member, soon becomes a recipient of Japanese largesse for the purposes of new oil exploration. As consumption drops worldwide due to tightened supply, smaller oil producers like Venezuela and Ecuador (both OPEC members) may find they no longer have the foreign currency brought in by oil exports to purchase the Japanese trucks necessary for Latin American transportation needs. Russians, flush with Japanese cash, head for European and Caribbean vacations, driving up prices in those economies while shutting out local consumers. In Dublin, a visiting businessman from Moscow buys a round of drinks for the house at the local pub. Enjoying a free Guinness is the Irishman who owns the petrol station around the corner. He is struggling to regain his equilibrium in the new marketplace.

Self-Interest and Global Equilibrium

In the cases above, decisions were made by individuals or small groups of people; those decisions had effects well beyond the immediate scope or intention of the original decision-makers. Local gasoline sellers give no more thought to municipal transport demand than OPEC members do to the fate of shrimp-buying Japanese housewives. Given time, general equilibrium will always be restored, as will the partial variety. Self-interest is usually at the heart of microeconomic decisions, but its overall impact is ultimately much larger. New decisions will—also given time—throw all of the markets out of equilibrium.

One of the hallmarks of modern society has been the ability to process information quickly enough to respond to imbalances before they cause major damage. As we will see in the section on macroeconomics, most of the global economic factors that were the primary causes of major wars in the past have been brought under a much greater degree of control in the latter half of the 20th century. A perpetual general equilibrium in global supply and demand has not been achieved (or for that matter deemed desirable) but large, catastrophic imbalances continue to be avoided. Advanced communications and increased information flow have greatly contributed to the duration of equilibrium and the avoidance of global conflicts.

CHAPTER 4

Basic Principles: Macroeconomics

IF ALL THE ECONOMISTS WERE LAID END TO END, THEY WOULD NOT REACH A CONCLUSION.

– GEORGE BERNARD SHAW

Macroeconomics

Macroeconomics is the study and analysis of the behaviors of markets in aggregate, as well as the behavior of governments that affect international and domestic economics. More precisely, it looks at total employment, production, consumption, imports, exports, and investment. Whereas microeconomics looks at how individuals or companies make decisions, macroeconomics analyses how municipalities, nations, regions and global markets formulate and react to governmental fiscal and monetary policy in order to achieve desired ends. While much of the remainder of the book will deal with these larger issues, some topics must be discussed beforehand.

As the quote at the beginning of this chapter implies, economists do not always reach the same conclusion, even when analyzing the exact same data. Even the advances in data collection and analytical tools (a.k.a. models) cannot bring about a single, definitive approach to how markets and government should interact. Currently, the biggest split in macroeconomic approaches is between the Keynesian economists and those of the New Classical Macroeconomics school (NCM). This divide centers around how each school views decision making, the role of government, and the efficiency of policy making.

KEYNESIAN SCHOOL

Briefly summarized, the Keynesian school makes no presumption that all consumers and sellers arrive at their decisions rationally—some do, some don't. Because of this view, the market forces described by Adam Smith as an "invisible hand" are not necessarily considered efficient or desirable. Government is a needed and welcomed controller of these two sometimes irrational decision-makers, resulting in outcomes favorable to the nation as a whole. Secondly, Keynesians believe that changes in the supply side only have a long-term effect, making government intervention necessary to control the short-term. Lastly, the followers of Keynes posit that the government, through fiscal and monetary policies, should control demand for specific products and for their subject economy as an aggregate.

NEW CLASSICAL MACROECONOMICS

Proponents of NCM are almost diametrically opposed to Keynesians on these matters. To them, consumers and suppliers are rational agents acting in what is ultimately an efficient manner, producing favorable outcomes. The "invisible hand" controls benevolently and efficiently. For new classical economists, a government should only intercede when a specific market failure can be discovered and only after proving that its intercession will actually lead to an improvement. Secondly, NCM sees short-term effects of supply changes but believes the rational forces of the market can effectively deal with such changes. Lastly, new classicists question whether government policymakers have the requisite tools to avoid doing more harm than good when entering the marketplace.

TO GOVERN OR NOT TO GOVERN

It should be clear that much of the difference between these two schools is a question of who is the better controller of the marketplace: government or the consumer/supplier. All of the different economic schemes discussed in Chapter 2 centered on how much, how often and where governments should intervene. Each school had very distinct views on government intervention and any economic discussion today—even at a cocktail party—will come back to that central issue. As readers progress through this book, a similar decision will have to be made by each.

Macro Theory

For many decades, macroeconomic theory was limited in breadth to the study of how individual nations reacted to each other's domestic economic policies, usually in terms of import/export ratios and monetary exchange. As we will see, international markets are today subject to a much broader range of decisions made by increasingly greater numbers of people. Let's look at some of the factors that trigger those policy decisions in brief before studying how consumers, businesses, nations and ultimately the international markets help formulate macroeconomic policy.

Business Cycles

Every economy, whether it be agricultural, industrial or technological, experiences fluctuations in activity. Periods of expansion are considered to be *boom phases*, while periods of decline are referred to as *recession phases*. Though every economy will experiences these ups and downs, the rate of these cycles will differ, along with their causes.

TRADE CYCLES

This is the cycle most commonly referred to under the banner of business cycles. Trade cycles represent fluctuations in the aggregate level of output and employment relative to long-term trends. Output is measured by *gross domestic product* (GDP = the amount of total goods and services produced by an economy, including that produced by foreign firms working within its borders, while excluding that produced abroad by its domestic companies). Under ideal circumstances, trade cycles are very repetitive in scope and duration. Actual trade cycles, however, are of varied length and severity due to the differences in time lags for making economic decisions from country to country. Economists struggle to predict these cycles with very mixed results.

REAL CYCLES

The term "real" is applied to a wide variety of economic terms to denote less theoretical factors, as is the case here. Real business cycles are based on economic shocks (unanticipated events) such as major geographical discoveries (oil), technical developments (the Internet) or social upheaval (war). These events make the prediction of trade cycles very difficult.

POLITICAL CYCLES

Because all nations have some governmental input into the economy, a theory has developed that these same governments manipulate their own economic cycles solely to maintain political control. In democratic societies, this can take the form of attempting to expand the economy just prior to elections, and making necessary retractions many years before the next election in hopes that the population will have adjusted. In one-party or totalitarian societies, economic expansion is used to quell unrest and potential revolution. Both types of governments recognize the impact of the economy upon politics, giving weight to the belief that people "vote with their pocketbook" even when there is no ballot box.

Inflation

The term inflation can be defined as the drop in purchasing power of a national currency, expressed as a persistent rise in prices. Countries try to track inflation by monitoring a set group of products in the form of a consumer price index (consumer goods only), a GDP deflator (consumer goods, investment products, government purchases) or a producer price index (wholesale prices). There are different types of inflation to consider:

SECTORIAL INFLATION

Prices of products within a market economy are always fluctuating relative to each other, as this is a natural function of supply and demand. Sectorial inflation occurs when prices of a particular set of products begin to rise rapidly, as is often the case with primary (agricultural, mineral or energy) commodities. These increases may or may not be part of a larger trend towards inflation. For example, a sudden rise in the price of sugar may be caused by crop failure, embargo or tariff increases and have little impact on the inflation rate of the economy as a whole.

COST INFLATION

This type of inflation results from cumulative cost increases being passed through the economy. Increased production costs in one industry (usually a key manufacturing sector, e.g., steel, automotive) cause the producers to raise prices. Workers demand higher wages to offset the price increases, which causes workers in other industries to seek higher wages to restore a balance in purchasing power. This cost-inflation-spiral can be very difficult to stop as each set of worker wage demands sets off a new set of price increases as costs rise.

DEMAND INFLATION

When demand far outstrips available supply, the result is a sharp inflation of prices. Since resources are not perfectly mobile within an economy, demand inflation can occur regionally or sectorially during the lag time needed to move production resources to the areas experiencing heightened demand. Wages increase as a response to the price increases that occur during this lag time. Such wage increases are difficult to rescind once resources are redistributed, thus setting off a cost-inflation-spiral as the increases ripple through the economy. Demand inflation is usually at the root of difficult to control cost inflation.

HYPERINFLATION

This is an aggravated form of cost inflation that has reached a level in excess of 50% per month in some countries. Several South American countries have suffered through this in the last few decades as had some European countries between WWI and WWII. Inflation of this size can overwhelm a currency, not only by greatly decreasing its value, but by eliminating it as a form of method of exchange. Visions of a population needing a wheelbarrow full of paper money just to buy a loaf of bread can strike fear into the heart of any government. Internationally, such hyperinflation also brings the specter of past wars and famines.

INFLATION TAX

This is the term used to describe the effect that inflation can have on the value of money and government debt. For instance, if the amount of money in domestic circulation equals 15%, and government debt 35%, of the gross national product (where GNP = national output produced, including overseas investments but excluding output by foreign companies producing domestically—see GDP above), what will be the effect of a 10% inflation rate? Money will decrease in value by 1.5% of GNP (10% of 15%) while government debt will lose 3.5% of its value against GNP (10% of 35%). Together this represents a 5% "tax" (1.5% + 3.5%) in the value of the economy. As we will see in the section on government regulation, this informal tax can conflict with the formal taxation system.

Investment

The word "invest" comes form the Latin word *investire,* meaning "to clothe," which is a suitable image of how business investment works. Investment enables a company, a national economy or a region to acquire the necessary (real) assets to produce goods and services, just as one would don proper attire to perform specific jobs from coal miner to surgeon. Investment comes in many forms and from many directions:

INVESTMENT GOODS

These are goods that are purchased for their potential to produce other goods or services, and not for direct consumption. For example, flour purchased for making bread in a bakery or the printer toner cartridges for use in the banking industry to print loan forms are investment goods. For accountants, these are short-term (for use in less than 12 months) assets.

GROSS FIXED INVESTMENT

This refers to the large capital expenditures made for equipment used to produce goods or services. In the bakery cited earlier, a large mixing machine would fall in this category, while the color laser printer would fulfill the same role at the bank. These are long-term (for use beyond 12 months) assets.

NET INVESTMENT

As gross investment declines in value due to "wear and tear" or obsolescence, the decline is subtracted from initial value to define net investment.

INVESTMENT ALLOWANCES

These are tax deductions issued by governments to firms that invest in favored sectors of the economy.

FOREIGN DIRECT INVESTMENT

In a national economy, this represents both the inflow of capital from foreign lands into the domestic economy as well as the amount of capital outflow invested overseas by domestic companies. Successful economies attract the greatest inflow, while laggard economies try to stem the outflow or "capital flight" through regulation. Wishing to invest in an attractive economy is not without controversy, as the Japanese found out when they attempted to buy into the U.S. real estate market in the 1980s. Their aspirations were seen by some as a form of modern-day colonialism to be fought off. Emerging markets, like Kenya and China, have installed tight regulation of foreign investment in certain sectors to avoid the same type of economic-colony status, from which many were only recently released.

RESEARCH INVESTMENT

Private businesses, national governments, and sometimes consortia of governments provide funding to develop new technologies or to train their workforces for new systems with this form of investment. Not all economies recognize this activity when calculating total investment.

EQUITY INVESTMENT

This is the purchase of stock securities from a company, resulting in the investor becoming a shareholder with rights to company assets equivalent to the investment plus profits or minus losses. Shareholders take *risks* with the hope of gaining high returns over time by owning a percentage of the company. National economies allow varying forms of foreign participation in private equity investment, though not all nations permit the public sale of stock even to their own citizens. China, which only recently permitted equity sales, offers different stock to domestic and foreign buyers. Major economies gauge their economic success by how the value of these markets fluctuate and accumulate return on investment (known as ROI) over time. In the mid-1990s, the U.S. equity market was producing an average 16% rate of return, while that of the second largest economy in the world, Japan, hovered around 2%. This came not from the profitability of the companies in the respective countries, but from the tight controls Japan places on its daily market activity, which restricts the volatile buying and selling that characterizes the relatively unrestricted American stock markets.

DEBT

Some companies, and virtually all governments, use the creation of debt (borrowing money) as a way to raise investment. Whereas an equity investment gives the holder rights to the profits in the form of dividends, debt gives the lender (the creditor) rights only to the amount of the debt plus a set level of interest, regardless of the profitability of the company. This creates a liability for the entity seeking to raise the investment, and this liability must be paid before shareholders receive their due. Both companies and governments issue bonds that stipulate when the debt will reach maturity (pay back date) and the amount of interest. Private companies try to limit debt and maximize equity, as the latter has less risk for the firm. The debt/equity ratio can attract new equity investors when it is low, although this does not apply to certain industries that are naturally debt intensive, such as banks and public utilities. Governments generate a great deal of debt through the sale of government bonds to both the domestic and foreign markets. This national debt can be the subject of much political wrangling and concern—some necessary, some not. It should be noted that some Islamic nations forbid the generation of debt—public or private—as part of a religious sanction against *usury* (the payment of interest).

Savings

Broadly defined, savings amounts to that portion of income not spent on consumption. Saving is a means by which to acquire, hold, and expand assets. The *average propensity to save* is defined as the aggregate ratio of savings to income, or how much a group on average saves. The *marginal propensity to save* is the portion of any added income that is saved. Savings has its own form of elasticity, known as *interest elasticity*, which measures how aggregates alter their savings-to-income ratio as interest rates change.

The word "savings" is applied to the activity of a wide range of groups:

- LIFE SAVINGS Personal assets stored up over time by individuals.
- SMALL SAVINGS The accumulated wealth of low-income earners.
- SAVINGS ACCOUNTS Interest-bearing financial accounts provided by banks to individuals.
- CONTRACT SAVINGS Accounts and series such as mortgages and pensions which accumulate over a specific period of time at preset rates.
- NATIONAL SAVINGS Government securities that have their value guaranteed by the state.

SAVINGS AND INVESTMENT

Savings are what generates investment (the creation of real assets). Even when an individual places his money in a savings account, the bank will use that money to invest in some form of assets (e.g., residential real estate, start-up capital for entrepreneurs). Profits from those investments serve to pay the interest to the account holder. On a national scale, a government will sell financial instruments in the form of savings bonds or treasury bills, which can be redeemed at a later date for a set percentage of interest (like bonds in the private sector). While a government's investments may not show a direct profit, they do contribute to the overall facilitation of the national economy. As the economy grows, this can be suitably taxed to recoup the monies necessary to pay off the bonds at maturity.

Household and national rates of saving do not always indicate the success of an economy, but they are good indicators of how investment is funded in a national economy. The following chart reveals many things about two of the world's largest economies:

Country	Household Savings Rate	National Savings Rate	Interest Rate	GDP Growth Rate
United States	4.2%	16.2%	4.25%	2.2%
Japan	12.8%	31.4%	0.5%	2.1%

(Sources: OECD / CIA / Reuters 2007)

THE JAPANESE SAVINGS MODEL

The chart above clearly shows that the Japanese as a group are excellent savers (in the developed world, only the Swiss come close); in contrast, it also shows that American consumers are spendthrifts. Yet, the United States and Japan experienced a similar GDP growth rate over the previous year. (Mature economies like the United States considered 2.2% GDP growth to be a slowdown caused by a weakening currency, while Japan viewed its 2.1% growth as a major move forward from the flat growth of the 1990s.)

Much of this disparity of outlook has to do with interest elasticity and the mobility of investment. The interest rate offered to savers in the very stable U.S. economy (four times the rate of Japan) was very attractive to Japanese investors holding their domestically generated savings. In most cases inside of a national economy, savings tend to increase in proportion to the rise in bank interest rates. When rates are low domestically, there is a tendency to consume, since there is also a corresponding freeing up of credit offers as lenders attempt to attract business. The comparatively high Japanese savings rate, however, seems to defy this pattern.

■ CONSUMPTION PROBLEMS

Japan's high savings rate, accompanied by low interest rates, occurs because it is difficult to consume in that country. Unlike the United States, where households will own several automobiles and three televisions, the Japanese consumer is greatly restricted by lack of space (Tokyo residents, for instance, must prove they have a parking space before they are permitted to buy a car) and the social taboos that exist against flaunting wealth. Japanese saving institutions are overflowing with cash that is loaned out at low rates (about 1/6 of U.S. rates) to domestic businesses. These businesses in turn often buy overseas assets unavailable in their home market (e.g., foreign real estate, high interest bonds). Japanese banks also buy a great deal of U.S. government bonds as well as investing in the American private sector.

Foreign stocks are also quite desirable (U.S. stocks average eight times the return rate of Japanese stocks), given Japan's rigid trading systems. While the mechanism has been somewhat simplified here, it does demonstrate how domestic savings flows across national borders towards the area of higher interest rates and expected growth. This flow affects growth in the domestic as well as the foreign market and is as much a function of how savings are treated as it is a willful investment strategy. Foreign investment—Japanese or otherwise—in the United States or any other economy is a sign of the recipient economy's strength, not, as many doomsayers would say, a sign of vulnerability.

THE U.S. SAVINGS MODEL

America is a consumer culture of gigantic proportions. Not only do its households resist saving, but they also use a great deal of consumer credit in the form of bank cards to finance purchases. While the average Japanese household may put away 30% of its income in savings, Americans are hard-pressed if they put away half that much and it is closer to a sixth. In academic terms, economists would normally praise the habits of Japan and denigrate those of the United States. And yet, the United States has economically outperformed Japan on a regular basis for the last two decades. As the thrifty Japanese languish in economic doldrums and have been surpassed by China, the prodigal Americans remain firmly atop the globe's economic heap even after the "credit crunch" of 2008.

Unlike many cultures, declaring personal bankruptcy in the U.S. when debt gets out of control is a common and accepted practice with little social stigma and only a mild economic one. High-rate mortgages on American homes bought up in "bundles" by domestic and foreign banks from 2004-07 became economic albatrosses to those same banks when hard-pressed Americans defaulted on the loans in 2008. Although the defaults represented less than 1% of all American mortgages, the massive dollar amounts brought weak banks to their knees and made the big banks fearful of lending.

■ ROOTS OF SUCCESS

Some of this discrepancy in economic theory versus reality comes from how each of these two countries has approached their international commercial efforts. Unlike Japan, which had fueled its economic "miracle" with a concentration on exports, the United States relies continually on domestic consumption balanced with a level of imports and exports suitable to its size. The United States always runs trade deficits (i.e., it imports more than it exports) with its major trading partners, simply because its population size, level of income, and living standards guarantee that it will outconsume its global competitors. American culture, in part, discourages domestic savings and its housing size (especially compared to Japan) ensures that there will always be space to be filled by new consumer goods.

It should also be obvious that when Americans decline to save and instead buy domestic goods, they are helping to generate jobs and incomes for their fellow citizens. But when they buy imports it is a somewhat different matter. Does buying imports not simply aid foreigners (e.g., Japanese car makers, Colombian coffee growers) to expand their own economies and job markets? Does the American aversion to saving prevent the United States from being able to afford to start new businesses at the expense of American workers? The answer to the first question is "yes" but "no" for the second, and is borne out by the preeminence of the U.S. economy. The details of these answers and their implications will be discussed in Chapter 8.

Recession

Recession occurs when overall demand becomes sluggish, and output (the growth in goods or services) fails to rise. Technically, a state of recession exists when an economy exhibits these symptoms for more than two fiscal quarters in a row, and it is accompanied by a drop in employment. Recession is economic retreat and in severe or prolonged circumstances it can lead to a full-scale depression. Recessions can be "mild" and easily corrected by the intercession of government central bankers and private enterprise. The early signs of recession are used as a signal to make changes in the supply and demand relationship, with attentive economic stewards being quick to recognize the problems.

CORRECTIVE MEASURES

"Deep" recessions, as occurred in Asia in the late 1990s, are more difficult to resolve, and are usually the result of unsound economic practices rather than competitive circumstances. In such cases, major economic reforms—statutory and theoretical—must take place for a nation to get back to a steady pattern of growth. After years of heady growth in the 1920s, a worldwide recession devolved into the Great Depression in the 1930s. The unrestricted growth of the former period caused the retraction of the latter period that could only be corrected by years of global austerity measures culminating in WWII.

Because of the international implications of recession and the modern-day speed at which such conditions can be spread (or corrected for), global organizations formed after the war offered aid to troubled economies in the form of advice as well as loans to blunt the effects. The International Monetary Fund (IMF) and the World Bank are not without controversy nor do they have a 100% success rate. They do, however, serve to demonstrate that recession—especially among the larger economies—is recognized as an international, rather than domestic, concern. A downturn in one economy will have an effect on its trading partners everywhere as the decline in purchasing power and production ability ripples from neighbor to neighbor.

POLITICAL FALLOUT

Recession is very much the bugbear of governments because it is taken as a sign of their poor stewardship. History abounds with examples of governments that were toppled (or at least voted out) when the "R-word" was bandied about. Readers should be cautioned to recognize real recession from a simple downturn or, for that matter, recovery. A nation on the upswing can still exhibit unemployment and lowered demand during recovery. Equally true is the fact that all economies experience temporary setbacks that can be quickly corrected if detected early enough and the proper political will is exerted. Observing the duration of the downturn and determining whether current statistics indicate an upward or downward trend will show whether a true recession is present.

Unemployment

In its broadest sense, unemployment is a measure of how many people in an economy who are of suitable age and capable of work are not working. But this is not the way that governments or private industry calculate unemployment figures. Some calculate it based upon how many people "want" to work, while others count part-time work equally with full-time jobs. It is not unusual for calculations to be based upon how many people have formally registered with government offices for unemployment benefits. None of these is accurate.

Some of this inaccuracy stems from the inability to gather comprehensive statistics due to time, money or logistics. Much is unfortunately the end-product of conscious manipulation. Because unemployment has a direct and evident effect upon the population, it is a very sensitive issue for both governments and business leaders alike. Governments are held responsible for the declining economies indicated by increasing unemployment, and businesses are taken to task for not supplying jobs to the populace. Also, as is quite common nowadays, when unemployment hits one nation severely, its population streams across the borders (legally and illegally) to find jobs in the international market. Some nations, like the Philippines, Bangladesh and Mexico, actually count the wages sent home by its overseas workers as a major component of their domestic economy.

MANIPULATING UNEMPLOYMENT

Some governments (like China and Russia) created "universal" employment schemes where people were placed in public sector jobs (state-owned industries), with little or no productive role. As was formerly done in Japan, some private businesses stave off criticism by instituting "lifetime" employment plans, with aging and unproductive employees kept on the payroll though no actual work is done. Still other nations, like France, put forth government mandates to private business that shorten the work week while maintaining the original payscale. By reducing an individual worker's hours, management is forced to hire more staff to maintain production. This artificially increased employment comes at a price that rarely contributes to long-term economic growth.

For economists there are several types of unemployment:

DEMAND DEFICIENCY OR KEYNESIAN UNEMPLOYMENT

This occurs because there is insufficient demand for goods and services in an economy. Governments or business can expand capacity, and thus employment, to cure this problem if funding is available. These new jobs, even makeshift government ones, spur demand among the newly employed. Emerging markets generally suffer from this form of unemployment and regularly seek IMF funding to "jump start" their economies.

CLASSICAL UNEMPLOYMENT

When wages prove too high or labor laws are too restrictive to enable a company to remain productive (profitable) if they hire more people, the labor force will not be fully employed. This is the leading cause of unemployment in western Europe. Wage reductions, labor regulation changes, or increases in productivity by those already employed will enable a company to expand its workforce in these circumstances. Political ramifications of taking these steps are often severe, especially in highly unionized societies.

STRUCTURAL UNEMPLOYMENT

This can occur when workers' skills are inadequate, or when they are located at too great a distance from the job vacancies. This is actually a labor shortage that can be remedied by training, or the physical relocation of either the business or the labor force (e.g., Microsoft's continual shortage of skilled programming engineers has resulted in both an importation of labor to its American headquarters as well as the opening of overseas programming centers).

FRICTIONAL UNEMPLOYMENT

This form occurs with the inefficiencies of connecting skilled employees with companies willing to hire them, or when employees are "between" jobs as they seek out suitable employment to match their skills. These problems are rectified by improving labor exchange mechanisms (job fairs, advertisements) or through a company actively recruiting skilled candidates.

IMPAIRED UNEMPLOYMENT

When potential employees are kept out of the workforce for reasons unrelated to the job itself, such as a lack of child-care, health deficiencies or discrimination, they are considered impaired. Improvements in working conditions and legal penalties for discriminatory behavior remedy this form of unemployment.

UNDEREMPLOYMENT

While technically employed, many people are working in jobs far beneath their educational or skill levels. They may also be only able to find part-time employment. Because these "underemployed" people are not contributing to national or regional productivity in the fullest possible capacity, they are considered to be part of the unemployment problem—at least for economists.

In technologically advanced economies, government officials are often accused of including the underemployed in the fully employed category for political reasons. (Critics deride them for treating these low-skill, low-pay jobs—sometimes called "McJobs" after the fast food giant, McDonald's—as acceptable forms of work. Like "temp" (temporary) jobs for some employees, such work is often used to bridge the period between leaving one full-time, full-capacity job and finding another.) In the emerging Asian markets, many rural workers flocked into the cities to fill the "3D jobs" (dirty, difficult and/or dangerous) of the booming construction industry. Such jobs ceased to be necessary during the economic downturn in that region in the late 1990s. These agrarian-turned-industrial workers are now being "encouraged" to return at much lower wages to the farms they left behind. While suffering a huge drop in wages, they are still counted as fully employed by their respective governments. (Indonesian officials even went so far in their "encouragement" as to raise the train fares to prohibitive rates for those workers seeking to return to Jakarta after having gone home for visits to their former villages during the 1998 Ramadan holiday.) Naturally, all types of governments want to avoid the potential for social disruption (or even coups d'etat) that can be caused by rising unemployment.

Macro- and Micro-Concerns

Macroeconomics and microeconomics are inextricably connected—the former cannot exist without the latter just as the larger is a natural extension of the smaller. Each is the concern of governments, private enterprise and individuals alike, though to differing degrees. Governments tend to concentrate on macro-issues while recognizing the impact on individual workers at the micro-level. These individual workers, who generally focus on issues that rarely go beyond their immediate households, will on occasion (usually during political campaigns) show concern with the larger issues. Caught in the middle, and driving both extremes, is private enterprise. The following three chapters will look at how these three groups fit into the world of international business and economics.

CHAPTER 5

Governments

THE PUBLIC IS A DEBTOR, WHOM NO MAN CAN OBLIGE TO PAY. — DAVID HUME, 1755

THE ENGLISH WORD GOVERNMENT derives from the Latin word *gubernare* meaning "to steer," with many governments and their leaders taking this definition quite literally (e.g., Mao was referred to as the "Great Helmsman," while deficient economies are often deemed "rudderless"). There is little doubt that politics in general and the brand of politics a nation subscribes to in particular can greatly impact economic growth. International clashes of political ideologies such as the Cold War, or politically inspired embargoes such as that used against apartheid-era South Africa can have both macro- and microeconomic effects on a nation. Even internal political and bureaucratic mechanisms can have a direct impact on a nation's international economic standing. This chapter will review the various ways in which governments consciously and unconsciously affect the economic standing of their nations.

Domestic Taxes, Global Ramifications

A tax is a compulsory payment collected from individuals or businesses by a government and it is one of the first rights a government, democratic or otherwise, claims for itself. Governments, like all ancient and modern organizations, need money to perform their functions and taxation is the source of that funding. For many centuries, being a tax collector was one of the most odious and dangerous jobs a person could pursue, as populations rarely saw a connection between taxes and the services rendered by the government. Even today, large nations such as Russia and China have a very difficult time collecting the majority of the taxes owed to them, the net result being a declining infrastructure and inefficient, underpaid bureaucracies prone to accepting bribes.

TAX EVASION INVASION

A nation's domestic tax system can have a very serious impact on its ability to compete internationally. High taxes can even keep a country from being able to hold onto the money made within its borders. The G-7 (Japan, Germany, France, Italy, Great Britain, Canada, the U.S.) has often formulated plans to stop what it calls "international tax evasion," which is defined as the movement of domestically taxable profits into other countries with little or no taxation. Such "tax havens" (though not the only suspect countries involved, Andorra, Austria, Belize, Liechtenstein, Panama, St. Kitts-Nevis and Switzerland have been nicknamed the "T-7") have attracted hundreds of billions of dollars to their banks. The G-7 members, especially those like France and Germany with expensive social programs to finance, feel they have a right to tax any and all monies made within their borders. The G-7 and the EU are both trying to make global tax-evasive maneuvers as illegal as the laundering of drug money. However, as long as companies feel there is no proportional connection between government services rendered and the amount of taxes paid, tax havens will be hard to shut down.

INTERNAL TAXATION SYSTEMS

Internal taxation can take many forms and is used in combination with other forms of taxation:

- DIRECT TAX This tax places the full burden upon the person or company paying the tax, and bars the payer from passing along the cost to others.
- INDIRECT TAX This tax can be passed along to customers or suppliers as part of a pricing structure.
- EXCISE TAX A tax levied on the domestic exchange of goods and services, sometimes called Sales Tax.
- INCOME TAX Personal incomes minus legalized deductions are taxed by national, regional, and local governments in this format. Some governments require that employers collect a large portion of what is owed, prior to issuing pay-minus-taxes to employees. These taxes tend to be proportional to the size of the income, and can be quite complex when attempting to tally a personal tax bill. Some nations, including the United States, are looking at simplified single-percentage "flat taxes" to replace the complex structures.
- VALUE ADDED TAX (VAT) As goods and services move through the distribution chain towards consumers, value is presumably added by each transfer, thus increasing the taxable value of the final sale. This tax is ultimately paid by the end-user.
- EXPENDITURE OR CONSUMPTION TAX These are taxes that are levied on income minus net savings and are used to encourage the population to save rather than spend their incomes. The consumption tax is a form of sales tax that is levied in lieu of any income tax so that the population transfers money to the government only when making purchases.
- INHERITANCE TAX These are special taxes that are levied on the estates of the deceased in order to diminish the wealth that can be transferred from one generation to the next. These taxes occur regardless of whether the estate has increased or decreased in value. Inheritance taxes are considered (like many other taxes) as a means to redistribute wealth in society. The United States is considering revoking all of their inheritance tax structure.
- CAPITAL GAINS TAX When capital assets (e.g., real estate, securities, equipment) are sold for profit, governments often call for a special tax on these "capital gains" above and beyond normal income taxes. These taxes have the greatest impact on the upper classes and serve to redistribute income to lower classes in the form of government-sponsored social benefits. More conservative economists decry capital gains taxes for taking money from savvy investors and putting it in the hands of profligate governments. Economists with more liberal agendas see capital gains taxes as a means to prevent the wealthy from becoming "too" wealthy.

- SOCIAL TAX Beyond the income tax, governments also levy additional taxes to cover the cost of unemployment, retirement or job-related injuries. Such taxes provide for social benefits in excess of those (e.g., health, housing) provided voluntarily by employers. Most governments make social taxes mandatory and compel employers to deduct the taxes directly from employee paychecks, as well as make matching payments to those of employees. As we will see later, the level of such mandatory benefits are a burden to business and thus have a great effect on a nation's or region's ability to attract and retain investment.
- SELF-EMPLOYMENT TAX These are taxes imposed upon entrepreneurs so that they make a contribution to the "social tax" system even when the entrepreneur is a sole proprietor without employees. The rates are generally equivalent to the mandatory benefits rate.
- POLL TAX (derived from *polle* meaning "head") This is a lump-sum tax levied on the citizenry, without regard to individual economic circumstance, exemption, or level of income. The UK's "community charge" during the period 1989 to 1993 was renounced as a "poll" tax, although its exemptions and lower rates for lower incomes defied the true definition. Because a true poll tax must be low enough to be paid by everyone, its ability to raise government revenue is very slight, making such taxes a rarity in modern times.
- LUMP-SUM TAX (a.k.a.-Specific) Some fees collected by a government, like those for a driver's license, may be the same for all regardless of income, though not levied on the population as a whole. Like poll taxes, lump-sum taxes must be very low and just barely cover the cost of providing the service.
- VICE TAX Some activities, such as gambling or the consumption of tobacco or alcohol, are subject to an excise tax much higher than the normal rate. The high rate is seen by some as an attempt to restrict consumption, though it rarely has that effect. (This same format is also used in the EU (European Union) for gasoline in an attempt to reduce the environmental damage caused by internal combustion engines.) Unfortunately, once governments find uses for these taxes they are loath to do anything that will discourage or completely eliminate further consumption.
- AD VALOREM TAX (proportional) Some taxes are levied based on the value of the goods and services under scrutiny. For instance, while a driver's license fee may be the same (lump-sum) for all drivers, the cost of getting license plates (government permission to use the roads) for an automobile is generally based on the value (and sometimes the weight or intended use) of the vehicle. The tax increases in proportion to the value of the goods or services.
- PROGRESSIVE TAX When taxation of income increases in a proportion greater than the actual increase in income, it is said to be progressive.
- REGRESSIVE TAX When the ratio of tax to level-of-income declines as income rises, this is said to be a regressive tax. Lump-sum, vice and poll taxes—regardless of size or intent—impact more heavily upon the poor as a proportion of actual income. Regressive taxes tend to be neither economically or politically sound unless implemented in small increments over a long period (e.g., fuel taxes).

Bonds

A bond is a security that establishes a debtor-creditor relationship between the issuer of the bond and its holder. Bonds usually have a redemption date in excess of one year, and may have either a fixed interest rate or a variable one tied to a financial index (e.g., inflation, prime lending rate). They may be issued by private firms, financial institutions or, as is our concern here, governments. These governments may be at the national, regional or municipal level.

CREDIT RATINGS

Like private citizens, different nations have different credit ratings that call attention to their varying ability to repay their debts. Standard & Poor's and Moody's, both based in the United States, are probably the most famous and widely used of the government rating services. Many national governments, and even some municipal ones, take umbrage at the fact that a private firm of unelected officials with no political oversight is permitted to "rate" a government's credit-worthiness. Nevertheless, they acquiesce to these ratings on a regular basis with the full knowledge that the ability of the nation to compete internationally can be tied to the government's credit rating. Since these bond debts often finance large-scale infrastructure projects like telecom or power systems, a nation's (or municipality's) entire economic future may depend on its ability to attract both domestic and foreign creditors.

The reason that governments sell bonds is simple: tax revenues are insufficient to cover the operating costs of government, which therefore require additional financing. Economists differ on the value and logic of governmental debt, with politicians adding a chorus of concern over how much of the debt is held by foreigners. Governments, like business, must often operate in deficit during a fiscal period; the accumulated deficits form a national debt, the subject of the next section.

National Debt & Interest Payment

For many centuries, governments shunned the idea of creating large amounts of debt through the issuing of bonds, unless it was under very unusual circumstances such as war or natural disaster. It was also true that such bonds were often restricted to being purchased only by the citizenry of the debtor government, somewhat like an interest-bearing form of taxation. All of that has changed, however. While some emerging markets keep foreigners from buying their government's debt, other larger economies encourage it. The United States, for instance, regularly and enthusiastically sells its treasury bonds and, its short-term treasury bills on the international market. (Note: As of 2008, Japan was the largest holder of U.S. treasury securities at US$583 billion, followed closely by China.) While the interest rates on these instruments are not high (about 5% over 30 years) by U.S. standards of return on private investment, they are often much higher than any rate many foreign buyers (e.g., Japan) could hope to get in their domestic market. This purchasing of debt is considered to be almost "risk free" to the buyer in the long-term because of the stability of the U.S. government and the size of its economy. But it is not necessarily "risk free" for the seller of the bonds.

PAST PERFORMANCE PAYS

Of course, if people are voluntarily investing in overseas government projects, then they are diverting investment from the private sector in their own domestic market. Governments must make themselves look attractive to potential investors when being compared to private industry. A good history of repaying bond debt leads to further sales, but not all nations have such a history. Defaulting on government bonds is not out of the question, as some South and Central American nations demonstrated in the 1980s and Russia did in 1999. Interest, as well as the principal, must be paid on the debt and governments—even the most stable—rarely if ever produce what could be seen as operating profits that could be used to service the debt. So where does the interest come from, and how is the principal of the debt utilized? What is the effect on a nation's position in the global economy if the debt is well utilized, or, alternately, poorly distributed?

GENERATING MONEY

Governments—at least those with legitimate ends—solicit international debt for the purposes of either improving their physical infrastructure (including equipment) or enhancing the employability of their population. This internal investment is the long-term means by which to repay the loans with interest. Enhanced infrastructure and an educated population lead to new private investment (domestic and foreign) and/or the expansion of the already existing economic structure. These new businesses, expanded businesses and well-paid employees can be taxed over the long term to enable the country to repay the debt. Like private sector indebtedness, government debt is an investment in the future earnings of the society. It should be noted, however, that unlike private industry, governments can set, increase and rigorously collect their "return" in the form of taxes as well as control the means of payment (currency printing) without undo fear of competition.

KEEPING BALANCED

Internationally, a government's ability to wisely invest in both its physical and human resources makes it ultimately either an economic leader or a follower. One set of resources pursued to the detriment of the other will not suffice. For instance, Vietnam has one of the highest literacy rates in the world (95%+) yet its physical infrastructure is so deteriorated as to keep it primarily an agricultural nation with a struggling economy. Italy, on the other hand, constantly finds itself lagging in the European market, behind Germany, France and the United Kingdom, due to its lack of widespread modern human resource skills (accountancy, programming). This occurs in spite of Italy's relatively up-to-date infrastructure. Other nations, like the Czech Republic, invest heavily in education and produce high test scores to substantiate the investment. However, the rigidity of the training system blocks the innovative skills necessary to produce marketable employees, especially managers, for a 21st century economy. All governments are now recognizing that the amount spent, where it is spent and how it is spent are all of equal importance. Balance is everything on the tightrope of global economics.

Military Expenditures

Even a brief inspection of a nation's expenditure of its taxes and loans will reveal that everything is not devoted to infrastructure and training. A key part of a country's status as a "nation-state" is its sovereignty over its physical territory, and its ability to protect its population from harm both domestic and foreign. This protective role takes the form of a national military force as well as a local constabulary (see below). It may be the citizen-army favored by the Swiss or a large standing military force like that in China. It may be the local policing of a county sheriff or a national police force like the Canadian Mounted Police. Many nations have a component to their security forces devoted exclusively to international concerns, with the America's CIA, Britain's MI5 and the former Soviet Union's KGB being the most famous. Even more global is INTERPOL and its devotion to cross-border criminal activity.

PAID PROTECTION

It is an economic reality that every government must be able to protect its citizenry and their assets. Such protection is paid for by taxes and debt with the same sense of the stewardship of the national economy as pertains to education and infrastructure. But few if any nations stand alone. In the modern world, national security is accomplished through a combination of sovereign military power coupled with an elaborate set of military alliances that center around joint economic interests. From medieval times, when border-sharing neighbors agreed to come to each other's aid when third parties attacked, military alliances nowadays wrap around the globe to link nations with thousands of miles separating their borders. Why does the United States pledge to come to the aid of Japan or Canada help to defend Germany, and why would Australian naval ships be put on the line for Kuwaiti interests? The answer is economics in general and trade specifically.

COMMERCIAL PROTECTION

Part of a nation's duty, and a good deal of its expenditure, is the protection of its citizens' right to conduct domestic business and international trade. As individual nations become more dependent on other countries for raw materials (oil), finished goods (trucks) or markets (places to sell oil and trucks), the need to protect trading lanes (air, land or sea) looms large. Equally in need of protection is a nation's ability to pay for goods and services. Such ability can be greatly diminished by armed conflict. Contrary to popular belief, wars are not major money makers for a cabal of big industrialists. Even arms dealers soon find out that nations at war operate dysfunctional economies that have little cash flow. Selling arms, chemicals and construction materials is much more lucrative during peacetime because buyers can actually pay. Post-war nations are, though seemingly ripe for the rebuilding of infrastructure, equally impecunious. Even the victors find that the price paid can be excessive, especially when the defeated have little left to confiscate. (Britain was so devastated by its "victory" over the Axis powers in 1945 that it had to maintain food rationing until 1954. It could only console itself with the knowledge that Germany and Japan were worse off.)

AVOIDING DISRUPTION

Because governments have come to realize that the scope of modern military conflict can devastate both domestic and international trade very quickly, such conflicts are commenced only after great diplomatic efforts fail. Using the 1991 Gulf War as an example, allied forces (paid for with joint funding) went to great extremes to allow Iraqi forces to withdraw from disputed areas in lieu of battle. Once forces were engaged, however, the war was prosecuted with deliberate speed with virtually all human and economic loss being confined to the losing side, Iraq. Iraq's defeat, loss of sovereignty and subsequent economic plummet show a clear link between conflict and its effect on a national economy. Even for the allies who experienced little direct damage, the billions of dollars, pounds and yen that were devoted to the conflict could have been invested elsewhere. But maybe not more productively given the circumstances.

THE LUBRICANT OF WAR

Cynical as it may seem, few serious observers believe the Gulf War was fought to prevent the killing of Kuwaiti citizens. As is the case in the vast majority of international conflicts, it was fought to protect economic interests, specifically, the free flow of petroleum from the Middle East. Similarly, Hitler's European expansion was a search for economic advancement, just as Japan's expansion into Asia was in the 1930s. America's revolution against Britain was over who would control the vast potential wealth of the colonies, just as the Battle of Agincourt (1415) was fought by the British and the French for the assets of Normandy. Even smaller conflicts such as the "ethnic cleansing" in the former Yugoslavia or the tribal wars in Rwanda are, at their base, fought over which group will control what assets. So close and highly recognized is the link between conflict and economic interest that when the United States sent a diplomatic mission in 1995 to Bosnia during a lull in the ethnic fighting, a major component of the contingent consisted of a group of private sector economic advisors. Their goal: help re-establish the local economy on an equitable basis to prevent further conflict. Ethnicity may have been a rallying cry for Bosnian combatants, but the base of the conflict (as in 1999 Serbia) was the control of assets.

CAN GUNS CHURN BUTTER?

Global alliances and huge military budgets draw a great deal of criticism, especially from poorer nations. The emotion-laden question is always, "How can we spend money on weapons when so many people are barely subsisting?" Societies have always had some form of this "guns versus butter" debate, though no government has totally disarmed. Some spend very little on their military, either in the belief that no conflict is imminent (Sweden) or because they are bound by domestic laws that limit such expenditures to a percentage of total GDP (Japan). Some economies (China, France, United States) use the sale of military goods to other countries as a major boost to their economy, and to a great extent encourage their allies to arm themselves to the teeth.

Manufacture of weaponry is today a major component of international private sector trade. Allies no longer just rely on each other's troops but allow the principles of absolute and comparative advantage to dictate how much and what they will buy from each other. All nations are now participants in the "military-industrial complex" that was once only the concern of America's post-WWII boom period. While military trade is either directly controlled or at least regulated by the government, we will see in the upcoming section on nationalization that it is only one of many industries with close government connections.

Black Markets, Black Economies and Organized Crime

A different kind of security issue is the presence in every society of some form of illegal trade, known as the "black economy." This is a blanket term for businesses that evade the payment of taxes, the use of licenses, social benefit deductions like Social Security, or the hiring of legal workers. The term "black market" denotes a less benign form of illegal trade usually set up to purposely evade government-established rationing or price controls put in place during periods of war or catastrophe. All of these illegal activities require policing, and that entails expenditure. When policing is slack, legitimate businesses suffer because their prices can be undercut by less scrupulous competitors. Stringent enforcement policies and "zero tolerance" programs are very expensive, thus requiring tax increases on legitimate businesses and citizens. Neither extreme is attractive to business owners or the economy in general. Consequently, all governments allow a tolerable degree of violation to go unchecked and unpunished, thus creating what is called the "grey market." Each nation has its own level of tolerance, and often that level of tolerance can affect the ability to attract foreign investment to governmental or private sector projects. The level of bribery and "under the table" business activity in many Middle Eastern and Asian countries, though considered common practice regionally, tends to stem the flow of investment from Western nations. In the West (especially the United States) business people are often bound by their domestic law from participating in such practices.

GOVERNMENTS LOSE CONTROL

Full-scale black marketeering can have more far-reaching effects, as it moves from common commodities into currency speculation. Governments can easily lose control of the market value of the currency, and therefore their international status, as the population moves to the black market in search of better deals. Each revaluation by the government is outmatched by the black market, until value has spun out of control. This happened to the Russian ruble in the months after the collapse of the U.S.S.R. to such an extent that the U.S. dollar became the de facto currency until the government could regain control. During this period, Russian importers and foreign companies based in Russia had a difficult time paying for goods and services from abroad since little "hard currency" was available as the population hoarded everything but rubles.

Even by 2008, very few people outside of Russia accept the ruble as payment without argument. Interestingly, neither China nor Vietnam has yet to "float" their currencies (the renminbi and the dong, respectively) against international currencies, primarily out of fear that both legitimate and black-market speculators will revalue them to the detriment of the governments. It should also be noted that currency speculation of all types was considered an offense worthy of the death penalty in many countries up until the 1950s.

ORGANIZING CRIME

In most countries, organized crime is treated as a local issue even when the organization is nationwide. The reality is that many such organizations are indeed international, and they can easily affect an entire national economy and its global status. Two examples bear this out. Colombia has an international reputation for selling two commodities: coffee and cocaine. Billions of dollars of each are sold worldwide, and yet the Colombian economy is hardly an attractive one for either its citizens or to foreign investors. Now saddled with one of the highest cocaine usage rates in the world (not all is exported), Colombia sees little of the billions of dollars brought in by its illicit trade and export. The profits have been spread globally to support other criminal activity, but Colombia retains all of the illicit trade's fallout in terms of political corruption, a stagnated economy, rising medical costs and related domestic crime. Half-hearted attempts to get coca leaf farmers to change their crop have had little success, and local government complicity in the illegal trade is well known if not openly acknowledged. Very few if any sectors of the economy or the citizenry are unscathed by this criminal activity. This is clearly a local problem with global connections.

CRIME GAINS CONTROL

On the other side of the world, in Russia, it is estimated that over 65% of all business is connected in some way to the country's criminal underground, the "mafiya." Once just a small and deeply submerged part of the Soviet economy, it has risen in the post-communist period to lofty and violent heights. Brazen daylight kidnappings and murders are now common occurrences and foreign businesspeople are not immune. The strong-arm tactics of the "protection" racket have sent a chill through the foreign investment community that only increased the revenues of bodyguard companies. The effect on the Russian economy is equally chilling, as even its domestic investors seek "safer" havens elsewhere, notably in Cyprus. Although it has a host of other problems, there is little doubt that the level of organized crime in Russia has contributed to its being ranked at the bottom of the industrialized nations for both competitiveness and investment potential. Only its "renationalized" petroleum and natural gas industry has saved the country from going under. In the cases of both Colombia and Russia, government laxity or even outright complicity in regards to organized crime has sharpened the effects of other deficiencies in the economy. All governments must deal with a degree of criminal activity, but it is the degree of efficiency in dealing with the problem that can separate globally successful economies from failures.

Nationalization, Expropriation, Domestication and Freezing

Governments everywhere seek to control the businesses that operate within their borders and sometimes even some firms that function externally. What varies from country to country is the degree of this control. Socialist governments seek total control and ownership of every business entity. At the other extreme are nations with a more laissez-faire attitude that own only those businesses considered "strategic" to the welfare or security of the country. The movement worldwide is towards less government control as populations have decided that the private sector is more efficient than government at generating wealth. Distribution of that wealth, however, is another matter entirely.

In this atmosphere, even communist-led governments like China are actively seeking to shed their state-owned industries. (Note: The Chinese government celebrated the traditional Workers' Day recently by asking its state-owned-enterprise employees to graciously accept the upcoming widescale layoffs—firings—for "the good of the country.") Meanwhile, democracies like Great Britain continue to expand their policy of regulation rather than ownership. Even though government seems to be getting out of the business of business, global investors still put "political risk" at the top of the list of concerns when looking at international projects. The reason for this is the historical precedent set by many governments of seizing businesses, both domestic and foreign owned, during periods of political crisis. They do so by several methods and not always when confronted with a true crisis.

NATIONALIZATION AND EXPROPRIATION

Nationalization occurs when a government transfers to itself the ownership of the assets of a private company operating within its borders. As long as "fair compensation" is paid for the assets, such a transfer is considered legal, even if the company protests every other aspect of the transfer. Of course, the concept of "fair compensation" is rife with the potential for political interpretation. *Expropriation* is essentially the same type of asset transfer as nationalization, but it lacks either fair compensation or compensation of any type. The revolutionary governments of Central and South America were infamous for their "liberation" of foreign assets (usually U.S.-owned) during the 1960s and 1970s. (The U.S.S.R., China, Vietnam, Cuba and other communist regimes took control of virtually all private businesses within their borders immediately upon seizing power, although the term "expropriation" was not used; these companies were "liberated.")

SELECTIVE NATIONALIZATION

The socialist-oriented labor government in post-WWII Great Britain also nationalized some major industries, such as the coal mines, which remained under government control until the "Thatcherite denationalization" of the 1980s. Britain's petroleum industry is still under government ownership and is one of the main sticking points in Scotland's bid for independence, since the North Sea oil fields would suddenly be under Scottish control. (Note: The U.K.'s control of the oil business actually predates the socialist labor governments of 1945. Winston Churchill, hardly a socialist, insisted that the government purchase a controlling stake in British Petroleum in 1911 when he was first lord of the admiralty. His reason: national security and the needs of the royal navy.) Even the United States, the bulwark of regulatory capitalism (oversight rather than ownership of industry), owns some businesses such as local mail delivery; it also subsidizes several others (railways, agriculture, aerospace).

DOMESTIC ACTION, GLOBAL REACTION

In today's "small government" atmosphere, few politicians, except those at the extremes, are willing to call for either nationalization or expropriation of foreign assets. Such actions by a modern government would result in an immediate downturn in foreign investment, as well as a downgrading of the nation's bond and credit rating. The effect on the domestic stock market and foreign exchange would also be one of devaluation. Governments seeking to take control of foreign businesses working within their borders now use a more subtle, less headline-grabbing method: domestication.

Domestication can be defined as the transfer of foreign assets incrementally to domestic private ownership, either through direct government intervention or behind-the-scenes regulatory pressure. Domestication usually takes place in less economically developed societies that have either a great fear of economic colonization or a loss of national pride. Greed is also not to be ruled out as a motivator. Foreign companies, especially those with desirable technologies or profit margins, can suddenly find that the government has supplied them with either a new local partner, or it has changed the status of the local partner already in place. The local partner, regardless of their investment percentage, may be given veto power on the board of directors, or simply have their investment (land, facilities) "revalued" by the government until it becomes a majority stake. The foreign firm has virtually no recourse in the court system since the domestication is legal by local standard.

DRIVING OUT THE FOREIGNERS

Another method of domestication is for a government to wait until the foreign firm has made a sizeable investment in the business before passing restrictive regulations or taxes on the operation. This can drive foreign firms to "cut their losses," leaving behind assets and processes to be scooped up by local firms at a discount. Vietnam's nascent manufacturing industry has seen the deleterious effects of this method of domestication. Once again, the courts can be of little help. A lack of stable legal protection for foreign companies is characteristic of emerging markets and can be a major stumbling block to economic development. It should be noted, however, that even highly developed nations such as France have used their legal system to force foreign companies out of local competition or joint ventures (e.g., aerospace, agriculture) when national pride or union jobs were thought to be at stake.

CROSS-BORDER CONTROLS

Another method used by domestic governments to control foreign companies and their respective governments is to freeze their assets. In this process a national government prevents a foreign company or a foreign government from gaining access to the assets kept inside of its national borders. This may be for political, ideological or legal reasons but the economic effect is the same regardless. The most common, or at least the most highly publicized, user of this technique is the United States. It can use this form of international economic control simply because it has the unusual distinction of having most, if not all, of its ideological adversaries as investors in American industry or depositors in U.S. banks. When Islamic fundamentalists in Iran overthrew the U.S.-supported shah in 1979 and later seized American hostages, considerable Iranian assets were "frozen" in U.S. banks at the direction of Washington as punishment. Many of these assets remain frozen to this day.

During periods of turmoil, as in central Africa or eastern Europe, the United States and its allies will place a freeze on the assets of the warring parties until clear legal ownership is established. No country, including the economically powerful United States, will invoke a freeze casually since the ramifications for its own overseas businesses and investments can be severe. Like nationalization, expropriation and domestication, the freezing of assets remains a powerful but blunt instrument in an international economy that, more often than not, requires an increasing level of finesse.

Foreign Investment

All governments are concerned about money leaving their country (capital outflow), but they are equally concerned about the quality, intent and origin of the investment that flows into their economy. One would think that if the source and intent of the foreign investment were legitimate, then a government would have no objections. Yet, an increasing number do raise objections via regulation. This apprehension is especially evident in developing markets where hard-learned lessons regarding short-term foreign investment have taken a toll.

CURRENT ACCOUNT BALANCE

The net inflow or outflow of capital is referred to as a nation's *current account*. Nations utilizing more foreign than domestic investment maintain current account deficits, while those that lend more than borrow have current account surpluses. These two categories do not necessarily correspond directly to the level of domestic savings (available domestic capital), as one might think. The movement of investment across borders (capital mobility) would, at least on the surface, seem to flow from nations with high savings rates to those with low rates. Spendthrifts would have large deficits as a percentage of GDP, while savers would have equally large surpluses. Alas, the statistics do not bear this out. The arch-consumer, America, only averages current account deficits of around 2% annually, just as fellow spendthrift, the United Kingdom, averages less than 1%. Japan, a top saver, runs between 1-2% current account surpluses while Germany, with relatively high national savings (approximately 21%), actually runs slightly less than 1% current account deficits. Plainly, other factors are at work.

SLOW CAPITAL FLOW

In the modern technological world, capital, in the form of money, moves electronically, but such speed of transfer does not necessarily imply frequency. Factors such as the exchange rate, financial risk assessment, political activity, legal guarantees and government regulation (of both inflows and outflows) can prevent the free movement of investment across borders. The decision-making process takes far longer than the actual transfer of funds. While it is certainly true that global investment has increased in recent decades (six-fold into the emerging markets in recent decades), it is nowhere near the levels supposed by the alarmist media. Nor is increased capital flow responsible for the seeming instability of some of the world's markets, as claimed by fretting politicians. Economists have laid the blame for the instability upon a lack of bank regulation, exchange rate inflexibility, insider deals and a lack of information available to investors (these topics will be discussed later). Rather than being erratic, capital flows somewhat cautiously into a promising market, and back out again when warranted.

THE CHILEAN INVESTMENT MODEL

Some national governments have taken a very aggressive approach to foreign investment, with Chile serving as a fine example of this "take charge" format. Chile, unlike many emerging markets across the Pacific in Asia, actually attempts to discourage short-term foreign investment by requiring that 30% of the money borrowed from abroad be put into a non-interest bearing (for the depositor) account for one year at Chile's central bank. This "tax" on investment (the government gets the interest and use of the funds during the account's duration) prevents the hit-and-run type of investment that plagued much of Latin America during the 1970s. Chile's regulations require a firm commitment to its economy, and prevents foreign investment from making a quick departure after taking advantage of low labor or property rates. Rapid inflows and outflows of capital can destabilize developing economies literally overnight. In fact, despite Chile's regulation and relatively steady growth (6%+), economists disagree over the direct impact of such investment controls. Many believe that it is the strength of financial institutions and general firmness of policy that dictate the impact of capital flows.

MAINTAINING FOREIGN INVESTMENT

There are some points on which all economists agree when it comes to attracting and maintaining foreign investment:

- TRANSPARENCY - Financial markets thrive on reliable information that flows in a steady stream. This is often referred to as "transparency" and its absence during the investment process can greatly limit the attention span of foreign investors (especially U.S. investors who prefer extensive due diligence).
- OPEN FINANCIAL MARKETS - Domestic financial systems must be released from direct government control and insider trading. Much of southeast Asia's problems in 1997 can be traced to private sector bank loans granted at the behest of government to favored companies. Even Japan's mighty MITI (Ministry of International Trade and Investment) has been severely chided for its once revered investment policies and directives to private industry.
- RULE OF LAW - Once banking has been released from government directives, economists still see a need for regulation, with legal recourse for both the foreign investor and domestic investee. Chile's policies prevent dramatic changes in the flow of investment while Taiwan has remained largely immune from the current Asian downturn due to its stricter banking procedures and more open financial system. Contrasted with Indonesia, where the deposed president's family controlled banking and investment alike, nations without extensive cronyism remain much more stable during periods of economic downturn.
- FLEXIBLE EXCHANGE RATES - Either a flexible currency exchange rate or one that is "pegged" to a hard currency via an independent currency board (as in Hong Kong) is generally considered to be another requisite for economic stability. Flexible exchange rates allow a nation's central bank to adjust interest rates (see "Central Banks and Currency Control" below) to prevent an economy from expanding too rapidly ("overheating"), since high interest rates on domestic

lending can inflate the currency's value. Meanwhile, currency boards, if implemented during stable periods, force a country to match its currency with an prescribed amount of foreign hard currency thus enforcing stability. Both systems prevent the kind of exchange rate uncertainty that can cause the flight of foreign investment, as happened to Mexico in the 1980s and Thailand in the 1990s.

Central Banks and Currency Control

A central bank is the institution that controls a nation's money supply and oversees national monetary policy. In some countries, it is also the bank that controls the operations of all other banks operating within the national borders. Political influence over a central bank is the subject of some contention. The United States makes an effort to immunize its central bank, the Federal Reserve, from political influence by making it difficult for politicians to dismiss its officials, who are appointed for lengthy terms. France, on the other hand, believes that politics and central banking are a good and desirable mix. It has even pressed this view upon the EU. (France has insisted that the current 8-year term of the EU's Central Bank presidency being served by the decidedly apolitical Dutchman, Wim Duisenberg, be cut by half so that a more politically sensitive French representative can be placed in his stead after four years.) Unlike the United States, where "the Fed" makes its decisions based primarily on economic data, France (and presumably, soon, the EU) puts greater weight on political fallout (e.g., labor union reactions, social strife) when setting monetary policy. It should be pointed out that those systems with the greatest political influence over monetary policy (e.g. Indonesia, Nigeria, Russia) are decidedly less nimble at resolving economic issues.

INTERESTING RATES

Monetary policy is the use by a government, usually via the central bank, of *interest rates* and the supply of money to influence economic growth and stability. Interest rates are the cost of borrowing money. These rates for interest are set by a central bank and, as such, are taken as a sign of the government's attitude toward the economy. This in turn will affect private sector lending rates. High rates make borrowing expensive, thereby restraining new investment and slowing growth. Low rates, conversely, encourage investment and spur the economy. Central banks, like the Deutsche Bundesbank, the Bank of England or the Federal Reserve, have not only great influence over their own economies but the international economy as well. This is not simply because their currencies are used worldwide.

Borrowing and lending also take place internationally with everyone seeking the most favorable rate for their respective endeavor. (When the interest required by a foreign lender is lower than can be found in the borrower's domestic market, capital moves across borders from foreign lender to domestic borrower.) Reverse movements of capital occur when the borrower's market drops its interest rates below that of its neighbors. Keep in mind that banks, both private and state-owned, lend out depositor's money so that the high interest rates paid by borrowers is reflected in higher interest paid out to those depositors. (Example: Country B may have members of its population that borrow heavily from country

A at low interest, while citizens of A might move their cash into country B's banks because they pay high interest. Country B's interest rates will be driven down as deposits swell and its banks are compelled to lend at more favorable rates. Rates will seesaw back and forth attempting to reach equilibrium.)

Money Talks

Favorable interest rates, coupled with a stable currency, make for a very attractive international economy. Money flows back and forth across borders, based primarily upon these factors. However, economists and governments have several definitions of what constitutes "money" and its supply in the economy. Below are the definitions used by Great Britain, although each country is apt to define money in various "broader" or "narrower" terms as suits their needs:

- M0 Includes currency notes and coins in circulation as well as that kept in balances at both the central bank and private banks.
- M1 This measure includes M0 plus any bank deposit accounts that may be transferable by check such as savings accounts or other demand deposits.
- M2 This is also called broad money and constitutes M0 plus non-interest-bearing bank deposits and deposits in national savings accounts.
- M3, M4, M5 These measures include M1, plus an ever changing variety of specialized bank deposits and other financial instruments that come upon the economic scene.
- EUROCURRENCY Originally, this was any currency held in a European country other than in the issuing nation, though not necessarily European in origin (e.g., euro-dollars, euro-yen, euro-pounds). It is now used to denote any currency held outside of the issuing nation's borders anywhere in the world. For instance, well over 35% of U.S. currency is held overseas, but even those dollars held in Japan are called euro-dollars. And, yes, now there are even euro-euros.
- LEGAL TENDER These are the notes (bank notes) and coins that are created and circulated by the government that must be accepted as payment. They may or may not have intrinsic value (gold and silver coins) or be redeemable for precious metals (silver certificates).
- LIQUID SECURITIES This covers a wide variety of other government-issued documents like postage stamps, postal orders, military scrip and even state-issued IOUs that can transfer value. They are usually considered in aggregate and can be a sizeable percentage of a national economy.
- FIAT MONEY This covers all forms of notes, coins or documents that governments issue and value by edict. Most modern currency has a value, set and guaranteed by governments, with no intrinsic value set in the currency or coins. (A single British pound is worth a pound because the British government says so and can guarantee that value.) Because money now moves internationally and even domestically via electronic means rather than physical exchanges of bills, the "fiat" (authorization for payment) now covers these computer transactions (digital fiat). Unstable economies have a "declared" value for money set by government and a "real" value set by international markets. During severe

instability, currencies from more stable economies can become de facto currencies for struggling economies. Loss of the monetary fiat usually presages political upheaval as populations lose faith in their governments.

Global Exchange Rates

The value of one currency measured against that of another currency is known as the *exchange rate*. Governments have become increasingly concerned about who controls the value of their currency on the international scene since their "fiat" does not necessarily extend across borders. Incidences of massive currency devaluation in the 1990s were not just confined to Asia. In 1992, Great Britain fought a desperate but futile battle to maintain the pound's value internationally. This sent chills through other EU nations, as the UK had to withdraw from the exchange rate mechanism that had been put in place as part of the European Monetary System to protect member currencies.

A government may set the value of their currency domestically, but it must convince other governments and a host of other global players that the value is correct. As mentioned earlier, some governments "peg" the value of their currency to that of a more stable economy like the United States. Hong Kong has set its currency value based upon the U.S. dollar for decades; it is even denoted as the Hong Kong dollar. It has remained within a few points of the HK$7.70 : US$1 ratio even after China's takeover of the territory in 1997. Hong Kong prints and coins cash, via their currency board, based upon that ratio while holding U.S. money in reserve proportionally equal to the currency issued. They are counting on the U.S. economy remaining stable.

THE FLOATING WORLD

Other governments float their currency on the open market and allow the marketplace to determine actual value. These currencies are convertible when exchanged for other floated currencies. The same U.S. dollar that Hong Kong uses for its peg has no backing in gold (not since 1971) or other metal. Instead, it reflects in market terms the value of the entire American economy. The U.S. dollar is considered fully convertible, since it may be exchanged by any holder for any purpose. Other currencies, like the Taiwan dollar, are partially convertible because the Taipei government restricts the cross-border use of its currency. This is done to protect the level of investment flow in Taiwan, and is also referred to as *current account convertibility*. Still other nations, such as China, have different exchange rates for different domestic activities, as foreign companies find out when they attempt to repatriate profits. The rate for repatriating profits essentially cuts the value of the exchange by half, thereby guaranteeing that foreign investment in China stays put. The Chinese *yuan* (or *renminbi*) is rarely, if ever, used externally. Finally, some countries have a currency value that has been set by their government at a rate far in excess of (or less than) what the market value would be if floated. These currencies, like the Vietnamese *dong*, function only inside of the nation's borders where the value of foreign exchange is arbitrarily set for visitors.

KEEPING AN EYE ON SPECULATORS

Currency speculation is the open market trading of national currencies based upon projected changes in value caused by economic or political forces or the speculation itself (e.g., demand for the currency). While government central banks engage in currency exchange with other central banks, currency speculation is for the most part a completely unregulated market that, at a brisk US$2 trillion per day, is the world's largest. Many banks make more money from their currency arbitrage (simultaneous exchanges in various markets to exploit value differences and time lags), than they do from their commercial loans. The size and lack of governmental oversight, combined with the 7-days-a-week, 24-hours-a-day nature of the speculation, have made such activity very controversial.

Some private speculators like George Soros (who made US$1 billion in profit in one month betting against the ability of the British government to defend the value of the pound sterling in 1992) have become global economic powers unto themselves. Reviled by the Malaysian government on one hand for allegedly driving down the value of the *ringgit*, Soros has achieved hero-status in Moscow for coming to the aid of the Russian economy. Soros has also been known to openly criticize the policies of central bank governors, which many view as warning shots of vigorous speculation to come, as his views often outweigh those of government officials. While private speculators like Soros and international banks can make or lose fortunes, governments are hard pressed to find a way to regulate currency speculation and maintain their individual fiats.

TOO PROUD TO PEG

Like taxation and maintaining an army, one of the activities a government reserves for itself is the issuing of money as a mark of its sovereignty. A nation and its citizens put a great deal of pride into having a strong national currency. Every nation uses coins and notes alike to depict its heroes, national treasures and accomplishments. This currency pride is not just harmless show, and it can greatly affect the domestic and international economy. The back and forth exchange rates of the world's two largest economies, the United States and Japan, are prime examples of this effect.

Immediately after WWII, the U.S. military oversaw every aspect of the destroyed Japanese economy, including the setting of the value of the Japanese *yen.* Two U.S. military officers very arbitrarily set the value at 360 yen per US dollar, based upon the 360 degree points in Japan's national symbol, the rising sun. The psychological impact of the rise of the yen against the U.S. dollar over the ensuing decades affected both economies. When the yen broke the 100 yen-to-the-dollar mark in the early 1990s, many believed that it signalled the end of American economic primacy: Japan had responded to the arrogance of those two American officers. Tokyo fought hard to maintain this exchange rate (it even strengthened to 88 yen per dollar), even when it became clear that the strong yen was hurting its ability to export and increasing the position of its rival across the Pacific.

ZERO PRIDE

Pride in the national currency and its effect on the population was also behind Russia's 1998 redenomination of the ruble. By lopping off three zeroes from every denomination (10,000 rubles became 10 but with the same buying power as before), the Russian government was relieving its people of the absurd exchange rates that plague other nations like Romania (14,900:US$1), Ecuador (8,700:US$1) and Vietnam (13,900:US$1). Exchanging at these rates generally signals a laggard economy, with only Italy and the much besieged South Korea counted among the developed nations exchanging in the thousands against the dollar. Italy's adoption of the Euro not only integrated it fully into the European Union, but finally put it on an equal currency footing with its neighbors who have long considered it a lesser among equals. The boost for Italian pride was enormous. Zimbabwe may have set the record in 2008 when it deleted six zeroes from its currency. Of course, its inflation rate at the time was just over 100,000%—and rising.

BAND TRADING

Many economies have adopted what is known as band trading, which permits their currency to be valued within a narrow range set by the government. There are two types of band trading being utilized today with varying degrees of success. The first model is fully internal and requires a currency board to peg the domestic currency to a stable "hard" currency (usually the U.S. dollar, although some African nations have used the euro). Once pegged, the board permits the local currency to fluctuate only within a narrow band in response to economic trends. Currency boards require political neutrality, as well as extensive reserves of the hard currency used for the peg. This system has worked well in Hong Kong for many years and was briefly proposed as the new model for the Indonesian economy when its economy took a nosedive in 1997. (Unfortunately for Indonesia, political will and hard currency reserves were deemed to be in too short supply. Malaysia, however, did opt for pegging and banding.)

MECHANISM SCHISM

The other format was used by the European Union as it made its way toward full use of the Euro currency (formerly the Ecu) for all of its members. In 1979, the Exchange Rate Mechanism (ERM) was established among the European Union members (minus the United Kingdom, which both joined and departed the ERM in the 1990s). The ERM limited the value of its members' currencies to 2.25% on either side of a central rate (some nations were given a wider band of 6%). The mechanism worked with only sporadic efficiency, causing recurring devaluations by France and Spain. The major speculation and devaluation that drove out the U.K. in 1992 also spurred the remaining members to expand the band to 15%. Though far from smooth in implementation, the ERM permitted the EU's membership (without Denmark, the United Kingdom, and Sweden) to combine their currencies and their economies for full integration in 2002. New members of the expanded EU observe a similar banding until they are deemed stable enough to become part of the "eurozone" currency club. A similar ERM format and a single currency have also been bandied about by ASEAN nations to decrease their dependence on Western currencies.

Foreign Reservations and Debt Doubt

As Europe moves toward a single currency and Asian nations consider similar integration, some economists have proposed a "world currency," while others say it already exists in the form of the US dollar. The reasons for this latter theory are elucidated by the following facts:

- Close to 50% of global bank deposits are denominated in U.S. dollars
- Half of all international trade is invoiced in U.S. dollars
- Over 45% of international bond issues are denominated in U.S. dollars
- Almost half of all foreign exchange transactions involve the U.S. dollar
- Over 60% of the world's non-gold reserves are denominated in U.S. dollars
- "Petro-dollars" remain the currency of choice for petroleum purchases.

THE SENIOR CURRENCY

This dominance by American currency has been a boon to the U.S. government. Washington receives 0.5% of its GDP in seignorage (the profit a government receives on issuing money) on those overseas dollars. However beneficial it may be for the Americans, it is a point of major concern for other nations. Governments keep large reserves of convertible foreign currency (and gold) on hand to protect the value of their own currency in the event of a major challenge by speculators. A government will, if its fiat is challenged, literally use these reserves to buy its own currency on the international market to protect the demand portion of the supply-demand-price relationship.

China, whose massive economy has a virtually inconvertible currency, maintains the world's largest reserves with over US$1 trillion on hand (Japan has slightly less). Similar to most countries with weak currencies, China must use its reserves for the day-to-day purchasing of imports, as well as long-term currency protection. Many countries have even begun to sell off their gold reserves (Brazil sold all of theirs in 1997, while the United Kingdom sold off 300 tons in 1999) in favor of holding reserves in hard foreign currency notes. Many countries have moved the majority of their reserves from dollars into "strengthening" euros.

A DEBTOR WITH CLOUT

Much of the concern regarding the U.S. position has derived from the amount of international borrowing that America does. It is currently the world's largest debtor nation. The dilemma for the rest of the world is that the United States incurs most of its debt in its own currency (those Eurodollars sometimes get called home)—the same currency over which it maintains a great deal of value control. America's creditors find themselves in the unenviable position of having a debtor that can control the value of the loan. In today's market, the U.S. dollar is still one of the strongest, hardest currencies and is much sought after for its guarantee of purchasing power. As long as it stays that way, America's creditors holding dollar-denominated debt will continue to invest and lend in the U.S. market in U.S. dollars. Some, like China, keep buying U.S. debt to protect the value of their own currency.

Purchasing Power Parity

Purchasing Power Parity (PPP) is an economic theory that claims that the exchange rate of currencies between two nations is in equilibrium when each currency's buying power is equal within their respective markets. This parity takes the measure of the entire national economy, not just in terms of total GDP. Instead, PPP looks at how much buying power each currency has in their respective local market. It works on the theory that similar goods purchased in different societies should cost the same, barring the influence of tariffs. For instance, the average GDP per person in actual monetary terms in China is far less than someone in Germany or the United States.

However, when total GDP is calculated on the basis of the internal purchasing power of a similar set of goods (e.g., housing, groceries) the story changes. Now, China ranks second in the world, while Germany takes fourth place, all relative to the United States which remains dominant in both real and relative GDP ratings. These figures show how PPP works and how exchange rates may not truly reflect living standards. They do not, however, change the fact that the majority of people in Germany and the United States are much better off than the average Chinese citizen. This is due to the fact that incomes in Germany and the United States are much more evenly distributed, with each of the two nations having a large middle class. China, for its part, has concentrations of wealth in the major coastal cities, a negligible middle class by global standards, and a primarily agrarian economy marked by subsistence in most of its territory. Purchasing parity or not, China is still a very poor nation, but making quick progress.

BURGERS AND BURGHERS

The UK's *Economist* magazine (they like calling it a newspaper) has developed its own system of figuring purchasing parity. Not content in using housing costs or grocery purchases, the editors use what they consider to be a near-universal product: the McDonald's Big Mac. Not only is the sandwich served worldwide, but it is exactly the same everywhere, whereas housing and groceries may not be. When the "Big Mac Index" (as the magazine lightheartedly calls it) is calculated, the United States and Germany almost achieve parity, for example, at US$2.58 and US$2.76, respectively, for the price of a Big Mac (+7%). Chinese Big Macs, however, are quite cheap indeed at US$1.27 each. This means that if China had a fully convertible currency, its current level would be almost 50% undervalued.

Subsidies

Governments take a number of actions to protect the purchasing power of their citizens. One of these actions is the subsidizing of producers. A subsidy is a payment by the government either directly to producers to compensate for losses in the marketplace (e.g., farm subsidies) or to consumers to enable them to buy goods (e.g., welfare food stamps). A subsidy may also take the form of a "tax break" to insulate producers or consumers from the additional costs of taxes. In any of these methods, the government is transferring money outside of the normal mechanism of the marketplace. The subsidy process is motivated more by politics than sound economic reasoning, and the effects can hamper both the domestic market and international prospects. Subsidies are also sometimes used in conjunction with a tariff to stave off foreign competition. A variety of subsidies and their effects are listed:

AGRICULTURAL

Food is a very sensitive issue in all nations and even more so when a nation is heavily dependent on imports or fears competition on a product that involves national pride. France heavily subsidizes its wineries and its cheese makers. Taiwan has similar subsidies for its fruit growing sector as does Canada for its wheat farmers. In the United States, where farming has reached almost industrial efficiency and productivity, farmers have actually been paid by the government *not* to grow food in order to maintain price levels. Farm subsidies tend to be a drag on the economy, as the money could be invested more wisely elsewhere. However, some of the subsidizing is strategic in motivation. This is true with island nations like Japan and Taiwan who wish to protect their food industries and thereby lessen their susceptibility to an easily enforced embargo. But even these strategic subsidies cause conflict with trading partners who also have food to sell.

When subsidies are coupled with protective import tariffs—and they usually are—trade wars develop that tend to spill over into other sectors ("Why should we buy your electronics if you won't buy our wheat?"). Developing nations, who generally have little else to trade but farm goods, always seek exemptions for certain areas of their agricultural sector when entering into trade agreements. Even technological giants, notably Japan and its rice farmers, still seek to stave off agricultural competitors, even when it means maintaining high prices for domestic consumers. Much of this is political (farmers have lobbyists, too) but part of it derives from governmental belief (perhaps illusion) that a sovereign nation must be able to feed itself.

INDUSTRIAL & TECHNOLOGICAL

Creating an industrial base is a major motivating factor for the governments of the developing world, though the motivation isn't always economic. Indonesia's attempt in the 1990s to create a "national" aerospace industry (and an auto industry) in a country still largely agricultural was done more out of pride than shrewd economic planning. This was similar to Malaysia's rush to build a "high-tech corridor" to rival Silicon Valley. Other nations, like Vietnam, attract industrial investors with tax breaks which are just deferred subsidies. The government then makes technology transfers part of the deal so that industrial growth, though second-hand, is externally financed by the foreign investor.

Subsidies may be used to compensate for the losses incurred by inefficient industrial operations (e.g., the "bailout" of Chrysler by the U.S. government in the 1970s). The causes and effects of industrial subsidies are not dissimilar to those of agricultural subsidies. Indonesia's aerospace efforts drained away investment that could have been used in sectors where it was more competitive. Vietnam has seen its foreign-financed automobile industry flounder since the domestic market cannot afford its products. Malaysian high-tech aspirations have fallen far short of expectations. The G-7 nations, for their part, try to transfer their support (both subsidy and tariffs) to technological sectors as they try to keep a few older home-grown industries happy in the meantime.

In the United States, for instance, software companies (a service sector) long ago exceeded the value of the nation's entire domestic auto industry. The strength of the technology industries has allowed them to bargain for government intercession. They clamor for the same protection from foreign competition (new copyright laws) and granting of subsidies (tax breaks from pliant municipalities and states) that their agrarian and industrial brethren sought in the past.

SOCIAL

No economy yet devised has been able to evenly spread wealth among its citizenry. Socialist and communist attempts have met with little success and much contempt. However, even the most capitalistic of economies make some effort to redistribute wealth from the upper echelons to the poorer citizens. Welfare (a.k.a., the dole), food subsidies, graduated taxes, educational subsidies, free medical care, transportation discounts, unemployment benefits, and subsidized housing are all means by which the wealthy, through taxation, assist the non-wealthy. While this is primarily a domestic activity carried out at both the local and national levels, these subsidies can greatly affect a nation's economic progress and ability to attract investment.

Like all subsidies, social ones are for the most part financed by taxes, and higher taxes tend to chase away foreign investment. Nations with high social subsidies, such as Germany and France, tend to have regulations that greatly restrict landlords and employers in their dealings with poorer tenants and laborers. Once again, investment tends to flow away from restrictive climates towards areas of less regulation. Both Germany and France can testify to that flow with their high unemployment rates. In the case of France, a good degree of "brain drain" has occurred as young entrepreneurs seek residency in the United States and the United Kingdom after finding that high social benefits back home limit profits and stifle progress.

INTERNATIONAL

The World Bank and the IMF have already been discussed earlier and their funding efforts can be seen as a form of global subsidy. Other specialized agencies (e.g., the Asian Development Bank, Islamic Development Bank) perform similar international/intercultural subsidization as well. There have been some attempts, however, to actually move wealth directly from rich countries to poor ones on a non-voluntary basis as opposed to the donor/recipient efforts of these agencies. Most of these attempts have focused on environmental matters, with the developed nations being taken to task for past industrial exploitation and pollution. Some poorer countries want the richer nations to pay for the environmental controls needed to move them out of agrarian societies into pollution-free industrial status. Thus far these attempts have been largely unsuccessful, since the developing world has no means to enforce their demands. This subject will be taken up again in Chapter 11.

EXPORT

An export subsidy is used by a government to keep its producers afloat when the overseas market for its products is in a downturn. Governments make up the difference between what foreign importers will pay and what domestic producers need to maintain profit levels. Direct subsidies are illegal by international agreement, but governments have found other means of keeping domestic businesses and jobs intact. These methods include reduced or refunded tariffs on imported raw materials, low-rate credit, preferential allocation of domestic materials, or tax breaks on land, capital expenditures and employee training. Companies producing similar products in the foreign importer's market may demand that their own government intervene on their behalf, with import tariffs or outright exclusion if the export subsidies are considered non-competitive.

IMPORT

Governments, on occasion, will assist their private domestic producers by paying for portions of high-priced imported goods or services necessary to build specific, government-sanctioned industries. Automobile manufacturing, high-tech industries, banking systems and chemical production in developing nations often receive import assistance. This can be both direct and indirect, dependent on whether their governments believe such subsidies will pay for themselves in the long-run with increased employment. It is not unusual for a government to use the monies collected in tariffs to finance such subsidies. This places the burden of the cost on foreign exporters, who may request assistance from their own governments in the form of export subsidies to offset these costs. This seesaw transfer of costs can become a source of contention between trading partners.

Import Tariffs

The word "tariff" derives from the Arabic for "notification," and was originally the name for the documentation of goods entering or exiting a port. Governments soon realized that there was an advantage to charging foreigners a tax for bringing certain goods into a port, as it provided a level of control as well as a source of tax revenue over which the domestic citizenry would not complain. The tariff soon became the name for the tax rather than just the documentation for levying it.

Over the centuries tariffs have become a complex and important issue among governments as each seeks to position itself to the greatest economic advantage without incurring the wrath and retaliation of its competitor nations. Trade "wars" usually have tariffs as the weapon of choice as the disputing parties restrict each other's products with escalating taxes. Rather than the outright banning of certain imports, a tariff barrier makes the import more expensive than locally supplied products of a similar nature, thus resulting in reduced importation. Import tariffs can be *ad valorem,* where the tax is a set percentage of the value of the goods, or *specific*, where the tariff is based on the number of units and not on the value of the import. The usual motivation for escalating tariffs is the economic protection of domestic producers against a more powerful foreign competitor. As mentioned earlier, sometimes the motivation may be more political or emotional than purely economic.

POWER PLAYS

Larger economies with efficient producers often feel they are often cut out of smaller foreign markets through the use of high tariffs and counter that exclusion with retributive tariffs. Smaller economies believe they must protect themselves from economic colonization with high tariff barriers, all the while demanding that the large economies open themselves up to the products of their poorer competitors. This is the basis of the United States / China trade relationship.

The theory of comparative advantage would seem to suggest that each country could specialize in whatever products it most efficiently produces. However, when put on a global scale rather than just between adjacent economies, some nations would not be competitive in any product line, thus making them little more than a source of raw materials, if in fact they had any to trade. Because of the emotional and political ramifications of international trade issues (including especially tariffs), an arena needs to be provided in which to objectively resolve disputes.

GATT & the WTO

In 1948, the United Nations tried to remedy centuries-old global trade disputes with a multilaterally negotiated trade agreement known as the General Agreement on Tariffs and Trade (GATT). The purpose of the agreement was to reduce tariffs over time for the benefit of both large and small economies alike. By the 1994 Uruguay Round of talks, GATT had 100 members and was in the process of converting itself into the World Trade Organization (WTO), to oversee international trade disputes. Like GATT, the WTO seeks to remove tariff barriers among its members while promoting the economic development of its poorer clientele. Membership is only open to those countries willing to accept strict accounting rules, legal obligations, and the eventual eradication or lowering of import tariffs. Disputes over unfair trading practices are litigated by a tribunal, and each member of the WTO has equal weight in such disputes.

The WTO does not cover every nation, nor is it considered the perfect mechanism by all of its members. Technological giants from the United States can find themselves on the losing end of a lawsuit filed by a tiny developing nation crying foul over trade. (Washington politicians tend to decry any unfavorable WTO ruling as an attempt to transfer wealth unjustly.) Meanwhile, a huge emerging market like China is denied membership because it can not (or will not) bring its accounting and banking practices into line with WTO guidelines. Such issues will be discussed in detail in Chapter 9.

Export Tariffs & Voluntary Restraints

One way in which a nation can seek to force a rival to reduce import tariffs is to restrict its own exports of other goods that the rival wants or needs. One form this ploy can take is an export tariff where goods leaving the country are taxed in an effort to slow their exodus, thereby reducing the available supply to the rival. Say country A finds the import duties levied by country B to be excessive on A's steel producers. Country A retaliates by taxing the export of wheat, which

B greatly needs. Country B's wheat importers petition their government to relax the duties on steel to free up wheat trade.

In another version, government A would ask for "voluntary" export restraints by wheat producers. This request would most likely be sweetened with compensating subsidies or be accompanied by legal threat. In either case, when nations trade a wide variety of goods or services, including competitive and non-competitive products, each side has potential leverage to overcome the other's tariff barriers, usually by governmental intervention. Reducing exports or even refusing to export is one area in which the WTO is helpless to intervene.

Wages, Prices & Inflation

One of the many fears that governments harbor—and rightfully so—is soaring inflation. Inflation is the "persistent" increase in wages and prices. A gradual and widespread increase in both wages and prices is usually deemed to be tolerable, but many economies have sudden increases in just one large sector of either category (e.g., transport wages, grain prices) which throws other segments of the economy into disarray. The wage-price spiral is the tendency for any increase in wages in one industry to be followed by an increase in the prices for the products of that industry. This then touches off wage increase demands in other industries to compensate for new higher prices. Hyperinflation occurs when prices increase so quickly that money ceases to have any real value.

The international ramifications of excessive inflation are numerous. Many 20th-century governments have been overthrown (Indonesia in 1998) and wars started (pre-WWII Germany) because the population of a hyperinflated economy suddenly awoke to find that it needed a sack full of cash just to buy a loaf of bread or a cup of rice. So potentially disruptive is inflation to global peace and prosperity that one of the first demands the IMF makes of a client economy is the acceptance of "austerity measures" aimed at reining in prices.

THERE GOES THE NEIGHBORHOOD

Because there is such an interlocking relationship among economies, when one nation descends into economic chaos, its neighbors are likely to follow. Populations flee from economic stress across borders in search of new opportunities, putting pressures on the recipient economy. Meanwhile, those left behind are no longer able to buy imported goods from neighbors because the currency is now deemed useless to the point of inconvertibility. Neighboring economies now start to experience sudden deflation in export sectors as supply builds up, while sectors hard pressed by immigrants, like housing and food, skyrocket in price. Overseas debts owed by nations experiencing hyperinflation go unpaid, which drives up interest rates in the creditor's economy, which may be on the other side of the globe. Bad loans drive creditor banks under and uninsured savings are lost. What started as a local problem begins to spread to all but the strongest and most alert economies. It is no wonder that the IMF likes to intervene as early as possible.

It should be noted that not all economic observers and client governments agree with the methods of the IMF. Many naysayers complain that the agency has one solution for all problems and that its record is not all that exemplary. Economic austerity plans, a favorite of the IMF, do not cure every ill, and these plans on occasion have done more harm than good. Countries like Malaysia, Russia and Indonesia consequently are trying to keep the would-be benefactors at arm's-length by trying to fix as many economic problems as possible on their own. However, the fact remains that if a nation wants the financial support of the IMF, it must accept rigid guidelines that can often have a political fallout.

Anti-Monopoly Laws

Most of the industrial and technological economies have laws set up to discourage the growth and power of monopolies. Emerging markets are a great deal more lax in this area, believing that monopolies and oligopolies are necessary if their economies are to advance. The basis for this reasoning is that, for the most part, this was how it was done by the developed world during their early stages of development. Even today, the developed world permits a fair number of regulated monopolies (utilities, postal systems) because of the efficiencies they can bring.

THE MONOPOLY MOVEMENT

The United States has the most stringent anti-monopoly (anti-trust) laws in existence, and has broken up monopolies that other developed nations may still hold dear (e.g., telephone, oil, railroads). Even today the U.S. Department of Justice regularly pursues some of the nation's commercial giants in court to keep markets open to competition. Once again, a governmental action that is seemingly domestic in scope can have global economic ramifications. For example, the EU government's finding that Microsoft (the undisputed leader in software operating systems) is an illegal monopoly may, in the long-term, result in more than just fines for Bill Gates and a victory for the competition. There is little to prevent this multi-billion dollar company from moving the majority of its European operations elsewhere. Jobs, along with the taxes and ancillary revenue generation they bring, can be moved to other economies that will welcome Microsoft with open arms. The penalties will be paid, but not only by Microsoft. As we will see in the next chapter, business is often ready, willing, and able to take advantage of the new "mobility of capital" when dealing with governmental interference.

War

Virtually every nation has had its borders created, realigned, expanded, contracted or imposed upon by some hostile act. The nation may have been involved directly in the hostilities or, as in the case of many African nations, simply assigned borders based upon the results of treaties signed between warring parties a continent away. Whatever the case, it cannot be denied that war and the potential for war have enormous influence on international economics.

MILITARY MIGHT

The 20th century has seen the greatest conflicts and devastation known to man, yet it has also seen the largest economic changes. Germany and Japan, both virtually destroyed as economies after WWII, are now two of the biggest economies in the world. The United States, a third-rate power in the 19th century, rose in part by virtue of its ability to win wars. Its production capabilities allowed it to become the 20th-century's leading military and economic power, with no sign of relinquishing its preeminence anytime soon. Russia and China, the largest and most populous countries, respectively, adopted communism after bloody internal wars, but they could not match their territorial and population size with significant economic success. The former British colony, India, achieved independence with minimal bloodshed in 1947, then descended into violent internal conflict to cleave off part of its nation into Moslem Pakistan. Each of these two impoverished nations has diverted enormous sums from their economies into armaments so that today they threaten each other with nuclear arms. Should they come to blows, the economic and nuclear fallout will be widespread.

PEACEFUL, AND NOT SO PEACEFUL, BOUNDARIES

But not all border shifts have been dictated by war. The European Union is well on its way to becoming both a unified political and economic entity through very peaceful means. Many of the former Eastern-bloc communist countries (Hungary, Poland, Czech Republic, etc.) have clamored to join the EU as full members. But even in this peaceful atmosphere the potential for conflict has risen. Russia rattles its sword out of frustration with its own economy as well as in seeing its former economic satellites side with old enemies in Europe. (In the spring of 1998, Russian ministers actually entertained the notion that Poland wanted to re-establish its ancient claim to Belarus and the Ukraine.)

Elsewhere as the world enters the 21st century, China threatens to forcibly take over the Spratly Islands situated in the middle of strategic shipping lanes in the South China Sea much to the chagrin of Taiwan, the Philippines and Vietnam. In the Middle East, economic development seems to be permanently on hold while violent religious fundamentalism and Arab-Israeli conflicts fuel investor doubts. In sub-Saharan Africa, internal intertribal wars and political instability keep this gigantic region on a subsistence footing, attracting less than 2% of the world's investment.

WAR AS AN ECONOMIC DETERMINANT

The violence of war has shaped the world's economies since the beginning of recorded history, with no end to its influence in sight. Most of the theories and principles of economics focus on peacetime economies, although economists have long studied the effects of violent conflict. The scope of this book will not permit a full exposition of those effects, but readers should be aware of war's influence when looking at the global economic picture. It was once said that war was "politics by other means" but the reality is that wars often have a very economic cause, cost, and effect above and beyond the political.

CHAPTER 6

Private Enterprise

HE WHO WORKS FOR HIS OWN INTEREST WILL AROUSE MUCH ANIMOSITY. — CONFUCIUS

IN THE PREVIOUS chapter the role of government and its conscious and unconscious effect on international economics was discussed. Governments seek to control what they often see as an adversary: private enterprise. Private enterprise, for its part, also sees itself in a relationship with government that is rarely ideal and, on many occasions, confrontational. Government relies on business to generate jobs and tax revenues, while business seeks government protection as well as a host of other services, including infrastructure and subsidies. This is true both domestically and internationally.

Change of Command

Government and private enterprise are always jockeying for control of an economy. Domestically, companies must deal with national, regional and municipal governments to comply with an ever growing list of regulations. Global companies now often negotiate with several national governments simultaneously, so that each nation is guaranteed its fair share of jobs and tax revenues. As they have done for centuries in their domestic markets, companies are not beyond playing one government off against another. Governments play a similar game when approached by several large corporations seeking to penetrate a new foreign market.

FIRST WORLD CHANGES

For many decades after the Great Depression of the 1930s, most economists and most of the general population were in favor of a strong role for government in determining the economic future of a nation. However, beginning in the late 1970s there was a major shift in the developed economies towards lessening government controls (now deemed "interference") over the activities of private enterprise. In the capitalist world of the West the greatest changes were seen in Great Britain. Here, Prime Minister Margaret Thatcher, with the aid of her "minister of thought," Keith Joseph, dismantled the state-owned industries and labor union hegemony that were driving the nation to penury. The homeland of Keynesian economics was throwing off decades of government control and privatizing everything in sight.

SECOND WORLD DECLINE

Even more dramatic was the 1991 dissolution of the purest of state-controlled economies, the Soviet Union. Once heralded as the savior of the working classes, communism lay in ruins along with virtually any other form of centrally planned economy. Around the globe, governments of all types were gradually being viewed as impediments to economic health. Downsizing, deregulation and capitalism became the order of the day. Even social programs such as public education, welfare and subsidized healthcare were tossed aside as examples of governments gone awry. Only privatization, it seemed, could save an economy.

THE COMMANDING HEIGHTS ARE TAKEN

Private enterprise had, for the time being, won the "commanding heights" of the world's economies. The term itself means the ability to control the overall direction and most important elements of an economy. The phrase, oddly enough, had been coined by Lenin in 1922 to defend his policy of allowing some small forms of private trade and agriculture to exist in an otherwise communal state. Lenin, who had risen to power decrying the abilities of market economics to create well-being, would have been shocked to see his disciples discredited by the 1980s. By the 1990s, the "commanding heights" of the globe's economies were firmly in the grip of market forces and the failures of government, not private enterprise, were regularly cited as the cause of economic weakness.

This chapter will deal with how private enterprise chooses to operate on an international scale. Its ability to retain control of economic growth will be determined by how well it can keep the globe's governments complacent.

Private Supply & Global Demand

One of the examples often used to explain how private enterprise operates is that of the Coca-Cola executive who was asked why his company wanted to go to all of the trouble of bringing its product to impoverished mainland China. Reflecting on the nation's population of 1.3 billion, he replied that he would be more than happy if everyone in China "just bought one Coke." It is not just large corporations that feel this way. As transportation and communication have improved, companies of all stripes and sizes have been able to take a larger view when developing marketing plans.

Private enterprise wants access to customers and when those customers are in another country the potential for company vs. government, as well as intergovernmental, conflicts to arise is great. Regardless of how much of the economic high ground private enterprise may hold these days, it never finds itself in complete control of the battlefield. In fact, many businesses often use governments when maneuvering for position against rivals.

THE FLAG FOLLOWS COMMERCE

Economic relations between countries nowadays can actually precede diplomatic relations, as has occurred between the United States and Vietnam. Private enterprise's desire to gain access to the 76 million consumers of the Vietnamese market (as well as its educated and low-priced labor supply) was the driving force behind the dropping of the long-standing embargo imposed by the United States after the Vietnam war. Other non-U.S. companies had been doing business in Vietnam for many years, but it was widely recognized that without access to U.S. markets, investment and technology Vietnam would remain at the bottom of the economic ladder. American companies had the supply of consumer goods and cash to match the demand of Vietnam's recently encouraged entrepreneurs. Only government wrangling stood in the way. Private enterprise (mostly, but not exclusively, from the United States) put pressure on Washington to drop the embargo. It did so finally in 1994—two years before full diplomatic relations were instituted with Hanoi. In the interim, the highest ranking U.S. State Department diplomat in Vietnam was, to no one's surprise, a commercial officer, a reversal of the old geopolitical adage, "The flag follows commerce"

A further and larger example of how politics has taken a back seat to economics can be found in the proliferation of trade agreements between historical belligerents. Every organization from APEC to Mercosur to the G-7 finds former enemies sitting across the table from each other discussing mutually profitable economic strategies. All of this is done at the behest of companies seeking to gain access to foreign markets. Governments have come to recognize and accept their role as facilitators, and not necessarily controllers, of international business. The result has been that, whereas an exchange of diplomats in past decades was done primarily to forestall the chance of armed conflict due to political differences, much of what embassies do today is related to keeping trade channels open.

Privatization of Industry

Governments have not only had to play second fiddle to private enterprise in recent years, they have had to suffer the privatization of many governmental functions as well. Populations around the world in political systems of all types have decided that they not only want their elected officials to keep their noses out of commerce but also to reduce the responsibilities of governments in general. The eventual effect upon international business may take years to recognize but it will certainly change the way money moves around the globe.

THE THATCHERITE MODEL

As mentioned earlier, the Thatcherite revamping of the British economy was one of the most sweeping privatizations of state-run business and it is still in process. In 1998, Whitehall officials were still contemplating how to bring free enterprise to the Post Office, the Forestry Commission and the Meteorological Office. The London Underground and the BBC, already equipped with privatized components, were also in the process of shedding themselves of government control. They are all hoping for the same success that accompanied the privatization of Britain's steel industry, British Airways and most of the island's utility industries. British Steel, once a recipient of a billion pounds a year in government subsidies, is now owned by Tata Steel of India and is one of the lowest-cost steel manufacturers in the world. Similarly, British Airways has become the world's most profitable airline. Telephone bills have dropped by 46% since privatization, just as natural gas (-31%) and electricity (-20%) have saved consumers billions. (To be fair, water and sewage rose 36% and 42%, respectively, due primarily to the increased expense of EU compliance.)

GLOBAL DUPLICATION

Some privatized industries in Britain have not fared well (e.g., British Rail), but overall the move was so effective as to draw attention and duplication around the world. Air France is trying to remodel itself based on its British competitor's schematic in a move considered unthinkable a few years ago in that highly socialized country. Hundreds of American municipalities and many of its states have rushed to privatize public transportation, sanitation and even prison systems. Russia's first major economic move after the breakup of the U.S.S.R. was to privatize thousands of state-owned businesses—many at bargain basement prices—through sales to former managers. China has also divested itself of some, but far from all, of its state-owned companies. Many economists and IMF banking officials have called upon China to privatize the last of their state-owned enterprises before these laggard firms pull their entire economy under. Even prosperous Singapore has relinquished its long-standing policy of subsidizing "executive condominiums" for local tycoons. Few economies have remained untouched by the drive towards privatization. Russia, however, has "renationalized" parts of its oil industry as a means of refilling the nation's tax coffers and addressing questionable deals given to "oligarchs" back in the 1990s.

PRIVATE CONCERNS

But not all privatization is heralded as economic advancement, nor does it always draw investors. Venezuela, an oil-dependent member of OPEC, made many attempts in the 1990s to privatize its national oil producer, PDVSA, as well as its "parastatal" aluminum conglomerate, CVG. Much of the successful opposition to these privatizations has come from unions and politicians decrying the loss of subsidies and jobs as well as the expanding role of foreigners. (This last cross-border factor is becoming an ever increasing concern of similar newly industrialized markets.) Venezuela's shift towards socialism in recent years has seen an end to any new privatization schemes.

For other emerging markets there are different concerns. Ghana in west Africa is facing the problem of being unable to attract foreign investors to its IMF-mandated privatization scheme. In ten years it has only been able to find investors for 120 of the 350 state-owned industries it wished to divest, even though the sectors range from oil to produce to pharmaceuticals. Pointing out that Ghana is politically stable relative to its sub-Saharan neighbors, investment supporters say that much of the lack of interest in divestiture is due to the availability of better deals in higher-growth economies. Privatization is so common nowadays as to give the private-sector investors a wide range of choices.

Privatization of Social Systems

In the waning years of the 20th century, few have been able to argue effectively against getting potential revenue-generating businesses out of government hands and into those of private enterprise. But what of those governmental functions that were never intended to have a commercial component? Should health care for the poor be privately financed? Can police or military functions be run as commercial operations? Could social welfare systems turn a profit? Will all schools become private, for-profit institutions? Should the population be subjected to privately owned highway systems?

REGULAR REGULATION

The United States is the leader in the move towards privatizing many of the areas previously thought to be the exclusive purview of governments. This is not surprising since the United States has always tended more towards regulating business than actually participating in it. Many American communities already have private police forces, and one of the areas of greatest employment growth is in the private security guard industry. Numerous state prisons and local jails are run by private firms with hearty profit margins. In some states, welfare is being converted to "workfare" where its beneficiaries must perform useful work in order to receive payments that are dispensed, in many cases, by private-sector administrators. The privately held Edison Company regularly places bids on state and county public school systems, guaranteeing both improved test scores and profit margins. The U.S. state and federal highway systems, long built by private firms under government contract, now have many administrative and maintenance functions contracted out in a similar manner. In Iraq, almost 50% of the American forces were private contractors, not soldiers of the nation. Privatization has many critics in the U.S., but a sizeable number of advocates.

PRIVATE GOVERNANCE, PUBLIC GOOD

Other countries besides the United States are moving in the same direction. Vietnam has made its once free education system into a pay-as-you-go process. Its medical and pharmaceutical industries have taken a similar turn. For the European Union, one of the many sticking points for several of its members, especially the United Kingdom, is how big or how small the social programs will be upon full integration. Several sub-Saharan African leaders currently employ private (mercenary) armies to train indigenous troops and to protect those same leaders from equally indigenous military coups. Highways, telecom networks, power grids and water systems among the emerging market nations are, in the majority of cases, put in place by build-operate transfer (BOT) contracts with private firms. With a BOT, private companies construct and operate what are normally considered "public" systems with a price structure that will guarantee an effective rate of return (profit) over a set period of time. Once this threshold is reached, the project is placed in government hands, usually with the private firm retaining a long-term administrative or maintenance contract. Most, if not every one, of these BOT contracts is handled by a foreign firm and that is where the international implications of privatization begin to arise.

National Subsidies Go Global

Privatization can initially be a hardship on both consumers and producers. The changeover usually results in the loss of jobs, as the new owners pare away redundant positions and eliminate excess production. Prices can actually rise to cover the loss of state subsidies. Though not true in every case, however, the long-term competition and more efficient use of personnel open up more opportunities than they close.

One factor that cannot be ignored regarding the role of the state in commerce is its ability to subsidize at very low rates the start-up of business enterprises. This subsidy may take the form of high purchase prices paid by state agencies for private-sector products, as is the case with the U.S. defense industry. Or it may take the form of the direct channeling of national investment into target industries, as occurs in Japan and Korea. Moves toward privatization have discouraged this interventionist activity. In many cases, however, such subsidies have allowed major industries (Japanese electronics, French aerospace) to develop a strength that might not otherwise have been possible.

INTERNATIONAL FINANCE

The vacuum left by the decline of individual state subsidies has been increasingly filled by international agencies such as the IMF and the Asian Development Bank, as well as by private investment groups. In the former two instances, individual nations pool funding and direct it to those economies experiencing difficulty. Russia and Indonesia are just two of the most recent recipients of this type of low-interest rate global subsidy. But such agencies dole out their funding in tranches (literally "slices") with strict guidelines for domestic disbursement (e.g., power supply, medical, water treatment) and economic austerity measures aimed at keeping a lid on domestic government spending.

Some low-interest loans come from private investors, as is the case with billionaire George Soros's multi-million dollar assistance packages to Russia throughout the 1990s to help prop up various sectors in that problem economy. (Oddly enough, Soros is considered a hero in Russia but a villain in Indonesia where his currency speculation is thought—incorrectly so—to have been a major factor in bringing down the value of the rupiah.) In an interesting combination of international agency and private-sector largesse, media mogul Ted Turner pledged US$1 billion to the United Nations to be redistributed by them for humanitarian-related subsidies worldwide. Plainly, subsidies, like trade, are going global and becoming increasingly privatized.

Tax Evasion or Invasion

As the role of government declines worldwide, many commercial enterprises are questioning the level of taxation levied upon their operations. Most of the developed nations have a top corporate tax rate of around 33% (see chart of some examples).

Australia	30%
Belgium	34%
Canada	35%
France	33%
Germany	30%
Italy	33%
Japan	30%
Sweden	28%
U.K.	28%
U.S.	39%

Emerging and newly industrialized markets tend towards similar declared rates that decrease via negotiation in inverse proportion to the size of the investment. Another approach in these newer economies is to have completely different tax rates for different economic sectors or varying degrees of local ownership. Kazakhstan, for instance, has a standard rate of 30%, unless the primary means of production is land, which lowers the tax rate to 10%. Neighboring Kyrgyzstan (Kyrgyz Republic) has a 70% tax on gambling winnings, but only 5% on profits derived from insurance. While these countries are trying to encourage and discourage various forms of business, others like the Bahamas and the Cayman Islands have made themselves extremely attractive to investors and corporations by having no taxes whatsoever on corporate profits or individual income.

TAX MOBILITY

Private enterprise has recently discovered that its capital and its profits are equally mobile. Tax rates (along with labor rates) are now used to determine where to set up shop as well as when to close shop. For decades the same criterion was used domestically to play one municipality or county off another. It is still widely used today as companies seek tax "holidays" and training subsidies from cities hungry for new jobs. Its movement to an international scale has become common only in the last twenty years, with even small manufacturers being able to extricate sweetheart deals to set up operations overseas.

Nations that maintain high corporate tax rates, like Germany's former average of 38%, find that investors pass them by to set up in places like Hungary at 18%, or in Poland where foreign investors can negotiate rates approaching 0%. There is little doubt that high corporate taxes in the past (and current "social" taxes) and equally high labor rates have been the main reasons for Germany's high unemployment rate. Russia has a much different problem. It does attract a good amount of foreign investment with a relatively low tax rate of 24%, but fails to collect most of the taxes due it. Moscow officials had rarely been able to collect more than 15% of the levies owed them by business—at least until recently. Corporations in Russia, both foreign and domestic, might feel little moral obligation to support the government, but draconian raids on corporate offices and the imprisonment in Siberia of formerly powerful "oligarchs" has made believers of them all. Russian businesses now pay their taxes early just to be sure.

CORPORATE TAX REVOLT

Internationally, companies often question the relationship between taxes paid and government services rendered. The mantra sounded among American corporate officers for decades, that "corporations should not pay taxes, we collect them," reveals their belief that they do a service for government by generating jobs, which will be taxed at the individual level. (In the United States, companies must also withhold taxes from employee paychecks on the government's behalf.) Recent attitudes towards transfer payments (see below) and the major growth in the global movement of investment capital demonstrate private enterprise's view that governments are being thought of as purveyors and not leaders. If anything, global companies often view governments as an impediment to success, and taxes as mere confiscation rather than payment for state services. Companies have packed their bags with capital and gone off in search of the best deal possible in the most cost-effective economies.

Mobility of Capital

Much of the success of international companies derives from their ability to shift their capital to whichever area is the most efficient. This fluid movement of investment across borders continues to be the hallmark of modern international economics, but it is not without controversy. Private enterprise has long been thought of as two steps ahead of its local government. It is becoming increasingly clear that international operations, especially those from the developed economies, are light years ahead of national governments and many trade blocs.

Global businesses look for low taxes, tax rebates, cheap land, inexpensive labor, flexible labor laws, suitably skilled workforces, and/or long-term leases. They seek unintrusive governments intent on fast, high-paced growth. Just like counties and cities before them, nations seeking such investment, and the jobs they bring, line up hoping to be picked for the latest auto plant, chemical processor or microchip manufacturing line. The IMF has assisted in this financial "beauty contest" by recommending that all of its clients open themselves up to the free flow of foreign investment as a prerequisite for assistance both monetary and consultative. The reader, however, should not get the idea that *only* emerging markets are targeted for investment.

TRANSFERRING PROFIT

The European Union and the United States both present excellent opportunities for capital investment. Yet even these financially sophisticated economies find that their governments are waging a running (and usually losing) battle when it comes to dealing with international companies. Global manufacturers will set up far-flung operations in nations that run the economic gamut from nascent to high-tech, then move profits to whichever locale presents the best taxation package. This is accomplished by transferring costs internally through making each subsidiary operation buy from another with prices set to make the best (lowest taxation) locale receive the greatest benefit (profit).

Global companies continue to keep their tax bills low via complex, often impenetrable, accounting. Since non-WTO nations can have whatever accounting standards they choose, it is difficult for each nation to determine if they are receiving their due. Even when national accounting standards are the same among a company's global operating locales, participating governments are fearful of being seen as too stringent. It is part of an all too realistic belief that they will become less attractive for future investment.

GOVERNMENTS FIGHT BACK

Such craven state behavior does have its limits. Elections or political turmoil can suddenly cause a backlash against foreign investment thought to be exploitive or evasive of government control. A good example of what can happen to foreign companies occurred in the Indian state of Maharashtra when the very global Enron Corporation (soon to have domestic problems of its own) was under contract to the state in the mid-1990s to build a multi-million dollar hydroelectric power plant. Having cut a deal with the local state government years before, and having spent millions on the build-operate-transfer style project, Enron suddenly found a new "nationalist," anti-foreigner government in charge after elections.

The original deal was declared "void" because, according to the new government, Enron had been given a "sweetheart" deal by the previous government, now decried as corrupt. Unwilling to abandon its investment, Enron renegotiated on far less profitable terms. This incident, along with the temporary closing of a Kentucky Fried Chicken (KFC) outlet in the same state, had effects beyond the locality. Besides resulting in a slowdown of foreign investment in Maharshtra specifically, it made foreign investors skittish about India in general.

Investment Tides

International companies know all too well, and client governments are discovering begrudgingly, that capital can flow out of an economy just as easily as it can flow in. Vietnam, which had enticed the Chrysler Corporation with promises of limiting access to that nation's car market to a select number of manufacturers, learned about the ebb and flow of capital the hard way. Hanoi officials were shocked to see one of the world's largest automakers pull up stakes and leave in 1997 after Chrysler discovered that eleven, not three, of its competitors had been given manufacturing deals. The effect on other foreign investment, especially American, was dramatic and downward. When big operators can't "cut a deal" that is profitable, medium and small investors see little hope for themselves.

POLICY AND INVESTMENT PLOYS

The effect of government policy on international economics is very forthright. Nations with liberal investment policies attract ever increasing amounts of capital, while those with restrictive or profit-busting regulations find themselves on the sidelines unable to get into the game. Some nations (e.g., Russia, China, Indonesia) have allowed high levels of government-condoned corruption to ruin otherwise attractive foreign investment policies. Investors see little point in financing an economy if the original investment, or its resulting profits, gets siphoned off by state-shielded criminals or political cronies. Information travels at lightning speed these days whether the news is good or bad. Economies with a history of shortchanging foreign investment or those that lack transparency in their business dealings find it difficult if not impossible to attract large-scale capital.

Investment, Not Investors

Some economies have found that their ability to compete globally has been greatly influenced by how foreigners are treated socially and legally upon arrival in the country. While the main goal of global investment may be profit, private enterprise and its personnel do not want to be reviled or endangered while pursuing an investment scheme. Populist politicians worldwide have gone on record declaring the need to avoid the "traps" set by wily foreign investors intent on overrunning an economy and its resident culture. These Jeremiahs come from the right wing as well as the left. They can be found in the United States and Japan as easily as in India or Indonesia, although in America or Japan the issue may be a single industry such as automobiles (Japanese demagogues were no happier about Ford buying Mazda than their U.S. counterparts were about Honda setting up factories in America). For Indian and Indonesian populists, foreign investment of all kinds is seen as part of a grand cultural conspiracy. Cries to keep the investment money but to send the investors packing can be regularly, if not convincingly, heard throughout the former Third World.

FEARING THE FOREIGNER

Though the anti-foreign-investor effect in the advanced economies is slight, it is growing in the emerging markets. The famous photo of the head of the IMF standing in a dominant pose over Indonesia's President Suharto as he signed an economic restructuring agreement triggered a severe reaction in the aging leader. Driven by a fear that he would appear to be too soft on foreigners, Suharto proceeded to stall on the agreed upon economic reforms and was in turn quickly driven from power by street protests. His misreading of both the photograph and his population's attitude towards foreign assistance will greatly affect the Indonesian economy and the level of foreign investment for decades. Suharto's departure did not help matters either as investors are as fearful of political instability as they are of over-regulation or corruption.

MAKING THE FOREIGNER FEARFUL

Other anti-investor activity can also affect the location and amount of capital private enterprise chooses when looking overseas. Terrorists with religious (Egypt) or political (Peru) objectives regularly target foreign businesses and their managers. This is done as a means to disrupt confidence in the local government, as well as decrease its sources of tax revenues. Once again, political instability can either shut down foreign operations or ward off new investment. Purely criminal activity that targets foreign investment, as occurs in present-day Russia, is usually aimed at "getting a piece of the action" rather than shutting down a business entirely. In both the terrorist and criminal scenarios, every tactic up to and including murder is put to use to gain control of or destroy foreign investment. Incompetent, weak or collusive governments that are either unable or unwilling to deter such behavior find that foreign investment—and economic progress—are hard to come by in such an atmosphere.

Venture Capital: Influence and Confluence

Venture capital (VC) can be briefly defined as investment in high-risk new businesses. It differs from standard capital because the degree of risk in VC is so high as to be unthinkable for normal lending institutions like banks, or even for the joint-venture agreements so common in international investment. Unlike bankers, venture capitalists become investors, not creditors, in the new business. Unlike joint-venture partners, venture capitalists want relatively short-term relationships with their new partners. Once a venture is up and profitable, VC specialists want to cash in their investment by taking the company's stock public with an IPO (initial public offering). Most of venture capital activity is confined to sectors that focus on innovative industrial processes and high technology. Invented by Americans for Silicon Valley start-ups, VC has now become not only a global activity but one that dictates regional economic prosperity.

GLOBAL VENTURES

Investment of this sort, long common in the United States, has spread increasingly to Europe. In both arenas it has been correctly cited as the leading cause of technological advancement and long-term economic power. European VC firms are second only to the U.S. in this form of funding, although the size and investment criteria is significantly different between the two. Britain, Germany, France, Ireland, Belgium, and the Netherlands all have thriving VC components. Each country also has a key factor which makes such activity possible: a stable, open, and legitimate stock market system.

Venture capital companies are not adverse to risk except in one area: when they decide that a client company is mature enough for its stock to be sold on the open market, they want immediate access to willing buyers with minimal restrictions. Obviously, economies with no public stock exchange will not be at all attractive to VC investors. Economies with restrictive exchanges, like China's, that greatly limit foreign participation have similar problems attracting venture capital-style investment. Stock exchanges that lack full disclosure rules, as in most of the crony-prevalent developing world, can equally deter VC investors. Venture capitalists in such circumstances are not always sure that market prices are freely arrived at, since they may be the subject of direct fixing by local financiers intent on getting a bargain via their good connections.

OPTIONAL WEALTH

Another area that greatly affects an economy's ability to attract international venture capital, or even the homegrown variety, is the local government's treatment of the wealth generated by the stock options. A VC project will lure competent managers to run risky operations with the understanding that they will be given such options that can be cashed in for millions at a later date. In the United States, where VC operations are behind most of the growth industries, governments only tax the options when they are cashed in as a capital gain. In Germany and France, these same options are taxed as income when granted to management, even though profit, if generated at all, may not be realized for many years.

In recognition of how this type of tax treatment can influence economic growth, the European Commission (the EU's financial overseer) has called for a review of its membership's tax laws for venture capital. It should be noted that many of the hot technology stocks traded on European bourses are companies started by European entrepreneurs headquartered in the United States. Much of the "brain drain" experienced worldwide is usually the result of entrepreneurs chasing the best tax regime and work environment available. More about this movement of human capital will be discussed in Chapter 7, "Labor Issues."

Trimming the Hedge Funds

Another private sector investment strategy that has greatly influenced the international economic landscape in recent years is the *hedge fund*. Devised a half-century ago as a means to limit the risk of private investment, these funds combined the capital of several people or institutions for investment as a group.

The strategy of hedging originally was to bet on both sides of a market (usually "on the margin"—the process of only putting up a portion of the actual funding needed for a completed transaction), hoping to profit regardless of whether a market rose or fell.

There are over 10,000 hedge funds worldwide worth close to US$2 trillion, including "macrofunds" that each control funds in the billions. The influence of the macro-funds has been particularly felt in their area of specialization: currency speculation. These big private players tend to locate themselves in tax havens, and are not subject to government demands for the asset and membership reporting common with public stock markets and mutual funds. The funds' managers, all of whom may receive as much as 20% of the fund's profits, are hawkish watchers of the technical indicators of the world's national economies; real-time information flow is their lifeblood. Weak economies have their currencies sold to buy those of stronger currencies, thus expanding the fund's coffers. Once a weakness or a strength becomes evident, they wager with their capital accordingly with little regard for the political fallout. Politicians seeking to put a good spin on economic data find that their speeches fall on deaf ears at the hedge funds: private sector analysis always supersedes that of the state.

THE HIGHWAY TO WEALTH

Former Prime Minister Mahatir of the oft economically besieged nation of Malaysia has referred to these funds as the "highwaymen of the global economy," blaming them for his currency's rapid decline in 1997. In reality, the greatest influence these hedge funds have is not in their actual buying power but in their ability to trigger similar investment strategies in the institutional investment community. The billions controlled by hedge funds pale in comparison to the US$20+ trillion that is put to virtually the same purposes by the globe's major banks and institutional funds. When it comes to the US$2 trillion-a-day global currency speculation market, major institutions take their cue from the hedge funds. As happened in southeast Asia in 1997 and in Europe in 1992, institutions will monitor the hedge fund's strategies, then pile into the targeted market, greatly amplifying the hedge fund's original foray. (In 1997, many of the Malaysian Prime Minister's own domestic bankers were selling the nation's ringgit in far greater amounts than the hedge funds.)

Hedge funds are often demonized for their unbridled investment habits, but rarely so by their clients. While many governments, usually those with propped-up currencies, call for the dissolution of hedge funds, the larger economies see no reason to rein in these financial bloodhounds unless there has been evidence of a fraudulent set of transactions.

Absolute and Comparative Advantage

As originally laid out by David Ricardo in the early 19th century, an economy, when left solely to the influence of market forces, will only purchase those goods from its neighbors which it finds too costly to produce itself. Sometimes the advantage a neighbor has will be comparative in the sense that importation of certain goods is done solely because there is a slight, but real, price difference. For instance, China may import Japanese luxury cars because their own auto industry cannot produce similar vehicles at the same (comparative) price. At other times the advantage is absolute because the neighbor produces something wholly unavailable in the domestic market. For example, China imports American jetliners because it has no aerospace industry capable (yet) of producing such machines at any price. The U.S. advantage is absolute.

CO-PRODUCING SUCCESS

While Ricardo's ideas work well in a completely free market, the real international economy is peppered with tariffs, national businesses, monopolies and subsidies. Many economies co-produce (e.g., Germany sells cars to the United States, which sells its own cars to Germany), while others sustain domestic businesses at a high cost to their own population (e.g., Japan discourages rice imports even as its citizens pay well above global market prices for this staple).

Private enterprise has not helped the situation, sometimes quoting vastly different prices for the same goods in neighboring economies. High-priced consumer goods and pharmaceuticals in one economy are marked down and shipped to developing markets where lower wages demand lower prices. The unfortunate result, especially in the relationship between eastern and western Europe, is that these same goods flow back across the original border at lower-than-domestic prices. This process is called *parallel importing*, and it puts a new twist on the theory of comparative advantage. In spite of its illegality, it is becoming an ever increasing problem for companies in the developed world that are forced to literally compete with themselves in everything from blood pressure medicine to clothing. It also raises the hackles of wealthy consumers who suddenly find out that they have been subsidizing the developing world by paying for the price differential—especially in pharmaceuticals.

One of the leading benefits that has come to Europe's consumers is that the institution of the Euro has made it easy to comparison shop inside of the EU. A side-effect of this has been that the participant nations will be able to determine if the role of advantage is real or one artificially influenced by private enterprise. Not only will the price of goods and services be easy to compare, so will the price of the factor that has had the greatest effect on the movement of global capital: the cost of labor. Fear of the movement of labor from less expensive Eastern European EU members to wealthier Western European economies has been much ballyhooed but has actually brought benefits to both regions. The Eastern EU gets monies remitted by its expats and the Western EU gets a ready source of labor for jobs its own people decline to fill.

Global Productivity and Local Business

Managers of private enterprise have long considered the cost of labor as a primary factor in controlling the costs of production. The productivity of that labor is the measurement of how well management is utilizing its human resources. Labor productivity can be defined alternately as the amount of output per unit of currency spent on labor, or the amount of output per hour of labor. Besides being an economic indicator, productivity is also a reflection of a nation's work ethic and attitude towards competition.

Germany has the most expensive labor of the developed nations, and its manufacturing workforce is considered to be one of the most productive in the world. However, besides having high unemployment, Germany's overall productivity does not approach that of the United States or even second-place Japan. Some of Germany's lower productivity comes from its acquisition of millions of less efficient workers from the former socialist state of East Germany, not just higher wages. Meanwhile, much of American and Japanese labor productivity derives from having sent many jobs overseas that had previously been devoted to low-ticket items. These two powerhouses, especially the United States, have reserved for their populations those jobs that add the greatest value to a product with the least amount of labor.

HARNESSING LABOR

Keeping the highest value-adding jobs at home can greatly affect productivity statistics. For instance, labor-intensive wiring harnesses may be manufactured in an emerging market country with pennies-per-hour labor rates, only to be transferred (internally sold within the same company) for US$5 to American stateside auto plants where employees making US$20 per hour install the harnesses via robotics in vehicles to be retailed for US$35,000. The emerging market measures its productivity against the transfer price of the harness, while U.S. productivity is a function of the sale price of the car, even though it is the same company handling both operations. This connection between where and how much value labor adds to goods and services has become a key factor in determining the rankings of nations in the international economy.

CHAPTER 7

Labor

EVERYTHING IN THE WORLD IS PURCHASED BY LABOR. — DAVID HUME, 1754

LABOR—THE VALUE it adds to products, its cost, its availability, and its control—has always been the subject of management and government scrutiny. For centuries people lived in a very limited geographic environment, working primarily for the benefit of themselves and their immediate family. Often, birth, a life to full maturity, and death all took place within a few square kilometers. In feudal society, people were tied, by law, to a particular piece of land or job. In post-feudal society, as people ceased to work for themselves and became employed (from the Latin *implicare* meaning "to fold or bend") by others, the need to move labor to specific areas became a means to increase productivity. Management (from the Latin *manus* meaning "hand") began to treat labor as another resource to be acquired, utilized, and put to the task of generating profit—the true goal of business. Once that resource is used or becomes too expensive, it may be discarded. Newer, less expensive resources may be acquired locally by management, or the job itself may be moved elsewhere—perhaps to another country. Labor in this scheme could be treated like any other commodity.

Labor can, for its part, refuse to work, change the company where its resource is applied, or even move itself across international borders (legally and illegally) in search of higher wages and better benefits. Like management, labor also retains a sizeable amount of political clout (e.g., Russian coal miners, French transport workers, Polish shipyard mechanics) and is capable of influencing government regulation. This chapter will look at how labor interacts with government and private enterprise to influence the global economy.

Technology & Mobility

Technical innovation has always been a major factor in the way people work and how much work could be done. Ancient man's invention of the animal-drawn plow freed up more people for other forms of labor (e.g., weaving, tanning). It greatly increased the amount (and types) of work a farm community could perform in one season. The impact of the Industrial Revolution (1750-1850), both good and bad, is well documented and forever changed the way people related to their work. The move from craftsman to employee was traumatic and complete. The technological revolution, which is driving today's labor market, is having perhaps an even greater effect on how individuals, national populations, private enterprise, and governments approach the concept of labor.

LABOR AND VALUE

As more and more manual labor is done with ever increasing effectiveness by machines—from the huge corporate farms of America to the pre-fabricated construction components of Berlin office buildings—the value of human labor is becoming more intellectual than physical. A trained mind in today's market draws far higher wages (at a minimum, double) than a strong back. Auto assembly-lines, long considered the archetypal form of mind-numbing labor, are nowadays populated with robots doing the jobs held just a decade ago by legions of manual laborers. Engineers no longer dream of building labor-intensive bridge projects, but of devising the next big piece of design software for the world's computers. These computers may design a bridge, fabricate its components and ship them to the job site where robotic-welders assemble the final product—all with a minimum of human supervision or participation. Work that once required thousands of people may today only require a hundred workers, or even ten.

BRAIN POWER

Most of this movement towards the intellectualization of labor has taken place in the developed economies of Europe and North America. It must also be recognized that, like other economic trends of the recent past, the less-developed world will pattern itself after the designs set forth by the wealthier nations. Evidence can already be discerned: while water buffalo may still pull the plows in much of agrarian China, the technology and the systems to replace them are being developed or adapted in Shanghai and Hong Kong.

When work becomes more of an intellectual process (software, finance) than a physical one (mining, farming), a labor force can be as mobile as it likes—just like capital. If I am a banker I can perform my job anywhere—perhaps even at home if I can access the Internet. However, labor has always been mobile to some degree (e.g., migrant farmers move to wherever crops need attention, miners have moved from one played-out shaft to regions more promising, often crossing national borders). What differs in today's labor market mobility is that technological workers control their own movement (whereas the itinerant farmers and miners never did), though the control is far from absolute. No matter how mobile the labor, companies still maintain legal rights to products and the structure of the supply/demand relationship.

THE RAISING OF THE BROW

The hallmark of the modern labor force is not so much mobility as it is exclusivity and disparity. The skills required to become a manual laborer are present in virtually every member of a society; those of an intellectual worker are not. Developed economies, and in fact the international economy as a whole, are experiencing a widening gap between the top and bottom of the economic structure. In the United States, 5% of the population controls 80% of the wealth. Internationally, Japan's GDP per capita is one hundred times that of Vietnam. Even Purchasing Power Parity cannot resolve the growing disparity between the haves and the have-nots. The difference is access to intellectual tools and skills, and observers from many different disciplines have concluded that human capital (managerial labor as well as employee) will either fail or succeed in today's market based largely upon education and training.

Education & Training

Economies around the world have experienced the consequences of the intellectualization of labor. Nations from France to India to Ireland have seen their best and brightest lured to other economies in "brain drains" that have altered their domestic ability to compete. Other countries like China, Taiwan and Mexico have purposely sent their children to other nations to tap into the intellectual capital found abroad for future use at home. Still other nations, like the United States and Russia, have made education—especially technical education—a priority as part of an overall economic and political strategy in post-WWII society. Class-based cultures, like the United Kingdom, found that a nation could become partitioned along educational lines and that the "old school network," not actual skill, was an economic or political ticket to success. Another partitioned economy, apartheid-era South Africa, was confronted with black students who refused education as an act of revolution and boycotted the schools provided by the white ruling class. That country's black leaders, now in political power, find that they are now confronted with a mass of uneducated adults unable to handle the job opportunities thrown open to them.

BRAIN DRAIN PAIN

The mobility of labor has tended to exacerbate the disparity brought by education. Thousands of Soviet engineers, trained at state expense, have taken advantage of relaxed immigration laws to create their own diaspora to wealthier economies. Israel alone has taken in hundreds of thousands of them in the wake of the U.S.S.R.'s dissolution. The CIS nations left behind by these immigrants are stuck in technological limbo having lost a good part of their intellectual capital. Israel's resultant sudden increase in the high-tech sector has created its own problem. Demand for technical workers now far exceeds domestic supply though the nation is reluctant to take in more immigrants. (The requirement of being Jewish narrows the pool and adds to the dilemma.) The Israeli government has instituted a plan to double the number of high-tech workers by 2003 but waiting for its schools to catch up with demand may leave this small nation, just like the former Soviet republics, on the developmental sidelines.

RIGHT IDEAS, WRONG CHOICES

Thailand, Malaysia and Indonesia can be seen as examples of nations whose lack of balance in educational strategy caused their reach to exceed their grasp. In the early 1970s these nations were essentially agrarian economies providing raw materials to the developed world. Intensive technical training, inexpensive labor and extensive foreign investment turned these three countries into high-tech powerhouses. Manual labor jobs formerly done by domestic personnel were, by the late 1980s, now shunned by those locals, only to be filled by immigrants from Bangladesh, Pakistan and the Philippines.

Having concentrated on technological hardware development, these "little dragons" of southeast Asia put little emphasis upon the rigors of modern finance, management or macroeconomic training (specialities of the West). They relied instead on traditional Asian business relationships, and the results have been painful. When the economies collapsed in the summer of 1997, the mobility of labor reversed itself, with high-tech workers returning to their farms and once-vaunted bankers resorting to selling food on the street. The middle-class disappeared overnight and the previously welcomed immigrants were sent packing back to their own troubled economies.

BRIGHT IDEAS VS. RIGHT IDEAS

Developing economies are not the only ones to suffer from misdirected education. The United States, generally seen as the inventor of the high-tech economy, has continued difficulty staffing its high-growth technology giants. Bill Gates, the head of Microsoft, is a regular petitioner in Washington D.C. to advance the cause of relaxed legal immigration. Hardly altruistic in motivation, Gates, along with other high-tech companies, draws many of his engineers from India, China and western Europe. Much of this need for immigrants is caused by the lack of technical interest shown by America's university students who prefer marketing, finance and banking to engineering. (India has 85 of every 1,000 of its graduates holding engineering degrees while in the United States the ratio is 15 per 1,000.)

Education has been duly recognized as a key factor in affecting how large companies decide where to locate their newest overseas operations and even their domestic ones (e.g., large American corporations, like 3M and Honeywell, locate their facilities in the frigid state of Minnesota primarily to take advantage of the high level of secondary education provided there). Of course, the education has to be of the right kind. Vietnam, which claims one of the highest literacy rates in developing Asia (95%+), is still essentially an agrarian society. It has very little technical training and minimal business training (not unusual for a communist-led government). International hotel companies located there have to train local staff members on virtually every aspect of service right down to basics. Foreign investors in Hanoi or Ho Chi Minh City can rarely fill all of the management slots kept open for locals due to a severe shortage of trained personnel. Similar scenarios are repeated in Kenya and Chile (with 69% and 90% literacy rates, respectively) and other economies worldwide. Finland, a high-tech leader, still has an unemployment rate of almost 7% because the jobless, in a nation with 99% literacy, lack the requisite technical skills. Literacy is no longer enough; numeracy, organization, and versatility are increasingly dominant factors.

AN EMERALD IN THE ROUGH

A poignant example of how education has both served and frustrated a nation's rise in the global economy can be found in Ireland. Two decades ago Ireland was the "basket case" of Europe with a dwindling population and a crumbling infrastructure. Its university-educated workers fled the island to seek top jobs in U.S. banks and British brokerage houses. Its disciplined (and Catholic) school system produced highly skilled and versatile graduates who simply could not find gainful employment related to their studies in this capital-deprived nation. Ireland was literally training its people for the exclusive use of other economies, thus further depleting its own scarce resources.

The downward spiral continued until Ireland's full acceptance as part of the European Union brought an influx of badly needed capital, especially for infrastructure. Improved roads, power and telecommunications suddenly made

Ireland an attractive place for foreign investors. Its high level of education made it particularly attractive to high-tech companies and large banks—both in the expansion mode. The latter were seeking to have many of their "back office" account clearing operations done by Ireland's skilled but less expensive labor force, while the former needed programmers and hardware specialists to supply the growing European computer market. By the mid-1990s, Ireland had a per capita income that rivalled the United Kingdom's and growth approaching double digits. This fruitful combination of investment and education led to Ireland's new moniker of "the Emerald Dragon" and the return of many Irish from their economic exile. (It should be noted that the economic downturn in the Asian "dragons" caused some problems for Ireland. As the price of labor has dropped in Asia, some hardware manufacturers closed their higher-cost Irish plants. Ireland's financial institutions, however, have remained steadfast.)

The Rise of Trade Unions

The legal ability of workers to bind themselves together as a single unit for representation when dealing with employers to decide wages and working conditions is the definition of a trade union. The amount of legal protection afforded to unions, their proportional control of the workforce, and their effectiveness in controlling the workplace are not just issues that affect individual companies. These factors can have an impact upon a national economy and greatly determine that nation's ability to compete globally.

Modern unions had their beginnings in the guild systems of medieval Europe, where specific trades (tanners, woodworkers, etc.) would establish standards for craftsmanship. The towns and city-states that were home to these guilds would then permit the craftsmen to oversee all activity related to that specific guild. For instance, all carpentry work performed within the city limits had to be performed by guild members. At this point, the guilds' members (master craftsmen, journeymen, apprentices) were self-employed, setting their own standards and wages. The economies they worked within were, for the most part, tiny and self-contained.

CRAFTING THE FUTURE OF LABOR

The dawn of the Industrial Revolution in the mid-18th century marked the beginning of the end for independent craftsmen and the rise of the employer-employee relationship. Owners and managers of private enterprise now determined wages and working conditions. Employees made parts for products without the satisfaction of producing an entire piece of work. Huge factories employed thousands of people performing repetitive tasks for twelve to sixteen hours a day, six days a week. They lived in squalid company housing and bought goods at company-run emporiums. By the end of the 19th century, conditions had become oppressive and the medieval seeds of unionization were set to germinate in this fetid environment. (The title of Émile Zola's 19th-century novel about the plight of French coal miners, Germinal, makes reference to both the growth of worker unrest and the fertile conditions in which it took place.) Union movements began in earnest throughout Europe and North America, with workers demanding to regain control of their economic future. Karl Marx (with Friedrich Engels) fueled the unionist fire with Capital and The Communist Manifesto as talk of "class struggle" became commonplace. The worker had greater concerns that just the immediate job environment: the scale was now global.

After the Russian Revolution in 1917, private enterprise was forced to reckon with the power and motives of much larger scale labor movements. Russia, billing itself as a "workers' paradise," would serve as a model, in part or whole, for other economies (not just socialist ones). Russia's socialist leaders would influence the union movement worldwide for decades. The cry of "workers of the world unite!" would presage the effects, good and bad, that labor unions would eventually have on the world economy.

Economies and Labor

Throughout the 20th century, the relationship between private enterprise and labor was, for the most part, adversarial, with regular mediation by government required. Each adversary believes itself to be the rightful controller of business activity, both from a moral and an economic standpoint. Since this book is primarily concerned with the interplay of national economies, it is best to look at how different countries deal with the establishment and activity of unions within their borders. The net effect of unions on a nation's economy will also help determine a country's global standing and ability to attract foreign investment. The following examples juxtapose national economies to show how unionization and labor-related issues have impacted upon the global standing of each country.

GERMANY VS. JAPAN

Unions are strong in both countries but it is a very different type of strength in each. German workers are the highest paid in the world and work the least hours of any in the developed economies (1,651 hours per year versus 2,201 in Japan). Union representatives sit on the controlling boards of German companies. Their input into decision making is on par with that of middle management. German workers can expect to have their jobs for a lifetime (with six weeks vacation per year) and productivity is rarely called into question. Training and apprenticeships are extensive. Though Germany is considered an industrial powerhouse, it still has unemployment figures over 10% with a social welfare system that does little to encourage people to get back to work. Germany's unions take to the streets in noisy and effective protests every time the government tries to cut worker or social benefits. This combination of high-priced labor, union strength, and generous social benefits financed primarily through corporate taxation has made it very difficult for Germany to attract foreign investment. The annexation of the post-communist East Germany has only added to the problem. New foreign investment in Europe streams toward the lower cost but reasonably efficient economies of eastern Europe.

■ FRATERNAL UNIONS

Though Germany is the world's fifth largest economy, its GDP is just about half that of Japan, which in turn has a GDP roughly a third the size of that of the United States. Even during the troubled 1990s, Japan's unemployment has registered only slightly above 4%. Much of Japan's economic size and strength is derived from its relationship with labor and unions. Loyalty of employees in Japan is legendary, and unions are formed on a company-by-company basis, not by trade sector, which ties them to the success of the company. As in Germany, Japanese unions have input into management decisions but upper level management maintains the lion's share of power. Workers in Japan observe a strict hierarchy and company management decisions are to be implemented dutifully.

■ PATERNAL MANAGEMENT

In return for this, management maintains a paternal concern for labor. Order is maintained and disruptive strikes or protests are rare. Contracts are renewed on a yearly basis (every April), and wage bargaining is a separate process from that for conditions and benefits. Though lifetime employment is on the wane, most of the 24% of the Japanese population that is unionized, as well as those without union representation, will remain with the same company for their entire working career. Until the early 1990s, Japan kept foreign investors at arm's-length, preferring to generate their own financing through exports. Like Germany, Japan is finding that its employment traditions combined with high labor cost relative to the rest of Asia have made it decidedly unattractive to direct foreign investment now that the country is in need of it. For Germany, now fully absorbed into the EU, and Japan, losing its hold on the top spot in Asia to China, regional competition in the labor markets will realign the rankings of these societies in the world economic structure of the 21st century.

FRANCE VS. INDIA

France and India are two nations trying to turn away from a recent socialist past. The status of each nation's labor force in general and unions in particular has been greatly affected by the move towards a more market-oriented economy. France's situation has been compounded by its integration into the European Union, which has its own regulations regarding labor. India has had to face a population fast approaching one billion that is still primarily agrarian and greatly impoverished.

■ UNION POWER

French unions have enormous power, and they represent vast sections of the population including many "professional" workers. Paralyzing airline and ground transportation strikes just prior to France's hosting of the World Cup soccer matches were reminders to the central government of just how much power and popularity unions retain. Unfortunately, it also sent the same signal to international investors, most of whom have found France to be a difficult place to do business. Far and away the biggest complaint that entrepreneurs, both foreign and domestic, have is the restrictive environment for hiring and retaining French employees.

Like workers' rights in many countries with a socialist past, those in France are extensive and rigidly held. Muscular unions represent most of the working population and they hold employers to the government regulations which bind union and non-union companies alike. Termination of an employee is almost impossible except for the most egregious transgressions. As in Germany, French vacations are generous and employers must contribute, by law, huge sums towards insurance for their employees. Because benefits are mandated and standard, they do not serve as incentives, as they do in the United States. Pay is similarly regulated, thereby making it doubly difficult for entrepreneurs to lure skilled employees away from established companies. As a further brake to entrepreneurs, employees must give lengthy notices when planning to leave one company to join another. The labor market in France essentially lacks competition.

■ UNEMPLOYED AND OVERREGULATED

France also suffers from very high unemployment (10%+), most of which is the result of government over-regulation of private business. Rather than spur job growth by encouraging entrepreneurs, the central government took the tack of subdividing already existing jobs by instituting a 35-hour work week in 2000. People would receive the same pay for less work with the lopped-off hours being used to create new positions and more payroll for the original amount of work. This move further staved off any foreign investment considering a move to the country. The government's Jobs and Solidarity Minister—a job title that reveals much about the nation's attitude towards labor—sent out hundreds of investigators to alleviate what it saw as a growing problem: voluntary overtime. After discovering that certain "cadres" (mostly consisting of executives and managers) were working overtime to achieve their incentive pay, the government went so far as to photograph license plates in parking lots to track who stayed after hours. There was even consideration given to monitoring laptop computers to make sure executives were not taking their work home at night. This applied to foreign as well as domestic managers. Japanese, Chinese and American executives would never tolerate such intrusion nor would they consider managers who worked just a standard 40-hour workweek (let alone 35) worth their pay. France eventually abandoned the 35-hour work week in the private sector in 2008 but retained it in the public sector, the nation's largest employer.

■ WORKING HARDER AND SMARTER

India, like many emerging markets, has had a love-hate relationship with foreign investors eager to take advantage of the Indian workforce. No one has ever doubted the ability and willingness of the Indian labor force to work hard. However, the New Delhi government has also taken measures to exploit India's ability to work smart. After reaching an economic crisis in the early 1990s, the new administration of P.V. Narashima Rao decided in 1991 to make a decided retreat from long-term socialist policies regarding labor and investment. The new model would not be based on the now defunct U.S.S.R. but upon East Asian models and British reform under Margaret Thatcher. Foreign investment would be encouraged, especially in the technology and infrastructure sectors. The Indian unions, though powerful, would be confined to traditional physical labor jobs and have little impact upon "white collar" and managerial positions. Consequently, unions have had little effect on the growth of the Indian economy, beyond the occasional disputes over the influence of foreign investors upon the cultures in India. Managerial authority is strong. Executives and managers can work as many hours as they choose. Unlike France, Indian job expansion will take place through the expansion of business, not the contraction of hours worked.

■ MINING BANGALORE'S MINDS

The city of Bangalore is a prime example of where India saw its future in the world economy. Top software companies from around the world use Bangalore as a programming center, transferring the data via high speed telecom lines back to their headquarters in Silicon Valley or Tokyo. Certainly, India's engineers draw far lower salaries than their Western counterparts but one of their greatest assets is their proficiency. India has the third largest contingent of scientists and engineers in the world. Neither of these segments of the labor force has ever been a hotbed of union activity in any nation. Add to this their fluency in the language of commerce and technology (English), and it becomes plain why post-socialist India is so attractive to foreign investors. While it should be noted that India receives only about one-eighth of the foreign investment flow of China, it should also be noted that India has not experienced the high percentage of failed foreign investments that has plagued China. India's far less rigid labor rules and less unionized atmosphere (China is essentially one big state-run union) have been cited as one of the main reasons for increased Indian success. China has struggled to attain the technical sophistication of India's workforce.

Like all economies trying to shake off decades of socialism, India's does have its drawbacks. The most salient of these is the remnants of the "Permit Raj," the nickname for the elaborate bureaucracy that once oversaw every aspect of Indian life. For the most part it was broken up by the Rao government's reformers, but the raj's licensing procedures, though greatly reduced, are still present in India.

INDONESIA VS. BRAZIL

Both Indonesia and Brazil are large countries with almost identically sized workforces (67 million and 65 million, respectively). Indonesia is a much more agrarian nation, with 55% of its population living off the land as compared to 35% in Brazil. Both nations are technically republics with a common law-based legal code. Indonesia is the world's largest Islamic state while Brazil is overwhelmingly Catholic. The GDP per capita of Indonesians is about a third of the Brazilian rate of US$9,700. Divergent in many ways, these two countries, however, have similar economic histories. Many of each nation's problems have come from attempting to move an agrarian workforce into industry and technology within a single generation.

■ FERTILE GROUND FOR UNIONIZATION

Between the summers of 1997 and 1998, Indonesia's leader of over thirty years, Suharto, was forced to step down, the country's economy began to experience double-digit negative GDP growth, and the currency (rupiah) had declined by 80% in value. A country that once touted itself as an example of the "Asian miracle" found that 40% of its population was now suddenly below the poverty level. One of the main demands of the street crowds that drove Suharto from office was the call for widescale unionization. While the nation experienced the high growth of the 1980s, business owners had few problems using their government connections to keep unions tiny and their expansion illegal. Individual "in-house" unions were legal but were subject to the control of a single, state-recognized labor union heavily controlled by government. This lack of union autonomy is very common in the developing regions of southeast Asia. It has served to make Indonesia attractive to foreign investors looking to keep the cost of labor, and therefore manufacturing, down.

Using the analogy of "rising tide raises all boats," the influx of foreign investments was welcomed as they provided hundreds of thousands of jobs. These jobs paid nowhere near what they paid in the West or in Japan, but decidedly higher than the amount that could be found in most of agrarian Indonesia. (Minimum wage in Indonesia, however, is recognized as being insufficient to provide subsistence for even a small family.) Meanwhile, unions were depicted as possible detractors from overall economic growth. Any call for higher wages, expanded benefits, or improvement of working conditions would be seen as an attempt to drive away the foreign money so necessary for the nation's success. Recalcitrant union organizers were detained and their organizations scrutinized by government officials.

■ GOVERNMENT COLLUSION

While this type of collusion between government and business may seem harsh to some readers, it should be noted that the theory, if not the practice, was sound at the time. Indonesia was in direct competition with other Asian nations seeking to attract a limited amount of direct foreign investment. As stated earlier, global companies see little value in investing in emerging markets unless they provide a broad basket of incentives from tax holidays to free land to low labor costs. Indonesia was unwilling to allow neighboring Malaysia, China, Thailand or the Philippines to soak up all of the investment funding. Presenting obstacles to investment, like high labor costs or strong unions, could have left Indonesia as an economic backwater in a part of the world that was showing some explosive economic growth.

■ PRESCIENT PRECEDENTS

Indonesia (like its emerging neighbors) could look to the models of Japan, Taiwan, and South Korea for precedent (and to some degree, China). These economic successes had kept a tight lid on labor activity during their developmental phase. All three models had allowed unions to take hold only after stable, positive economic growth had become a predictable reality. Even after union acceptance, Japan and Taiwan had effectively limited the power of the unions while South Korea made its unions subservient to the needs of the very powerful *chaebols*. Unfortunately for Indonesia, it has yet to experience the long-term stable growth that the "Asian Tigers" have enjoyed in decades past.

■ FOUNDERING FOUNDATIONS

When the economic crisis of the late 1990s hit Asia, Indonesia and her developing neighbors (as well as the "Tigers") suddenly found that economic growth had been built on shaky ground. Rather than blame themselves for poor economic strategies, government officials (Suharto, quite vocally) now blamed the foreign investments once thought to be the lifeblood of success. Foreigners, not the government, had undermined the people. Luckily, the Indonesian people found the excuse implausible and blamed the cronyism of government business decisions for the downturn. While Suharto faced removal from office, companies were not held blameless and union organizers were some of the first to man the barricades in Jakarta's streets. Union activity is on the rise and once the economic crisis has been alleviated, business will undoubtedly find that the price of wages and benefits has increased. If this also occurs in the rest of southeast Asia, then the effect on Indonesia may result in stable but lower growth rates. If, however, only Indonesia becomes heavily unionized in the future, then foreign investors will focus on more cost-effective environments. Should this happen, the Jakarta government can expect GDP stagnation and public unrest for many years to come. Some nation, maybe Indonesia, will have to accept the title of "the sick man of Asia" and the rise of unionization may be the most obvious symptom.

■ BEEN THERE, SURVIVED THAT

Brazil has already experienced many of the economic problems that are currently plaguing Indonesia. Up until the 1950s, this former Portuguese colony (Indonesia was a Dutch colony) was the great economic powerhouse of South America. Moving from agriculture to industry, however, brought many problems to Brazil's economy. The lack of fiscal discipline common in agrarian cultures takes its toll on capital-intensive industrial projects. Industrialization also brought greater calls for protectionist legislation, accompanied by the distrust of those foreigners willing to invest in (maybe exploit) the country. Through the 1970s and 1980s, hyperinflation, political unrest, and social instability made Brazil the archetypal Latin American basket-case economy. Renegotiation of international loans, denunciation of foreign interests, and IMF intervention led to austerity measures aimed at putting the economy back on track. Today, Brazil has found a level of stability that is reflected in its economic statistics and its labor laws.

■ FATHERING STABILITY

Brazil is the star of Latin American economies and ranks ninth in the world and first in Latin America according to the World Bank. Brazil is considered an up-and-coming world power and is mentioned alongside Russia, India and China in the "BRIC" designation of "nations to keep an eye on" by investors. This prosperity can be seen in the generosity of the labor legislation. The national Consolidated Labor Law calls for collective labor agreements with definite and indefinite contracts. Employees can choose between two different benefit regimes, both of which allow for significant termination payments. Brazilian regulation oversees vacation, holiday and overtime pay as well as retirement benefits that require contributions from employers and employees alike. While Brazil's system of mandatory benefits is more akin to France's than to that of the United States, it is still more indicative of a stable, growing economy than the Indonesian system. (Argentina and Mexico, both economic leaders in their own right, have labor legislation that is equally paternalistic as Brazil's—a reflection of a regional tradition. Centuries of political "strong men" have ingrained the idea that the top portions of the hierarchy will provide for the lower echelons as long as loyalty is assured.)

■ FAVORITE CHILDREN AND DOTING FATHERS

Indonesia has a similar tradition of strong, paternalistic leaders (it has had two since independence, Sukarno and Suharto), but any patronage thus far has been showered on business owners, not workers. One piece of fallout from the Asian economic crisis of the late 1990s was the shift of investment dollars from the promising Far East to Latin America. Auto manufacturers, convinced that parts of Asia were dead ends, have rushed to countries like Brazil. Steel, chemical, and petroleum companies (even software firms) have all shifted their attention to a country that only a decade before was considered by most investors to be an economic black hole. This is less a tribute to the fickleness of the investment community than to the resilience of the Brazilian economy. Its attractiveness and current stability are both a cause and a result of an increased partnership among government, business and labor. Government-enforced austerity measures that brought great hardship to companies and workers alike have paid off handsomely. International investors have seen that Brazilians have the market discipline that is called for in today's economic environment.

The same discipline has been found lacking in Indonesia, where even the successive governments that replaced Suharto have failed to respond to the full scope of that nation's economic problems. Foreign investors meanwhile have found Brazil to have a stable political environment, a supply of cheap and plentiful real estate, an educated workforce, competitive wages, and *reasonable* union activity. These last three attributes are fast becoming important economic factors that companies consider when reviewing opportunities for overseas expansion.

Minimum Wage, Minimum Effect

A great deal of pressure is placed upon international companies working in the emerging markets to pay wages that are comparable to those paid in the industrialized markets. Governments in the developing societies are similarly pressured to enact legislation that guarantees a minimum wage for their citizenry. Even when global companies pay in excess of local minimum wages, they are still taken to task by activists for paying significantly less for labor than in the developed world. It should be obvious that the low labor costs found overseas are one of the main attractions for overseas expansion. It should be equally plain that those lower costs are reflected in the prices paid (even by activists) for the goods and services produced. Debates over wage disparities generally have more of an emotional and political emphasis than an economic one, as markets presuppose that some groups will prosper more than others. What we will discuss here is the value or lack of value that minimum wages provide to an economy in the international marketplace.

LABOR AS A COMMODITY

In his treatise on wages, Henry Hazlitt wrote that it "is unfortunate for clarity of economic thinking that the price of labor's services should have received an entirely different name from other prices." Characteristically, people attach an emotional value to the price of human labor (wages) that they do not apply to the price of other component prices such as materials, utilities, or advertising. Wages (from the same German root as the word "wed," meaning "to pledge") represent an agreement between labor and management for compensation for work performed. Wages are even considered differently from salaries (derived from the tradition of paying Roman soldiers with salt, *salarius*), from both an accounting and a social standpoint. Wages are for laborers, and salaries are for supervisory personnel.

Once unions gained acceptance and a powerful voice, the opinion was promulgated that while ownership and management were suitably paid, somehow the mass of the labor force was getting short shrift at pay time. Governments responded by instituting the form of price controls called the minimum wage. Long accepted in the West, this concept is rapidly spreading to the emerging markets. As we will see, this is occurring in spite of the fact that no economically sound argument can be made for instituting a minimum wage.

WAGES AS COSTS

Minimum wages in a market economy are self-defeating, as they presuppose that labor is underpaid and not subject to the forces that determine the price of other goods and services. When wages (and labor) are viewed as the commodity that they truly are, the argument against government wage controls is the same as that for other price interference. Artificial prices (those not determined by supply and demand) force consumers to pay more than the goods or services are actually worth. This results in either reduced consumption or no consumption at all. The jobs provided by the producing company are either reduced in number or eliminated altogether.

When an artificial pricing scheme is applied to wages, the number of jobs available decreases and therefore the benefit to the labor force is nil. Those potential employees (the unskilled, the young) whose labor is not considered worth the mandated government-established wage remain unemployed. Companies prefer not to hire at all rather than pay wages in excess of potential productivity. (For example, the unemployment rate in France for workers under the age of 25 is 28%. Those in the same age bracket in the United States are three times as likely to be unemployed as other American workers. Oddly, this under-25 age group is most often cited as potential beneficiaries of minimum wage legislation.) This process has international as well as domestic implications.

MAKING FOREIGNERS PAY

Many emerging markets (Malaysia, Chile) have established minimum wages not as a result of the behavior of their domestic companies but in response to the arrival of foreign firms. Some countries, like Vietnam and China, have two-tiered minimum wages with higher rates for firms with foreign investors than for those with purely domestic ownership. Though these wages are not by any means excessive (Vietnam requires US$40 per month for rural labor and US$60 for urban employees of foreign, not local, companies), they do reduce the competitiveness of the subject companies. When a two-tiered system is used, it also sends a message to foreign investors that they will be treated differently by government officials—a prospect few foreign firms relish.

A common myth surrounding minimum wage regulation is that such intervention drives up all other wages and therefore is a benefit to the workforce. Such thinking is wrong on two counts. Firstly, minimum wage regulation is based upon the prevailing average wage already present in an economy. Calls for increasing the minimum wage come after the average wage has increased. Even those nations with two-tiered systems establish the minimum wage below the average made at the foreign firm. The reality is that minimum wages do not drive wage increases in market economies but follow them. (Note: In socialist economies all prices, including wages, are artificially set by regulation.) Secondly, as time progresses, the market price of goods rises to reflect any net increase in costs that companies may incur, wages or otherwise. When and if employees are hired at the artificial rate, their buying power and that of all workers is brought to a new parity level as prices adjust. Unless their skills improve and they move out of minimum wage positions, they will not see a true increase in pay. If anything, increases in the minimum wage will only further reduce the jobs available for the unskilled.

AVOIDING OVERPRICED LABOR

Much of the desire by companies to pursue overseas prospects comes from the need to avoid the wages that their domestic governments mandate for unskilled labor. High-paying, high-skilled jobs tend to stay within wealthy economies. On the other hand, many manufacturing jobs requiring little more than basic literacy have been moved into the emerging markets by producers from Japan, Britain, and the United States over the last two decades. A day's wage in the developed world could buy a month's worth of labor in the emerging markets. Just as companies sought out cheap commodities like oil and minerals in the former "third world," they now seek lower prices for the commodity of labor. As both minimum and average wages rose in the newly developed markets in Asia (as occurred in Taiwan and South Korea in their early stages of development), global companies sought less expensive labor in economies like Thailand and Indonesia. As these nations in turn became expensive by the 1990s, China became more attractive. When China's wages exceed its workforce's productivity, another region will be sought out and jobs will be "exported" as they were in the big industrial nations. (Note: There is pressure on China to keep its currency weak in order to keep its labor force cheaper than its neighbors'.)

Minimum wages set in the domestic economy will determine for some companies whether or not they will seek production overseas. Jobs that can be easily transferred as well as readily and cheaply filled overseas are the first to be exported. Because wage regulation is usually targeted at a society's least skilled and least productive members, the adverse consequences of job mobility are potentially the greatest for them. The unskilled will be left behind usually to become part of the welfare subsidy problem. The increased taxation placed upon companies to pay for these subsidies acts as another spur to move into the international economy and leave high costs—and the labor pool—behind.

CHAPTER 8

International Trade

IT IS MUCH EASIER TO GET GOODS THAN IT IS TO GET MONEY. — JEREMY BENTHAM, 1789

ALL NATIONS HAVE found it necessary to trade with their neighbors at some point. Most have found it to be of great advantage. Initially such trade was in raw materials that were bartered, but over time finished goods and then services became part of the exchange process. Eventually, money, in the form of coined precious metals that had originally been traded for their intrinsic value as decoration, became the medium of exchange. Now goods and services were valued separately from a one-to-one bartering, and transactions became more complex. Precious metal currencies were eventually superseded by government guaranteed paper money, along with other forms of payment like checks, credit cards and electronic transfers. Besides enabling multi-party transactions, the development of money had the problematic effect of creating a scoreboard by which each nation could easily measure its imports against its exports.

Trading with the Enemy

As discussed in Chapter 2, many nations during the mercantile phase of their development chose to see gold as a commodity to be taken in exchange for goods exported to rivals, both economic and political. By maintaining this gold surplus, nations like England hoped to "beggar their neighbors" and thus make themselves the only nation financially capable of building and paying a large military. The amount of gold was, of course, limited, and keeping neighbors in a constant state of deficit proved problematic. Nowadays few nations maintain large gold reserves, and currency is given market value based on a national economy's overall strength, not just imports and exports. Without gold, however, trade surpluses and trade deficits still occur, but for many different reasons. The political and economic ramifications of deficits and surpluses also remains important.

The Japanese–American Trade Conflict

A country like Japan, with few natural resources, must import the majority of its raw materials. Japan, however, has an extraordinary manufacturing capacity for making finished goods. These value-added products are then exported to an eagerly awaiting world. Japan's domestic market imports few finished goods from overseas, resulting in an overall surplus of trade of billions of dollars per year. The Japanese, in monetary terms, sell more than they buy when it comes to manufactured goods. Even though they are very wealthy on a per capita basis compared to the rest of the world, Japanese consumers save much of their money.

They have been discouraged from buying imports through formal tariffs, lack of space, and informal restrictions, as was discussed in Chapter 4.

The United States, with the largest economy in the world, has a very different approach to its trade balance. Unlike Japan, the United States has massive amounts of raw materials matched to an active value-adding manufacturing sector. Although many large manufacturers have "gone global," most of America's manufacturers have remained within the nation's borders. Compared to Japan, the U.S. market is wide open to imports, while American culture and living conditions encourage consumptions at all levels. Even for those citizens considered to be living below the "poverty level" in the United States, the majority own their homes as well as automobiles, cable television, mobile phones and air conditioning. The United States buys more goods than it sells resulting in trade deficits of hundreds of billions per year.

GOODS AND SERVICES

Trade surplus and deficit figures, which occupy the thoughts of politicians everywhere, are usually only stated in terms of manufactured goods. Services are rarely included in these discussions even though for some economies like the United States, such services make up a large chunk of the export economy. The interminable wrangling between the United States and Japan (and nowadays, the United States and China) over trade deficits ignores three factors. One, the United States has twice the population of Japan with roughly the same per capita income but with higher domestic purchasing power parity. (The U.S. has one third the population of China but over eight times the purchasing power per person.) Even if Japan's markets were as open as those of the United States, it would be very difficult for the Japanese to buy as much as the Americans. Secondly, much of what the United States exports to Japan is in the form of services like financial services, software, movies and music. The United States has few rivals in some of these sectors, and none in others. When these services are factored in, the American trade deficit with Japan shrinks considerably. Lastly, some of what the United States imports from Japan comes from American companies exporting from Japanese territory. The facade of a troublesome trade deficit is maintained by both sides because the U.S. politicians need the villain of Japan (as well as China) to take the blame for the decline in unionized American manufacturing. Japan for its part ignores the service sector figures rather than admit to its complete lack of competitiveness in those areas.

Imports = Exports

The economic, and very apolitical, fact is that technically no nation can export more than it imports. This is because money is the basis of trade. If the United States imports US$1 million in cars from Japanese companies, then the Japanese will be paid in American currency. The Japanese can either exchange those dollars for yen at a premium from foreign exchange banks or they must spend that currency in the U.S. economy. That could be done by directly purchasing U.S. goods or through exchanges with third party nations. Either way, that US$1 million should return to the American economy eventually through U.S. exports or investment. International trade is really an elaborate form of bartering and as long as the market sets fair prices, the equilibrium of trade is maintained. The lagtime between transactions and currency devaluations during these delays also plays a part in creating this façade of surplus and deficits.

The continual U.S. trade "deficit" (not just with Japan, but overall) is partially caused by the fact that, unlike other "hard currencies," U.S. dollars are used as a secondary and, sometimes, primary currency by other nations. Both Russian and Vietnamese citizens, for instance, use the "greenback" for daily transactions alongside their own currencies. Approximately one-third of all U.S. dollars in circulation are held off-shore either in the currency reserves of governments or as "real" money being used by private citizens living in troubled economies. It may never return to the U.S. economy although it still represents American wealth. More on this topic will be taken up when global debt is discussed in Chapter 9.

Import / Export Failures

The trading problems of wealthy nations are well publicized if not fully understood. But trade issues are an important part of the emerging economies as well. Many readers might assume that all poor countries are net exporters because per capita incomes would prevent the purchase of expensive imports. This is certainly the case with China and its 1.3 billion population. While pockets of extreme wealth can be found on the coastlines, the greater part of China's population exists at almost a subsistence level. While cars might dominate Beijing, Shanghai and Shenzhen, the rest of China looks to bicycles and oxcarts for transport. On paper, China is operating with a trade surplus because its raw materials and cheap manufactures flow outward much faster than foreign goods flow into the countryside.

However, China does not have a convertible currency. When China exports goods, it receives foreign currency. But its own currency (the renminbi) has no value on the international market for making import purchases. They must buy foreign goods, like computers or sometimes even rice, with a currency (yen, pounds or dollars) that does not obligate the foreign seller to make future purchases in the Chinese economy. Whereas the United States or Japan can pay its bills with a currency it controls, China must pay with a currency that is controlled for the most part by the sellers. Consequently, China's trade "surplus" is as ephemeral as the U.S. deficit. Though the Chinese aversion to convertibility keeps them immune to the type of direct currency speculation attack experienced by other Asian nations, its trade is completely subject to the whims of the "hard currency" nations. Such a trade surplus has great domestic political value for the Chinese but little global economic worth as China remains essentially an economic colony of the hard currency nations.

Emerging Importers

Some nations that should technically be net exporters by way of their impoverished populations are actually not. India, another massive nation with a crippling level of poverty is a net importer, though hardly by choice. Poor agricultural planning, a middle-class consumerism far in excess of China's, and a clumsy manufacturing sector have put this former socialist nation in a continual state of trade deficit. Even when its growing service sectors (40% of the domestic economy) are added, the result is still a deficit because its services (e.g., banking, films) have little export value. Groaning bureaucracies, protected but inefficient industries, and a countryside incapable of feeding a massive population have made India seek solace outside of its borders. The result: a "trade deficit" financed by international loans. Like the United States, India has significant external debt, but unlike the United States, Indian indebtedness has done little to advance the economy as a whole. Its trade "deficits" merely allow it to subsist.

EXPORTING WEALTH, IMPORTING PROBLEMS

Russia shows signs of another type of import/export problem. Russia's vast countryside is desperately poor yet chock full of natural resources (oil, gas, minerals) that became the focus of a major export push. Even the more wealthy urban areas with a history of manufacturing began capitalizing on the technological advances that Russia made for much of the 20th century. However, governmental bungling and outright malfeasance prevented this former superpower from being considered little more than another chaotic emerging market for many years after communism fell. Instead of exporting its natural wealth (even with the declining oil prices of those early days) Moscow officials spent most of their time soliciting foreign aid. Throughout the 1990s Russia was unable or unwilling to stockpile the massive amount of foreign reserve currency to allow it to function globally. What foreign currency that did arrive was spirited offshore all too quickly. The rising oil prices beginning in 2006 and foreign investment in drilling finally allowed Russia to amass hundreds of billions of dollars (petrodollars) for its reserves. Of course, now Russia's economy is too attached to a single commodity, oil, which can drop as quickly as it rises. If the new-found wealth is not used to diversify, trouble lurks down the road. Ironically, much of the increase in oil prices of this period was due to demand for fuel during rapid expansion by China, one of Russia's old adversaries.

THRIVING ON CHAOS

Both China and Russia have weak national currencies, an industrial base, cheap labor, and a host of other economic factors that make them huge exporters. The former exports manufactured goods while the latter exports commodities (oil and gas) that get "value added" elsewhere. China, through careful control of its currency reserves, can afford to buy what it needs from abroad and even advance its technical base. Russia is spending its money on beefing up its military and sinking money into infrastructure for communications and mineral extraction. China uses its most abundant commodity, labor, to advance the economy. Russia relies on its natural resources, many of them strategic, to fill its coffers. As these two nations go from being poverty stricken behemoths to becoming enriched mega-economies, the rest of the world will have to make room for them and pray that they will start importing more than they export.

Import and Export Policies

Nations like China and Japan have consciously made choices to engage in export promotion as a means to control their domestic economy. Both keep enormous foreign reserves (China first, followed by Japan) and have both formal and informal means of limiting imports. They use these choices to protect themselves from more powerful competitors like the United States and the ever expanding European Union. These Western economies have aggressive approaches to both imports and exports based on the principle that growth can be best facilitated by exchange rather than the hoarding of cash characteristic of mercantile economies. For them, the pursuit of balance rather than surplus or deficit is the ideal.

In all four cases, the choice or lack of choice about trade has greatly influenced the status of each player in the global marketplace. No "invisible hand" of Adam Smith made the determination of how these economies assembled the building blocks of their trade policies. It was either done by domestic government policies, or imposed, as in the case of Japan after WWII, by external agencies. These strategic trade policies, chosen by some and felt by all, are imposed by governments but formulated with the assistance of business, and even military, leaders.

TARIFFS

Governments will regularly impose import tariffs on foreign products that are also produced domestically. Besides generating tax revenue, this is done in an effort to either keep that market exclusive for domestic businesses or to offer them some competitive protection from more efficient foreign manufacturers or service providers. Export tariffs are imposed to keep important goods and services from leaving a country's borders. This might include valuable minerals like gold or militarily strategic goods like computer chips or plutonium. Such tariffs are also imposed in cheap labor markets to "tax" a foreign producer operating domestically who intends to export the value-added goods or services for increased profits.These are certainly domestic issues but the impact can be globally strategic. By imposing (or threatening to impose) greater or totally restrictive tariffs, a nation can force rival economies to lower their own tariffs.

STRATEGIC SUBSIDIES

The same result can occur when a nation decides to set up a system of import and export subsidies. Governments, usually at the insistence of business, will actually help defray the cost of imports with tax dollars as a means to gain a technology transfer, lower the cost of food or fuel, or assist a trading partner with an eye towards future trade concessions. Domestic manufacturers considering export can also be financially assisted with low cost export processing zones (EPZs), subsidized transport or labor, refunded tariffs, cheap credit, access to scarce materials, or even government-funded infrastructure like roads, harbors or airports. EPZs may be offered to foreign manufacturers as well in an effort to create domestic jobs or gain technology transfers.

For both imports and exports the result of strategic trade policy is the same: costs per units produced are lowered relative to competitors. It should be noted that "direct" export subsidies are illegal under international law. The examples cited here are considered indirect. Both subsidies and tariffs are taken up in detail in Chapter 4 and are mentioned here only for their strategic impact on trade.

Exporting Your Imports: The Grey Market

Often, producers in developed economies will attempt to gain market share in emerging economies by lowering their prices significantly. This is used by manufacturers whose product prices would otherwise be out of reach of the targeted population. Such reductions are also used for products that the target society (rich or poor) has come to consider low cost through previous government subsidy or local custom. This occurs regularly with pharmaceuticals in Europe or with Western beer in southeast Asia. Sometimes this largesse backfires on the exporters by creating what is known as parallel imports.

PARALYZING PARALLELS

In the *parallel import* scenario, a manufacturer exports goods to an emerging market at a reduced price with the hopes of making up the losses over time as the target market develops. Instead, these goods, often consumer products with high demand in the manufacturer's domestic market, are exported by the target market in direct competition with the original manufacturer. The goods may return directly to the market of origin at a lower price. This particular problem has blossomed in borderless Europe where expensive economies are a short truck drive away from emerging economies not governed by European Union laws.

Western and northern European goods of all types, from eyeglass frames to antibiotics to candy bars, are sent to developing eastern European nations or the CIS at reduced, market-acceptable prices. Once there, they are bought up en masse and reshipped to their original EU markets where eager retailers snap up bargains for their customers. Within a matter of weeks, the high-priced brand-name product is available for full price at the expensive German boutique and for 20% off at the discount competitor across the street. Many retailers, rebuffed by high-end producers for being too down market, hail the grey marketeers as heroic "price busters." Manufacturers find parallel imports to be the source of lost income. The impact upon the value of the brand-name should be obvious. The effect upon international trade has much more telling by-products.

EXHAUSTING LEGISLATION

Under current EU law, the manufacturers' concern about the cheapening of their brands and trademarks is countered by rules on trademark exhaustion. These laws declare that once a product is sold (that is, within the EU), no restriction can be placed upon the resale of the product or its price. Such regulation was put in place specifically to safeguard the free movement of goods within the EU, where individual state or municipal governments have been in the habit of price-setting for products like fuel and drugs. Arbitrageurs, those willing and able to take advantage of known price differences, have long exploited these laws. Such arbitrage was accepted, if not beloved, by EU manufacturers as long as it took place entirely within the EU. Non-EU "grey marketeers" are another matter entirely and the subject of ongoing European Court of Justice legal battles.

DIMINISHING BRAND NAMES

The United States, long a champion of free markets, keeps itself wide open to parallel imports from all directions. The idea here is that the free movement of products spurs competition and all competition is good. The American position is that once a product is sold the producer loses any right to restrict further sale under the original brand unless the product has been altered to mislead or defraud customers (e.g., refilling liquor bottles with cheaper distillates). The counter argument to this concept is that parallel importers profit by cheapening a brand-name without adding any value to the final transaction. Furthermore, such trademark diminution discourages manufacturers from investing in quality control or from developing new products. It may also make them resistant to shipping innovative products to the emerging markets in the belief that no trade is better than the long-term crippling of the brand. The reader will note that, currently, there is no fully international law covering trademarks, copyrights, brand equity, or other intellectual property rights.

Exporting and Importing Crime: The Black Market

Not all international trade takes place within a legal framework. Much trade is intentionally illegal and derives its price structure primarily from its illicit nature. Some products may be cheap because they do not include the cost of taxation, inspection, or customs control. Other products may be expensive because they reflect the risk involved in cross-border smuggling. Whatever the case, the black market of international trade is enormous, ancient, and shows every sign of being a growth sector for centuries to come. Another characteristic is that it is often accomplished with the complicity of government officials.

TRADING IN CRIME

All countries suffer or tolerate some degree of criminal activity in their trade with other nations. The most notable and newsworthy of these activities is the drug trade. It is a multi-billion dollar business that contributes enormous amounts of hard currency to the economies of Afghanistan, Myanmar, Colombia, Turkey, Mexico, and a host of other developing nations. The wealthy developed world, where most of these illegal substances are consumed, sees the diversion of these same billions from more productive uses in their own economies. However, as in all trade, that money finds its way back to its home economy when it is used to pay for the cars, planes, and consumer goods purchased by the drug dealers and their underlings. Some of the mounds of cash are actually used to invest in legitimate global businesses. Even the illegal drug trade must submit to the principles of international exchange and no currency is of use unless it is in circulation.

The drug trade and other "underground" economies have long been recognized for their effect on domestic economics although the profits rarely appear when assessing the level of poverty in a nation. The impact on international economics, however, garners little attention and remains somewhat of a dirty little secret when discussing the machinations of world trade. Most of the illegal trade that occurs does not involve anything nearly as reprehensible as narcotics or gun-running. Most cross-border smuggling involves food products, cigarettes, textiles, shoes, construction materials, vehicles, fuel and even labor.

LEAKY BORDERS

As an example, the border between Vietnam and China is a veritable sieve for everything from cement to clothing to even cat meat. The border could easily be closed to such trade by the military garrisons on both sides. However, smuggling has a long tradition in the region and its benefits are shared on both sides of the border. On occasion, the Chinese and the Vietnamese will arrest, try and penalize (usually by firing squad) smugglers and complicitous border guards, but the illegal trade continues. It flourishes, like all black market trade, because the benefits far outweigh the risks. In this case, many of the products would be otherwise unavailable or would be otherwise rendered too expensive if standard tariffs were imposed. China's rate of smuggling, across all of its borders, is so great as to actually cause international bankers and economists to readjust their statistics on China's import demand when assessing growth potential. (Note: There are many ramifications of criminal cross-border trade. The cat meat mentioned above, a delicacy imported by China, was declared contraband by Hanoi after Vietnam became infested with free-ranging rats that had devastated crops.)

CONTRABAND LABOR

The problem is hardly confined to poor economies, however. The United States has unprotected borders with both Canada and Mexico. Every year thousands of illegal immigrants cross those borders to find work in the U.S. economy. (While most such migration comes via Mexico, Canada's population has also started moving south due to a severe drop in the value of the Canadian dollar.) This "black market labor" is no less a commodity than Chinese cement, and the same consideration of mutual benefit applies to North America. Farms, restaurants, offices and construction sites all over America benefit from this source of inexpensive labor that requires no additional company-provided health benefits. America's two neighbors reap the benefit of billions of dollars of hard currency that flow into their economies through either the postal service or directly out of the pockets of returning emigres.

The governments of the United States, Mexico and Canada make little effort, relative to the size of the problem and the amount of money involved, to stem the flow of people or cash. Since the advent of the North American Free Trade Act (NAFTA), even less attention has been paid to such contraband labor in North America. The United States even educates the children of illegal immigrants in public schools, provides some social benefits, and on occasion grants amnesties to long-term unauthorized residents.

Unlike the Asian example, where governments turn a blind eye to keep potentially rancorous peasants supplied with consumer goods, the North American scenario has developed with the notion that all three governments will gain economically, not just politically. For Mexico and Canada, U.S. dollars will return and be used locally to spur the economy. They will be taxed locally as well, as either sales levies or personal income. Stateside, illegal labor helps keep some U.S. industries competitive (e.g., fruit growing, restaurants) while the sales of those companies using the labor will be taxed in lieu of the lost payroll taxes of those illegals being paid "off of the books." And, in line with the principle that imports spur exports, the U.S. dollars eventually find their way back across the border when they are exchanged at a premium or used to buy American goods (autos) or services (software).

Crime Controls

In the examples already cited, the black market is at work in only a small percentage of sectors of the economies examined. In most nations, illegal activity including all crime, domestic and cross-border, makes up less than 5%—at most—of the entire economic picture. However, 5% of some economies (the United States, for instance) represents a great deal of money. Less successful nations, those countries undergoing economic restructure, or those suffering through war or revolution, have far higher rates of black marketeering. In extreme cases it sometimes evolves into institutionalized thuggery. The effect on the international status of such economies usually worsens the domestic problem, as is the case with Russia and Myanmar.

GOVERNMENT COMPLICITY

Russia's transition from Marxism/Leninism to capitalism was an unusually bumpy one. Unlike Poland, which swept communist politicians from government ranks in the early 1990s, Russia simply allowed long-term apparatchniks to rename themselves and remain in power, albeit by elective office. Part of the result was that the former secret police structure, notably the KGB, reinvented itself into a massive and powerful black market system that was just as willing to use a gun as a computer program to make a profit. Currently, a vast majority of Russian businesses, including joint-ventures with foreign firms, have a black market (mafia) component. The bodyguard business is flourishing and more common illegal activities like prostitution and drugs have reached epidemic proportions in major cities.

Criminal elements are not solely to blame for Russia's well-publicized post-communist economic problems. A disastrous privatization of state industries along with ongoing commercial cronyism have also helped bring this former superpower to its knees. What the black market dominance is doing, however, is preventing global foreign assistance from coming to the aid of Russia's legitimate economy. So widespread and violent is the mafiya that international agencies like the IMF or even private investors have seen their money disappear into a maelstrom of corruption. Banking and investment reforms are met with intense opposition because they endanger, even eliminate, the potential profits of entrenched black marketeers. The global economy sat helplessly by for years as a major nuclear power began to spiral into chaos, in good part because of its lack of attention to the rule of law. A good deal of the chaos (and, to some degree, the poverty) has been relieved by Russia's success in the oil and gas industry, but day-to-day life in the cities still contains a large component of criminal commercial activity. Foreign investors remain reluctant to pile into this potentially vibrant economy. At the base of the problem is a Russian black market that has come to dominate rather than serve as a minor augmentation to the economy.

STATE-SPONSORED CRIME

The nation of Myanmar (formerly Burma) is another problem altogether, for here the state actively sponsors the black market. The military government, brought into power by a rather murderous coup d'etat and maintained by repressive tactics, keeps an iron grip on the political and economic structure. Its black market cross-border trade in timber, sex, drugs, and precious stones has enabled the government to finance one of the largest military budgets in Asia (including a 300,000 man army) in one of the world's poorest nations. State-sponsored black market activity at first glance appears to be just a dubious way for the state to seek revenue. Myanmar has also shown that by directly controlling all business, legitimate and criminal, it can keep a tight political control on the nation. The reaction of global investors to Myanmar's activity has been strongly adverse.

This poses a number of problems for Myanmar's people and the country's potential for future economic growth. Although Myanmar was grudgingly admitted to ASEAN it has effectively been cut off from most of the development aid that would normally be placed at its disposal. The government's heavy-handed political activity, such as placing its main opposition leader under continual house arrest, further marginalizes the nation and prevents major investment from the West. Adding to the problem, Myanmar's ASEAN co-members are currently in no position to offer economic aid. Even if they were, they would be loath to do so out of fear of the West's reaction. Only China has stepped forward with sizeable loans, mostly for military hardware. This was done primarily so that the Chinese can maintain better surveillance of a long-time enemy and Burmese neighbor, India.

INVESTOR AND CONSUMER BACKLASH

Having turned instead to black market activity to cover the costs of keeping itself in power, Myanmar's military government has only exacerbated the development problem. The private international investment community looks beyond the initial level of official corruption found in any nation to focus instead on the top fears of international companies: political instability and expropriation. Cutting investment deals with government officials who live by violence and deceit usually means that the deal will be subject to numerous "changes" over its lifespan. Investors can never tell when a new "partner" will come into political power. It is also almost assured in such a corrupt atmosphere that should the business become profitable, every means will be exploited to either increase the "fees" the company pays or to oust the foreign partner entirely. Murder or imprisonment are not out of the question. Such prospects are hardly attractive to investors.

Added to this mix is the pressure that companies are under from their domestic market consumers (especially in the United States and Europe) to avoid doing business with unsavory governments like the one in Myanmar. Heineken and Pepsi-Cola both withdrew their high-profile investments from Myanmar after being chastised and threatened with boycotts by Western consumers. It should be noted that, like all international investment in emerging markets, the potential for helping the local population break out of poverty is a real result of attracting foreign firms. Rarely has the poverty-stricken population in any emerging market

(Cuba, North Korea or Myanmar) objected to foreign investment on the grounds that such investment may further the cause of a despotic government. It is generally forces outside of the country that bring pressure to bear with little regard for how their political intervention will adversely impact a local economy. In Myanmar, the local opposition to the government by Nobel prize winner Aung San Suu Kyi means little without the backing of American and European sympathizers willing to make their opinions known at the cash register.

Politics as Unusual

The obstruction of international trade in the name of influencing domestic politics can keep a national economy paralyzed for decades, just as the U.S.-backed embargoes against Cuba, North Korea, and (until 1994) Vietnam have done. However, Western political self-righteousness is not applied to every government that has black market financing and a jail full of political dissidents. Although China has far more political prisoners than Myanmar, Western companies are under little pressure to abandon their investments in this land of over one billion consumers. The same is true when viewing the West's approach to Russia's "crony" economy and her heavy dependence on black-market operators.

These two nations would be normally considered "rogue" economies (as are Myanmar and North Korea) if not for their size and economic potential. Realists in the international political community have decided that global economic impact outweighs local political concerns. Whereas Myanmar never has been, and probably never will be, a major economic player, Russia and China are large, populous, and well educated. They also have the added advantage of being major (if not super) military powers. The West, with little fear of Burmese military might, does see China and Russia as potential disrupters of international trade should they decide to expand their borders (in China's case, to Southeast Asia) or to reacquire old ones (if Russia rebuilds the once powerful Soviet Union). A good flow of investment and increased trade are seen as a form of insurance to protect the international economy from potentially violent disruption. China has been allowed to join the WTO, while another WTO applicant, Russia, has decided that perhaps the WTO is not that important to its goals.

Doing the Global Laundry

International criminal activity of all types generates huge sums of cash, and cash is what fuels further ventures in the global black market system. Criminal trade must maintain "cash flow" but legitimate governments constantly pursue crime-tinged assets in an attempt to take the profit out of nefarious activities. (Many governments use the seized cash as a supplement to tax revenues to finance their law enforcement activities.) Black marketeers have found that keeping large sums of cash stashed in suitcases or strongboxes is just too risky and too difficult to transport internationally. Like all profitable global companies, these criminal organizations have sought to invest their profits, not just in new inventory, but in other—legitimate—industries that show signs of potential growth.

DOING THE WASH

This process of international "money laundering" (a term derived from the famous American gangster Al Capone's habit of hiding his profits from the government by investing in a chain of laundries) first began with international banks. Money was simply placed on deposit with no questions asked about the source of the funds. The banks would invest the money in legitimate business, and the criminal organizations would reap the interest. Looking for much more lucrative investments, crime groups began to use their deposited money to finance the purchase of low-priced goods overseas. These goods, bought in good faith with bad money, would then be exported globally with the original nefarious monies effectively covered up by the transactions. The criminal elements succeeded in this because cash is very hard to trace, especially internationally. The bankers were under no legal obligation for many years (and felt no moral responsibility) to ask depositors about the source of their funds. Some national banking systems, with Switzerland's being the most famous and now infamous, actually built reputations based upon secrecy and "discretion" regarding the identity of international depositors and account balances.

CASH-FLOW CONTROLS

For many decades into the 20th century this situation was allowed to persist until the United States decided to crack down on the drug trade that flourishes within its borders. Unable and unwilling to secure its massive borders to cut off supply, the U.S. government-enacted legislation requiring that its banks report all transactions, deposits or withdrawals in excess of US$10,000. It then pressured other nations—usually through threat of trade sanctions—to enact similar legislation. Now, legitimate international trade had become a weapon to help control illicit trade. Banks suddenly became legally obligated to track their depositors' activities and report them to government officials. Though far from being 100% effective, the move was the first of many to attack illegal global trade activities at the "bottom line" rather than on the street.

The laundering of money does not only occur in drug transactions but in a whole host of illegal and quasi-legal import/export activities. From bootleg music to stolen computer chips to rare animals to untaxed cigarettes, nations around the world found that significant parts of their economy and cross-border trades were part of the black or grey markets. These same nations also found that they were several steps behind the criminals who were growing more and more sophisticated and their crimes more complex. Besides the international division of domestic police forces, like the FBI in the United States or Britain's National Criminal Intelligence Services, global police forces like Interpol were designed to tackle this problem. On a wider scale, the International Chamber of Commerce (ICC) has a Commercial Crimes Division, while the G7 has created the Financial Action Task Force on Money Laundering.

GLOBAL CRIMINAL CONSORTIA

For all of this attention from police forces, governments agree that criminal trade activity actually appears to be growing rather than contracting. The reasons are diverse. First, crime consortia take advantage of the lack of truly international laws. Squabbling over jurisdiction and the fruits of prosecution once crime crosses borders plays right into the hands of perpetrators. The crimes themselves and the resulting profits are spread over as many nations as possible, resulting in confused and warring governments. When nations have weak governments, like Albania or Nigeria, they become special targets of criminal activity. (The Nigerian government has to place full-page ads in international newspapers warning people not to fall for the numerous scams that are headquartered within its borders.) Secondly, absence of global accounting standards makes it difficult to distinguish a legitimate trade from a criminal one. Assets have no standard of valuation or categorization, making it easy to hide shady deals from auditors.

Thirdly, advances in technology such as computers, the Internet, and mobile telephony have made the long-distance movement of money and goods across borders simple and often anonymous. Sadly, governments are lagging the most behind the criminals in this technical area with no signs of being able to catch up anytime soon. Fourthly, the physical borders between nations have been made easier to cross in the name of advancing legitimate trade. While this is surely true, these same porous frontiers serve the black market just as readily. Fifthly, an international currency like the U.S. dollar or euro allows criminals to transport and spend their profits virtually anywhere in the world. (The 500 euro note has replaced the 100-dollar bill as the preferred means of "transferring" money through the black market system.)

THE CRIMINAL CONTRIBUTION

Lastly, it is a sad fact of international economics that many nations are dependent on black market activity to support their national treasuries. Though the G7 (sometimes called the G8 when including junior-member Russia) may form a task force to help thwart money laundering, there is little hope that Russia will be willing to take on its own mafiya that dominates its economy. To a much lesser degree, doubts about fellow members Japan and Italy can be raised concerning their ability to deal with the yakuza or the mafia, respectively. The United States and France also have long-established criminal organizations operating within their borders that have built both economic and political support. Outside of the G7, countries as large as China, India or Brazil down to tiny ones like Cambodia, Ireland or Colombia have segments of their economies that could be labeled "criminal," "black market" or "underground" in nature. Concern, both domestically and internationally, begins when the illegal economy starts to dominate legitimate commerce.

CHAPTER 9

International Trade Issues

THE EXCHANGE RELATION IS THE FUNDAMENTAL SOCIAL RELATION. — LUDWIG VON MISES, 1949

ALL NATIONS HAVE come to see the benefits of cross-border trade in the form of potential profits and new products. However, trade brings with it the competition that naturally occurs when two economies exchange goods and services for money. Each side of the exchange hopes to maximize their own benefit, although, as was discussed earlier, sometimes that maximization is purely psychological. As trade grows, national economies become concerned about their status in the global economy and the long-term effects on their domestic well-being. What was at first seen to be a mutually beneficial trade program between two friendly nations can suddenly be viewed by either side or both as a pernicious attempt to take advantage or even subjugate. Large economies claim that the "playing field" is not "level" and demand equal access to all markets. Small economies view free trade demands as attempts by the developed world to "economically and culturally colonize" them. Though much of the conflict is political, it is hard to separate politics from economics. Trade barriers, tariffs and economic advantage have been discussed earlier, but there are other issues of global economics that need to be resolved if nations are to enjoy the full benefits of international trade.

Intellectual Property

One of the hallmarks of the modern global economy is its increasing dependence on information flow. No longer can a nation's growth potential be measured just in terms of population, geographic size, or natural resources. Not even growth in manufacturing facilities serves as an indicator of future wealth. Physicality has taken a back seat to intellect—mind has triumphed over matter. The educational level of a population and its access to information has become the newest and most important indicator of whether a nation will succeed or fail in the global economy. However, it is not enough to only have access to information—the real money is in owning it. Ownership of information and charging for its use are the source of numerous and expensive conflicts.

Patents, Trademarks & Copyrights

The developed economies (e.g., United States, Japan, Britain, Germany) have devised a great deal of intellectual property law to protect inventions (patents), brand names (trademarks), and written materials such as books and software (copyrights). Holders of these intellectual property rights have the exclusive ability to produce or license the production of their "ideas" for a set period of time, which varies from nation to nation. After that period expires, these ideas become part of the public domain and are open for use by anyone, anywhere. Currently, there are no international intellectual property laws so intellectual products must be registered in each country individually, and therein lies the problem.

Commercial law in the developed world is very explicit and the means for enforcing the regulations are in place. The four nations mentioned above, for instance, have all seen the need for and monetary value of protecting their intellectual property, since most of the world's commercially applicable inventions and ideas flow from them. They respect and uphold each other's rights because it is mutually beneficial. But not all nations agree with this concept of owning "intellectual property."

STEALING THOUGHTS

Most of the world's emerging economies see intellectual property rights as just another means to keep their economies in a constant state of backwardness. They may give lip service to developing their own domestic regulations but enforcement is rare and usually done for show. Probably the most egregious violator of intellectual property rights is China. One cannot walk down the streets of Beijing without being accosted by street vendors hawking "bootleg" music CDs and fake designer clothes. Computer industry analysts estimate that over 95% of all software in China has been copied without license or payment to the companies that developed it. Similarly, the film industry loses billions in revenue from illegally copied videos. Though its laws are explicit, the Chinese government does little to stop this commerce and only acts when threatened with trade restrictions. Even then, enforcement is temporary and done only for public consumption. Similar abuse of intellectual property rights is repeated in Vietnam, India, Egypt, Brazil, and, to some degree, even in the highly regulated, developed economies. The lawsuits against file-sharing websites like Napster were successful but did little to stop the illegal copying of music and videos online.

For some emerging nations, these so-called "property rights" are just another despicable attempt by developed economies to maintain supremacy now that the "first world" has successfully exploited numerous ideas that were not originally their own. After all, who has ever paid the Chinese for the rights to gunpowder, or India for inventing the zero? Other nations just see the cold, hard facts of the situation: their population cannot afford modern products at their current level of development. They must either circumvent the law or forever remain poor.

GOOD IDEA, BAD EXECUTION

Opinions about the legitimacy of international intellectual property rights have not been helped, for example, by bio-medical companies who claim to own the rights to several species of plants. Similarly, Harley-Davidson's attempt to obtain the rights to the "sound" of their motorcycles has engendered much international press about the sanity of U.S. trademark laws. While the opinions of the "haves and the have-nots" differ, it should be noted that membership in the World Trade Organization (WTO) requires the recognition of intellectual property. The WTO is also taking steps to develop fully enforceable international laws to cover this aspect of trade.

Mergers & Acquisitions

Mergers and acquisitions (M&A) have long been a part of the economic landscape of many countries. It is one means by which small companies become large companies. Direct competition is either bought outright (acquisition) or two competitors combine to form a new, larger company (merger). Sometimes the companies involved are not even competitors, but share common business interests. National governments usually have a regulatory body to oversee domestic M&A activity and are given the task of making sure that the new business entity that emerges does not constitute a monopoly or create other unfair advantage. In Great Britain, where acquisitions are referred to as "takeovers," the City Code of Takeovers and Mergers oversees this activity (takeovers in this sense should not be confused with expropriation by government). Problematic M&A transactions can be further regulated by the Monopolies and Mergers Commission (MCC). This all works well and good until companies decide to merge or acquire across national borders. Suddenly, jurisdictions as well as national interests conflict.

MERGING TRADE, ACQUIRING PROBLEMS

As with much of international trade, mergers and acquisitions are subject to both political and economic concerns. When a U.S. aerospace company wanted to "acquire" France's largest helicopter company in the early 1990s, the deal was scotched, not because the economics was bad but because a vocal sector of the French population was offended that the Americans were buying into France's defense program. Trade at this level involves not just products, but entire companies. No longer just a simple purchase, the transaction took on symbolic importance far in excess of the real effect on French autonomy. Many acquisitions cross borders quite easily and are used to gain immediate access to larger markets or to circumvent future regulatory problems.

Such was the case when Sweden's Electrolux acquired Italy's Zanussi, another electrical appliance firm. Since Sweden is outside of full-EU (and euro) integration, Electrolux was positioning itself to take advantage of the euro market economy. In a further attempt to gain market access, Electrolux's acquisition of Britain's Thorn Refrigerators (the United Kingdom is also a euro-currency abstainer) and America's White Appliance Company was done swiftly and quietly to the satisfaction of everyone. Obviously, helicopters raise more hackles than washing machines.

SIZE MATTERS

Mergers tend to present fewer problems because they generally maintain the identity of each company involved. Mergers are a kinder form of acquisition as both sides have agreed to combine assets (as well as liabilities), although one partner will dominate the new entity. When mergers occur across borders they do, however, raise the specter of the "international conglomerate." Public concern increases based upon the perception of how vital the products involved are to national pride or sovereignty. When Chrysler and Germany's Daimler-Benz merged, the only consternation was over what the new company would be named. The result was Daimler-Chrysler, with Daimler as the clearly dominant partner, though they have since dissolved the merger. However, when British Petroleum (BP) merged with Amoco, or when Deutsche Bank took on Bankers Trust, many in the United States found the prospect of the new entities too indicative of global monopolization. This was especially "suspicious" because the American partners were the junior members of both the mergers and the subject was oil. Although these two mergers went through as originally designed, subsequent consolidations like the domestic American merger of global giants Exxon and Mobil received greater scrutiny.

Concern over the adverse economic impact of mergers and acquisitions has more to do with psychology than objective economic analysis. Many people, private citizens and government officials alike, are very willing to avail themselves of the benefits of globalization (new products, cheap travel, expanding markets) but fear the loss of local control that the process involves. Governments, even a large government like that of the United States, often believe that global companies and merger activities are designed to usurp political power. Unwilling to allow private enterprise the potential of the upper hand, governments the world over regularly delay and derail M&A activity. Sometimes this is done with the sole motive of showing who is boss.

MERGING COMPANIES WHILE DISTRIBUTING BENEFITS

While most M&A deals are designed to lower operating costs or to gain more efficient control of global market share, national governments do have legitimate concerns. Most international mergers and acquisitions result in layoffs (redundancies) into the thousands. Since the benefits derived from the efficient new business entity may only flow to a single nation—usually the headquarters of the dominant partner—some government may be left "holding the bag" of unemployed citizens and reduced tax revenues. Since any government that is involved in the M&A process has the potential to put a quietus on the deal, wise global companies make sure that the economic benefits and drawbacks are fairly distributed. (Note: The Japanese and U.S. governments have agreed to "mutual administrative intervention" in order to uncover unfair mergers, tie-ups, and cartels. It will permit either country to request investigations and penalties in the other country based upon their own anti-monopoly laws.)

Foreign Direct Investment

Investment is actually a form of trade in which the potential investor seeks to purchase part of a company or part of a market. On a global scale, foreign direct investment (FDI) is the procurement by residents of one country of real assets in another country. These capital movements from one country to another may take the form of real estate purchases, plant construction, infrastructure projects, or the whole / partial acquisition of an existing business in the foreign market. Although Chapter 5 covered the attitudes that various governments take towards FDI and their current account balances, it is necessary to review FDI as an international trade issue and how political attitudes towards it affect the international economy.

CAPITAL EBBS AND FLOWS

The 1997-98 downturn in Asia was blamed—wrongfully so—on the fickleness of foreign investors. FDI from all quarters certainly did "pull out" of the region but it was merely reacting to poorly managed economies, not creating them. As southeast Asian economies crumbled, several governments, like Malaysia and Indonesia, put the blame on foreign investors. Some of these "pirates" were supposedly part of a grander conspiracy to humiliate an emerging Asia. Of course, none of these governments balked as the investment flowed into their economies—only when it flowed back out, for rather legitimate reasons. The reactions of Asian governments have varied with equally diverse results.

South Korea and Thailand quickly (relative to their neighbors) admitted to the problems in their respective economies and made attempts to correct them. Indonesia stumbled into political chaos, resulting in new leadership but making few real economic changes. The hastily rigged "capital flow controls" imposed by a politically embattled Malaysia initially made that nation's problems even worse. Though making it easy to put money into Malaysia (but difficult to remove), officials in Kuala Lumpur have not corrected the intrinsic problems of their economy (weak banks, cronyism, high public spending). Jakarta has been similarly lax in attending to its problems. As a result, investors are finding Thailand and South Korea far more attractive than Indonesia and Malaysia. The former two are recovering much quicker than the latter, although Malaysia's restrictions are proving far less cumbersome than projected.

POUND WISE, FRANC FOOLISH

Driving out foreign investment is not just a phenomenon of Asia at the end of the 20th century. The socialist Mitterand government of 1980s' France did so with policies of nationalization, as had many Latin American countries in the 1970s. In all three decades, those economies that shunned FDI quickly had reason to regret their policies. Soon, their neighbors with more welcoming attitudes shot ahead developmentally, with tax revenues to match. Such was the case in Europe. Just when France was showing foreign investors the door and expanding government ownership of business, Britain and Margaret Thatcher were privatizing state-owned enterprises and courting FDI. The results of both nations' policies are still evident today. Though matched evenly in population (around 60 million), France has nearly double the unemployment rate of the United Kingdom. The still-powerful pound sterling is controlled by London, while the euro used in France is controlled by the European Central Bank in Frankfurt, far from Paris' control.

FOREIGN INVESTMENT AS NECESSITY

For all nations (including the greatest attractor of FDI, the United States) the ability to find adequate foreign financial resources has become just as important as the ability to access and trade for raw materials. Growth requires financing, and those economies that are considered "good investments" will see the highest growth. Of course, FDI is betting on potential and some nations have failed to live up to their own sense of promise. China, for instance, with its billion-plus consumers, has become a "black hole" of foreign investment funds. While China itself is successful, fewer than 25% of foreign-invested projects in China have shown any kind of profit and the ability to repatriate their profits is still greatly restricted. As the failed economies of southeast Asia begin to recover and South America blossoms, China will see fewer and fewer FDI packages heading its way. It can take as long as a decade before FDI can even reconsider an economy that has failed to deliver in the past, unless serious restructuring (usually regulatory and taxation) has taken place. Russia, South Africa, Kenya, and India all face similar prospects. The mood will remain positive but cautious for some time to come. More on the motivations behind global investment will be discussed in Chapter 10.

Exchange Rates

The effect of exchange rates upon international trade has been at the basis of almost every economic crisis in recent memory. The global economies "communicate" with each other via currency. The tone and tenor of that communication is set by a variety of factors. How well an economy will function and what its function will be in the global stage are determined by its ability to control the exchange rate of its currency. Nations with strong currencies and stable exchange rates can purchase whatever they need, whenever they need it. However, the exports of hard-currency nations will be considered expensive by weaker economies and can cause trade imbalances like that which currently exists between the United States and China.

The weak-currency economies will also find it difficult to purchase raw materials from overseas to feed domestic manufacturing, thus causing problems in what should be a very productive export market. This is the position that Indonesia found itself in when its currency "crashed" a decade ago. Indonesia had cheap labor and a decent manufacturing base but no means with which to buy materials to feed the system.

DUELING CURRENCIES

The role of maintaining control over the exchange rate has traditionally fallen to a nation's central bank. (The other roles of those banks are a subject to be discussed later in Chapter 11.) It is not unusual for nations to use what control they have over exchange rates (and it is diminishing yearly) to enhance their own trade position or to diminish a rival's. The United States and Japan regularly spar over their exchange rates in an effort to adjust their respective trade balances. When the yen is strong, Japanese exports are weak because of their expense. Since it is usually measured as a function of the US dollar, the yen's strength entails the dollar's relative weakness and therefore strong U.S. exports. During such a period the Japanese government will attempt to influence the U.S. government to "strengthen" the dollar. The EU does the same to boost its exports. As we will see later, such intervention is subject to a growing number of private-sector influences.

DOMESTIC CONCERN, GLOBAL IMPACT

But these back and forth currency movements do not just affect the two currency markets involved. For Japan and the United States, the stakes are global, not local. When Japanese exports are down, Japanese companies will be unwilling to expand manufacturing capacity and their overseas investments will be the first to be pulled back, in order to preserve their domestic jobs. Emerging economies in Asia, Africa, and South America will see Japanese FDI curtailed or dry up completely. Those economies in turn will see a drop in middle-class incomes that are needed to buy much of what Japan produces. This will cause another drop in Japanese exports and another round of FDI contractions.

Meanwhile, in the United States, the weak dollar is promoting exports, but now Americans find it difficult to travel overseas and buy European or Japanese imports as the dollar has just too little purchasing power outside of U.S. borders. Currencies directly "pegged" to the U.S. dollar, like the Hong Kong dollar, or economically linked, like the dollar of NAFTA partner, Canada, will suffer similar drops in purchasing power when it comes to imports or international travel. When U.S. imports drop or its tourists stay home, less of the nation's currency is in circulation worldwide. This situation makes it unnecessary and potentially impossible for foreigners to "buy back into" the U.S. economy. This further reduces global output because the size of the United States economy has made it the traditional "buyer of last resort" for most of the world's exporters. (When everyone else is poor, the United States can always be counted upon to pick up the slack.) Manufacturers worldwide, not just in Japan, find that their goods and services are just too expensive for the United States and that they cannot buy cheap U.S. exports because the needed American dollars are not in the marketplace.

THEORY OF THE WEAKEST LINK

This scenario has played itself out many times as the two economic giants—one dependent on exports and the other addicted to imports—try to find an optimal exchange rate. Both are attempting to not only maximize their own economies but also help stabilize those of the rest of the globe. The exchange rate is not just an indicator of economic strength but a tool for both political and economic stability. Russia, South Africa, Indonesia, and Brazil have all seen the political fallout that can occur when a currency becomes weakened. The hard-currency societies must use all of their resources, both private and public, to maintain proper balances in their own economies as well as in their more vulnerable neighbors. Exchange rates have become the links that form the chain of global trade. And, like all chains, the weakest link will determine overall strength.

Tourism

Tourism is now the world's largest business and a major focus of most national trade policies. As an umbrella industry it includes airlines, hotels, restaurants, museums, car rental agencies, travel agents, and virtually any other business that sells goods or services to tourists. Developed nations, like France, as well as emerging markets, like Cambodia, want to be tourist destinations. In some cities, like the top international tourist destination, San Francisco, the tax revenues generated from tourism amount to one-third of the local tax structure.

While the developed world hopes to maintain the flow of tourists to cities like London, New York, Montreal, Stockholm, and Rome, the emerging markets of Cambodia, Chile, China, and Kenya struggle to make themselves attractive to ever more discerning travellers. However, unlike Londoners who are just as happy to see tourists from Cornwall as from Tokyo, cities like Phnom Penh or Nairobi set their sights on visitors from wealthy foreign economies only.

The reasons for this exclusive approach to the tourist trade are two-fold. The first is the need for hard-currency. Even when an emerging market has a convertible currency, its real use outside of national borders is quite limited.

For instance, no matter how many Chilean pesos may be on hand in the national bank in Santiago, it does not change the fact that all oil imports are priced, and must be paid for, in U.S. dollars. Even Hong Kong, once the tourist capital of Asia, is having problems attracting foreign visitors now that it has become part of China. Its latest problem is the onslaught of "brown bag" tourists from mainland China who come to see the sights but bring their own food and often sleep at relatives' homes or on the street. What little they do spend in Hong Kong is done with the renminbi—a currency virtually useless in the global economy. (Note: Mainland China permits foreign firms to bid on local projects in Chinese currency but only for 50% of the amount of the foreigner's bid. The rest must be paid in a "hard" currency.)

KEEPING HARD CURRENCY AT HOME

In some nations the flow of hard currency from tourism is one-way only—into national coffers. Vietnam requires that its businesspeople wishing to travel overseas obtain letters of invitation from foreign firms that include a statement from the foreign host that all expenses will be paid for by the company issuing the invitation. Leisure travel overseas is strictly forbidden. This is not just symptomatic of a totalitarian socialist government. Since Vietnam does not have a convertible currency, any overseas expenditure is a drain on the national hard-currency reserves. In a country where the average wage is the equivalent of less than US$300 per year, a US$5,000 two-week trip overseas is a major expenditure.

In somewhat of a gamble, emerging markets have built luxury hotels and beach resorts for the exclusive use of foreigners. Foreign investors (FDI) tend to invest only in those areas they find attractive and welcoming. They also need to have a fair degree of experience with a nation and its culture before they are willing to invest millions. The emerging markets of Asia did an excellent job of welcoming and pampering tourists for decades before investment flowed in during the 1970s and 1980s. Sub-Saharan Africa, on the other hand, has (with the exception of South Africa) done little in the way of making itself attractive to full-scale foreign tourism. The economic consequence of failing to participate in the "beauty show" of tourism has been the general perception that much of sub-Saharan Africa is just too developmentally primitive to warrant serious consideration by investors who have friendlier, less risky prospects elsewhere.

Infrastructure

An old adage of business is that one "must spend money to make money." This has never been truer than now, as seen in the effect of suitable infrastructure upon a nation's stature in the global economy. Those economies willing and able to put in place, renovate and maintain the latest power supplies, roads, airports, telephone systems, computer networks, offices and housing are those reaping the benefits of the globalization of trade. Those that do not will languish at the bottom of the economic ladder with few prospects of climbing up. This is not a case of the rich getting richer and the poor poorer but one of overall success by paying attention to what is necessary. Any visitor to Poland and Russia will see what a difference intelligent spending can make on an economy.

RUSSIAN RECKLESSNESS

Post-communist Russia, once the greatest debtor to the International Monetary Fund at US$19 billion, squandered its loans on corrupt companies and hopeless attempts to protect its crumbling currency. Meanwhile, its ground transportation system, airports, seaports, power grids and telephone systems of regions outside of the major cities of St. Petersburg and Moscow are little better than they were in the Stalinist 1950s. Foreign firms wanting to exploit Russia's natural resources in Siberia find that they have to start virtually from scratch as local infrastructure for communication, transport, and power is quite primitive. The effect on the population was even more telling. Every winter Russia faces food and fuel shortages caused not by lack of supply but inadequate transport. This dearth of modern infrastructure, combined with Russia's growing political problems, put the former "superpower" at the bottom of the list for potential foreign investment. It was saved from collapse by "restructuring" (renationalizing) the petroleum industry and the fortuitous rise in oil prices starting in 2006. The billions in new funds were used to repair infrastructure and retool the national pride. For the next few years, Russia will extract its FDI at the gas pump.

POLISH PRUDENCE

The story in Poland is somewhat different. Warsaw's leaders have used their post-communist time and IMF loans well by making major improvements in the nation's communications and transport infrastructure. Poland has taken advantage of its proximity to Western Europe and membership in the EU to boost its GDP to several multiples of 1989 levels. The ease of road and rail transport has been behind Poland's trade growth, and investors have flocked into Warsaw, Krakow and Gdansk to take advantage of the modern communication systems deemed mandatory for global business. The virtue of wise infrastructure investment and its effect upon trade can also be seen in the nation's US$84 billion hard-currency reserves.

Education

The United Nations Children's Fund (UNICEF) recently estimated that close to one-sixth of the world's population is illiterate. Not surprisingly, most of these one billion people referred to by UNICEF live in the poorest regions of the world. The global disparity of wealth will be discussed in detail later in Chapter 10. It bears mentioning here that, like infrastructure, quality education is a necessary building block in determining a nation's advance in the global economy. However, it must be linked with stable politics and accessible capital to have its full impact.

Education by itself is no guarantor of economic success. North Korea and Vietnam have very high literacy rates, but plagued economies. India, now the world's largest producer of engineering graduates, has carved itself a significant niche in software development, but its elitist education system still keeps most of the population at subsistence levels. Japan has reached an educational crisis where the system has found that while it can produce highly educated graduates, it has not provided them with the innovative skills needed for the modern economy. This has greatly stunted high-tech entrepreneurship in Japan, adding to that economy's problems. (Note: Of the G7 nations, Japan has one of the lowest rates of computer use.)

AN EDUCATED ECONOMY

In the United States, an education system that promotes innovative thinking has kept the American economy at the global forefront. Even domestically, the impact of education is evident. Even secondary school graduates (high school) make around half the wages of college graduates. Masters degrees in business administration (MBAs) are now becoming mandatory for anyone wishing to advance in management. Because education—the right education—is driving its high-tech economy, America has become the number one destination for students looking to study overseas. Though many stay on to work in the entrepreneur-rich (or rich entrepreneur) American economy, most of these foreign students return home hoping to bring back the skills needed to jump-start the economies of their homelands.

Another telling fact about education and economic impact: The same week that the UNICEF report cited that the vast majority of the globe's 1 billion uneducated, impoverished people are female, the United States released a report of its own showing that women are beginning to outnumber men on American college campuses. Plainly, nations unwilling to tap all of their human resources—male and female—will be unable to compete in the global economy.

Credit & Capital Access

A nation with a highly educated workforce and serviceable infrastructure is well positioned to succeed on the international stage. However, the accessibility to capital is still vital to economic development. The inability to procure long-term financing, domestic or foreign, can keep any economy from growing beyond its present level. This problem, known as a "credit crunch," can occur for a number of reasons. Often, if a nation has been profligate in the past, its government and private businesses can expect to receive poor credit ratings from such agencies as Moody's or Standard & Poor's (S&P) whose job it is to determine credit-worthiness. It can take as long as a decade of good financial controls to overcome a bad credit rating (Chile), but only a few months of poor performance to ruin a good one (South Korea). The causes of a downgraded rating can range from political instability (Croatia) to corruption (Belarus) to improper banking controls (Malaysia), or all three (Indonesia).

TURNING OFF THE CREDIT TAP

Sometimes the access to loans and credit is intentionally limited by a process known as a "credit squeeze"; this can be a part of a government's domestic economic policy. Governments will limit the money supply, raise the interest rate for loans, restrict by law the level of lending by particular banks, or even restrict the number and types of transactions or businesses for which domestic loans would be available. Japan used this form of "credit rationing" to curtail the easy lending practices of its banks that had resulted in widespread defaults on loans when their "bubble" burst. These bad loans in turn had a major impact on other Asian economies. In response, the Japanese government highly regulated the lending process. Consequently, Japanese banks had so much money in their coffers (Japanese are big savers, not spenders) that they were technically able to offer some loans at negative interest rates wherein the borrower was actually paid to take the loan. However, other restrictions actually discouraged borrowing, and domestic manufacturers decreased production accordingly, keeping prices high and supply low.

While Japan's domestic economy has been in a decades-long malaise, the government was able to lend billions to its Asian neighbors. This international largesse, however, came with some strings attached. Projects funded by Japanese loans must involve Japanese manufacturers and services working in the target economies. These "tied" loans enable foreign markets to buy locally made Japanese products, while the credit squeeze back home keeps domestic Japanese producers from having excess capacity. In turn, Japan imports goods made by its companies manufacturing overseas to the detriment of its domestic operators. (Note: The other Asian markets cannot afford to buy Japanese goods sold as exports—except used cars—because of the high cost of Japanese labor.)

DEFENDING YOUR CREDIT

Not all economies voluntarily restrain credit, as Japan has done. Taiwan, originally thought to have avoided the economic problems of the other Asian nations, suffered its own unique credit crunch. Taiwan's private banks took it upon themselves to decrease financing when they became concerned about the nationwide downturn in export levels. Where once credit flowed to Taiwanese producers, private banks were forced to cut back for fear of never being repaid by failing manufacturers. The banks had, in the words of one Taipei analyst, "gone from aggressive lending to defending their balance sheets." The cause for the "crunch" was that other Asian economies could not afford Taiwanese exports, although the effects are likewise international.

Taiwan is one of the biggest investors in the emerging markets of Asia (China and Vietnam, in particular). Any reduction in domestic financing will immediately impact a Taiwanese company's ability to expand overseas. Such a banking/credit problem is really a "crisis of confidence" since it has resulted from the Taiwanese forecasting a bleak future rather than dealing with their present good fortune. Taiwan has very little foreign debt and close to US$275 billion in reserves. It has GDP growth regularly above 5% (small compared to China, yes, but quite respectable compared to the EU or US economies), yet its private banks are fearful of greater downturns in Asian economies where Taiwan is heavily invested.

LAISSEZ FLOW

Unlike Japan, the Taiwanese government has stepped in to shore up confidence and promote lending for its exporters. It has created a US$8.7 billion fund to stabilize the Taiwanese stock market and maintain prices. The government also issued an official directive to private banks to loosen their lending practices, and, more importantly, for the central bank to significantly reduce interest rates. The effects will be felt long-term, but it was plainly a recognition of how domestic credit and access to capital can in turn drive the global economy. Money loaned on the streets of Taipei and Taichung finds its way into the trading rooms of Jakarta, Hong Kong, Kuala Lumpur, and Bangkok, as well as into the factories of Shenzhen, Ho Chi Minh City, and Manila.

Environment

Much has been made of the United States' reluctance to sign on to the international accords regarding industrial pollution controls and their costs. The American position is that all nations should reduce their industrial pollution on an equal basis. Emerging economies have a different take on environmental controls. Their position is that industrialization is a dirty business and one that the developed world went through in the 19th century during the Industrial Revolution—long before the concept of pollution controls came into existence. Emerging markets either want to be left alone to pursue development without restriction, or they want the rich, technological economies to finance (for free) the necessary pollution controls. Poor nations recognize that if they have to abide by the same environmental restrictions as the United States or the advanced economies of the EU, the ability to "catch up" to the rich world is greatly forestalled if not eliminated. They have a point.

LOOKING FOR LESS GREEN PASTURES

Just as they pursue low-cost labor in the emerging economies, international manufacturers and potential polluters (e.g., paint manufacturers, chemical makers, petroleum refiners) from the "first world" regularly seek out foreign economies and have set up shop in southeast Asia and Latin America where they are not fettered by expensive capital-consuming environmental controls and restraining orders demanded by "green" activists. Or they have taken over smokestack industries in the very polluted former Soviet Union states like Belarus and the Ukraine.

These struggling economies have welcomed the investment funding for the resulting rise in exports and local jobs. What they have not welcomed is the attention of environmental activists bent on closing down factories with poor pollution controls. Even the tourism industry has been touched by these concerns as new golf courses and hotels become the focus of concerns about fertilizer run-off and waste disposal controls. The hacked-out forests and heavily polluted beaches of Thailand's resorts are often cited by environmentalists as being the products of the international economy run amok. They, too, have a point.

THE POINT OF NO RETURN

Foreign investors see potential markets everywhere they look in the developing economies. However, those new markets are very expensive and risky to enter even without the demanded environmental safeguards. When those controls are in place, or the possibility exists that they will be, foreigners see little value in pursuing direct investment in a market that may be as expensive in the long run as their own domestic markets. They will either cut off investment altogether or greatly curtail it. This prevents the population of the developing economy from gaining access to either jobs or potential technology transfers that would lift their nation as a whole. While the environmentalists of the West are happy to prevent the trade-off of jobs for pollution, the impoverished workers of the emerging markets are not so keen to remain in poor, though non-toxic, conditions. Foreign companies say there is little point in setting up an investment that cannot show a profitable rate of return. Like the emerging economies and the environmentalists, the investors have a point.

COMPROMISING POSITIONS

What generally occurs to assuage all sides is a good deal of compromise. Each of the three groups must learn to do with less of what they would like to have, although not in equal proportion. The foreign investors are likely to get the majority of what they want. Money does, after all, "make the world go around" and unless commercial interests are kept reasonably happy, nothing—not even pollution controls—will be financed. Emerging economies consequently receive a little less investment than they would like and a lot more environmental controls than they feel they need. Environmentalists receive the least of what they were looking for and they can only hope that improved economic conditions in the developing world will bring about greater environmental awareness in the future.

REGULATING THE ENVIRONMENT

Much of what plagues the cause of environmentalists is that they are completely reliant on governments to enforce their proposals. Unfortunately, in the last twenty years governments have been greatly discredited regarding their ability to effectively control economic success. This shift has left private enterprise in control of the "commanding heights" of commerce (see Chapter 6). Added to the general distaste for government controls is the fact that environmentalism is viewed by emerging markets as a "Western concept" and potentially a form of cultural imperialism. Rather than an improvement, "green" programs and their proponents are taken as roadblocks to achieving success in the global economy. This subject will be discussed again, in purely economic terms, in Chapter 10 which looks at regional disparities and the transfer of wealth.

Strategic Trade Policy

It has often been said that business is akin to war and much of the terminology of commerce has martial overtones. Companies "penetrate" markets, "seize" market share, "marshal" resources, set up "task forces", and "roll out" products on a regular basis. Just as wars are fought between and among nations, so, too, international trade and investment take on the tone of conflict. Governments around the world have all adopted in one form or another a set of strategic trade policies, usually at the behest of private industry.

Unlike the protectionist measures discussed in Chapter 8, *strategic trade policies* (STPs) are designed primarily to have their greatest effect upon another nation's trade policy. Rather than simply relying on legal restrictions such as tariffs, subsidies, or quotas, strategic policies rely on economic finesse. These policies are considered "strategic" because their goal is to benefit the policymaking country indirectly by influencing the behavior of the targeted country. The pressure may be economic, political, or a combination of the two.

BATTLING OVER BANANAS

An example of a strategic trade policy writ large is that of the United States in its wrangling with the European Union over the importation of bananas. The United States has threatened the EU with a 100% tariff on selected EU exports because the EU's import policy regarding bananas gave preference to former British and French colonies in Africa, the Caribbean and the Pacific. Although the United States does not grow a significant number of bananas itself, Washington was supposedly acting on behalf of its global fruit distribution firms. The WTO agreed with the U.S. stance and ruled as such. The EU promptly revised its "banana regime" in an attempt to avoid being the subject of both U.S. and WTO sanctions. The United States replied by saying the revisions were too little, too late. But all of this was a smoke screen for larger international economic issues.

The real issues—the strategic issues—were the large EU subsidies, not just for the agriculture sector but for even more important industries such as aeronautics. The EU trade ministers struggled to get a resolution to the banana issue before attending an international trade summit in Vienna. At the summit, the United States was expected to press the EU for more financial information about Airbus Industrie (Europe's heavily subsidized airplane manufacturer and main competitor to the privately owned American company Boeing Aircraft). The United States has its own form of corporate subsidies for Boeing but they are nowhere near the scale of the EU membership and only kick in when the planes are exported. Because the EU and its euro-currency give the United States serious economic competition, American lawyers are seeking to make sure that the competition is on a more "level playing field." By protesting EU trade violations to the WTO on issues like bananas, the United States is sending a message that the EU government HQ in Brussels better get its trade policies in order quickly unless it wants to find itself in one of America's favorite venues—the courts. If the United States is willing to apply 100% import tariffs over commodities it only distributes—like bananas—then Europe can only imagine how far the Americans will go to protect the export of their own produce or multi-million dollar aircraft. Note: The United States took up the challenge again in regards to the EU's restriction on "genetically altered" foods—an area in which the United States has a virtual monopoly. The EU replied with accusations regarding Boeing. These issues will be played out over decades in the courts rather than in the marketplace. As one lawsuit closes, another opens.

CHAPTER 10

Growth and Development

YOU CANNOT FEED THE HUNGRY ON STATISTICS.
— DAVID LLOYD GEORGE, 1904

THE EBB AND FLOW of the global economy has made some nations rich and others destitute, with the vast majority of countries somewhere in between. Formerly wealthy and powerful economies have been driven down to near subsistence levels, as can be seen in the cases of ancient China and modern Russia. At the same time, tiny nations like Kuwait and Brunei have gone from being economic backwaters to experiencing fabulous wealth within a few generations, all because of a single commodity like petroleum. While nations rise and fall economically as well as politically, wealth is redistributed throughout the globe with little regard to need or egalitarianism.

Money—like power, natural resources, or weather—has always been indifferently distributed among the world's inhabitants. While that is unlikely to ever change, it is worth investigating how and why those disparate pockets of wealth and poverty occur.

The West and the Rest

Any look at economics statistics will reveal that the majority of the globe's wealth is found to be concentrated in western Europe, Canada and the United States. Of the members of the G7 (the world's seven largest economies and, some say, the designers of modern wealth distribution), six are "Western-style" economies (Japan is the seventh). This would imply that the world is divided *economically* into the Eastern and Western hemispheres. The fact is there are many different economic zones, not just two. Some economies are a function of their geography, others of their politics, race, religion, or culture. All of these factors combine to determine how well a nation will do economically.

Dominance in the international economy has been held by the Western economies for centuries. France, Germany, Italy (in the form of the Catholic Church), and Britain have all taken turns as the economic leaders of the world. At the beginning of the 20th century, the United States saw its economic star rise, partially by virtue of two destructive European wars. Gifted with a strong manufacturing base and the isolation provided by two large oceans, America found itself to be the only functioning major economy after 1945.

THE OCEAN OF WEALTH

Trade had been very much based around the Atlantic Ocean during the 19th and 20th centuries, although many raw materials were shipped from Asia across the Pacific. Until the 1960s, most of the value added to products was added in the United States or in the rapidly recovering nations of post-WWII Europe.

America's postwar Marshall Plan of economic rebuilding was aimed squarely at Europe, the continent most culturally tied to America. Asian economies like Japan, Taiwan, and the Philippines were assisted by the United States mostly in the form of very relaxed tariff structures, but with very little direct investment as compared to Europe.

Communist China and the Soviet Union were political enemies but both had centrally planned economic systems that were antithetical to the global capitalist markets the United States was intent on building. Politics and economic reality demanded that the communists be treated as opponents, not as the allies they had been during WWII. They were left to fend for themselves during the Cold War and each side of the conflict tried to economically outdo the other. Khrushchev claimed he would "bury" the West but his shovel was made mostly out of doctored statistics. Mao drove his nation over the economic precipice with his attempt at a "Great Leap Forward." And while Kennedy tempted nuclear war, West Berlin was turning into an enviable shopping mall.

ALL THE THIRD WORLD WAS A STAGE

While all of the economic restructuring and headbutting of the 1950s and 1960s was going on in Europe and Asia, the continents of Africa and South America were given short shrift. As large as they were and however well stocked with natural resources, these two giant continents were treated as economic and political sideshows—a blockade here, a ground war there, perhaps a coup d'etat on occasion. But little was given in the way of industrialization or long-term investment. Both continents were considered to be too culturally explosive and economically unstable to warrant serious attention. Like parts of eastern Europe and southeast Asia, Africa and South America were just stages upon which the capitalists and communists would fight mostly inconclusive battles until the mid-1980s.

When the Soviet Union finally unraveled, communism as an economic policy was officially declared dead, although its party and politics carry on to some degree today. Capitalism and market economics had won. Lenin and Marx had their statues pulled down and their treatises rebuked. But all was not going according to the capitalist plan. The "second world" was gone and its adherents plunged almost immediately into "third world" status. Embarrassment was covered and face saved by the application of the terms "emerging" and "developing" to both old and newly poor nations alike. The reality, however, was much starker. The world found itself by the early 1990s divided into what economists call today "the West and the Rest" with a major economic chasm between the two. This phrase has a soothing rhyme to it and is meant to replace harsher predecessors like "the haves and the have-nots," "the first and third worlds" or, simply, "the rich and the poor" of the international economy. By using the term "the West," commentators are implying a certain geographical determinism. As the world enters the 21st century, they may be right.

North versus South / Hot & Cold

Unlike the distinction of East and West, which has both cultural and geographical implications, North and South rivalries conjure up distinctions of temperature and temperament. In his book on economic disparity, *The Wealth and Poverty of Nations*, David Landes posits that climate has a lot to do with how nations develop economically. Compared to countries with moderate or cold climates, nations that spend much of the year in heat have very low productivity because such conditions tend to limit the desire to expend both mental and physical effort. For humans, cold is far easier to deal with than heat.

Even within a single nation this productivity divergence can be found. It is a recognized fact that in the United States the sultry Southern states were grossly behind the chillier Northern state economies until the advent of air-conditioning. It is also no coincidence that vacation times for school and work in the United States (and elsewhere) were granted during the heat of summer when productivity nationwide was likely to be at an ebb. (Even in the European Union, the southern economies of Greece, Spain and Italy are laggard when compared to Germany, Britain and France.)

DISEASE, DEATH, AND DEVELOPMENT

But heat has had effects on productivity other than simple discomfort. Hot climates, especially those that are hot year round, tend to produce an array of organisms hostile to human life. Colder climates have winters that greatly reduce or even eradicate these viruses and their carriers. From malaria to dengue fever to typhus, hot weather is found as the root cause or as a promoter. Even AIDS has been traced to that great incubator of human suffering, the steamy jungles of central Africa. Nations continually ravaged by microbial diseases lose people and productivity in huge numbers. Even when the wealthy of the northern economies arrive to invest, exploit or assist, they have fallen prey to the same disorders. If they don't perish, they return home with tales of woe and well-heeded warnings for would-be investors.

Such microbes and warnings have kept an enormous swath of the globe in a state of perpetual underdevelopment. Most of the poverty in the world can be found in a wide belt that runs around the globe centered on the equator. Roughly encompassing the tropics of Cancer (0° to 25° north) and Capricorn (0° to 25° south), this 6,000 km-wide band contains poverty in proportion to its excessive heat and virulent diseases.

CENTRAL ISSUES

Although cold and heat are associated with north and south, respectively, the design of the Earth has really placed its hotter climates centrally. The continent of Africa is a good example of how this central swath of heat has an effect upon economics. The equatorial band described above slices through the continent in the region normally referred to as sub-Saharan Africa. The countries north of this region (Egypt, Morocco, Libya, Tunisia) are by no means economic giants but they are decidedly better off than the sub-Saharan nations, at least in terms of per capita GDP. South Africa, the continent's "powerhouse" economy, is located south of the Tropic of Capricorn and has never been subject to the pestilence and drought that have afflicted sub-Saharan Africa for centuries. Of course, other factors, such as colonization, tribal disputes, corruption, and the lack of infrastructure investment, have affected growth in sub-Saharan Africa. It should be pointed out, however, that these factors have come into play in the history of the more productive regions of Africa as well.

Heat and Servitude

Hotter climes are also given to one of the great economic and cultural scourges of mankind: slavery. While this form of human bondage has existed in every region, both hot and cold, it has persisted longest in those nations where excessive heat has made certain forms of work grossly undesirable. Even today, though technically outlawed by every nation of the world (Mauritania held out until 1980), people are taken into permanent servitude in parts of central Africa, as well as into temporary "forced labor" conditions in Myanmar and Cambodia. Even the caste system of India, an ongoing form of permanent categorization of labor, finds its roots in climatic conditions that make some jobs undesirable and other positions simply unhireable at any pay rate.

WOMEN AND CHILDREN LAST

With regard to gender, those nations with low status for women, high occurrence of forced marriages, and enforced social servitude are also, for the most part, located within the equatorial band. South and Central America, south and southeast Asia, and sub-Saharan Africa all experience the highest levels of female servitude. In these areas where food-gathering, farming and water procurement are made extremely arduous by the climate, the tasks have fallen to women when titular slaves cannot be found.

Added to the burden of female servitude in these hotter regions is the greater propensity for death during childbirth as well as the highest rates of child mortality before the age of five. In these regions children tend to be viewed as chattel, as well as guarantors of care for aging parents. Male children are considered the least burdensome during childhood and most useful as adults, so the rate of female infanticide is very high. Women who produce only female children must continually expose themselves to the risks of childbirth in order to produce male heirs. Coupled with the educational discrimination mentioned earlier in the book against women in most emerging markets, it is plain that in this equatorial heat-band, a potential resource is being poorly utilized due to a tradition of servitude. Many economists believe that the economic liberation of women has been a key factor in the success of the cooler Western nations. But other factors beyond climate can have their effect upon an economy.

Racial & Cultural Factors

Earlier it was stated that much of the world's riches were held by the Western economies. The majority of those capitalist economies are Caucasian and rooted for the most part in European cultural traditions. But, as the Japanese have shown during their meteoric post-WWII rise, those attributes are not requirements for success in the international economy. Racial connection may, however, dictate the level of investment required for future development.

ASIAN VALUE, ASIAN VALUES

Throughout the 1970s, 1980s, 1990s and well into the 21st century, the highest rates of economic growth were found in Asia. Of these, the most spectacular change of fortune has been in China, where double-digit GDP growth is standard, although Beijing's statistics are uncorroborated and rightfully suspect. Leaping from near the bottom of the economic standings to the Top 10 within 20 years was accomplished with a great deal of foreign investment and know-how. Where the majority of this money and acumen came from breaks down along clear racial and cultural lines.

China's greatest benefactors were other Asian nations as well as the millions of "overseas" Chinese scattered around the globe. While the United States, Canada and Europe invested in China's growth, it was her Asian cousins—Japan, South Korea, Singapore and Taiwan—that provided the lion's share of financial inputs. This was not necessarily by virtue of a lack of interest on the part of the Western economies. The Chinese made it very clear early on in the "opening up" of their formally socialist economy that they were much more at ease dealing with Asian, rather than Caucasian, economies. The Western, Caucasian economies made it equally clear that they were unfamiliar and uneasy with the cultural and ethnic baggage of the Chinese.

RACIAL RETRIBUTION

The economic slump that hit southeast Asia in 1997 was blamed by some on the quick retreat of Western (read: Caucasian) investors. Prime Minister Mahatir of Malaysia and other national leaders as well went so far as to claim that the Eurocentric West had plotted the downfall of the Eastern economies because it wanted to keep Asia and Asians in their place. This hardly attracted the return of Western investment funds nor were there apologies forthcoming when the factual evidence showed that Asian investors had been the first to bail out of the troubled region.

To a greater degree, Africa, Central America and Latin America are all suffering from this same type of anti-ethnic approach to investment. It is not that the wealthy Western companies do not want to invest in these regions, but they are unwilling to accept the responsibility for centuries-old deeds they did not commit or necessarily profit by. They also see no reason to have terms dictated to them when there are so many better investment opportunities available worldwide. While there is no denying that past generations of Western companies and governments committed acts that were highly unethical by today's standards, developing economies will find it near impossible to attract funding with too many historical strings attached.

South Africa, once the darling of human rights activists, is a good example of how the attachment of too many cultural and racial provisos to investments can subjugate even an economy with the highest potential. Post-apartheid South Africa has continually rebuffed foreign investors by demanding local black control of companies even when local investment in the firm is minimal. The results of the "black empowerment" program were at first spotty and then, by 2001, it was an acknowledged failure. Foreign investment has been skimmed off by a few government cronies and the masses remain just as impoverished as they were twenty years ago. New investment is nowhere to be found. The country has, as one observer put it, "simply traded a white elite for a new black elite."

While such "empowerment' schemes may be politically palatable for some, it is economic suicide in a global economy where much better deals can be found elsewhere just for the asking. Vietnam, India, and China have suffered from this same situation in the past but are making steady gains towards correcting it. While the largely Caucasian West has begrudgingly learned to curb its patronizing attitude toward negotiating with emerging markets, some regions of the developing world have been slow to check their racial and ethnic biases when pursuing foreign investors. Emerging market cultures that insist on keeping this type of cultural retribution on the negotiating table will find themselves left out of the growing flow of international capital.

Religion and the Growth of Capitalism

For centuries the pursuit of wealth through commerce and the charging of interest for loans (usury) so necessary to that commerce were considered unworthy pursuits for the followers of Catholic Christianity and Islam. In Asia, money was the strict purview of monarchs and not the common folk. In all areas up through the 17th century, merchants were considered a necessary evil and trading not a career to be sought after by the righteous. (Judaism did not proscribe such activity, resulting in a clustering of Jews over the centuries in the merchant classes and a concomitant bad reputation among non-Jews.) Even in the wealthy technological economies of today, a favorite villain in entertainment circles is the avaricious, scruple-free businessman. In less developed economies like Somalia, the non-nomadic merchant-traders are called "sab" (low) to denote their departure from normal, acceptable Somali life.

CHRISTIAN COMMERCE

Regardless of these examples, there can be little doubt that business and the pursuit of wealth in reasonable amounts are today considered admirable pursuits in much of the world. It is also an observable fact that those regions of the world with the greatest degree of religious fervor tend to have less prosperous economies. In the West, economists have seen a clear link between the religious Reformation of the 16th century, the rise of Protestantism and the eventual success of the Industrial Revolution. Britain, Germany, and Scandinavia surged ahead with industry while deeply Catholic Spain, Italy and Portugal saw their fortunes decline. The United States, founded by European religious exiles, went on to dominate the world economy. As Catholic fervor faded and populations began to concentrate on this world over the afterlife, economies and physical well-being advanced. (Note: Catholic countries were also hindered by having held on to the restrictions on usury much longer than the Protestant sects. Over time, usury in the West has conveniently come to mean charging "excessive" interest, not its original meaning of charging any interest whatsoever.)

ISLAMIC, JUDAIC AND CONFUCIAN COMMERCE

In the Middle East and North Africa, the secularization of populations has had the same result. While Islamic fundamentalist nations like Iran, Algeria, and Syria compete for the title of "most stagnant economy," less pious Moslem cultures like Egypt and Turkey make steady economic gains. Judaic and largely secular Israel, the only technology producer in the region, shows remarkable growth and receives the resentment of its neighbors in return for both its political and economic status.

In Asia, the merchant classes, long held in low regard by peasant and warrior classes alike, became unfettered in the late 19th century in response to Western expansionism and technological superiority. Japan subjugated (but did not obliterate) its national religion, Shinto, to pursue Western-style development and succeeded dramatically. China tried to maintain old Confucian imperial structures only to have them replaced after WWII with the fundamentalism of anti-profit communism (a godless religion, but a religion none the less—and only recently reformed!). Its more secular cousins, Taiwan and Singapore, put economic growth ahead of philosophical purity to become, along with South Korea, three of Asia's economic "Tigers."

SAME CONTINENT, DIFFERENT ECONOMIES

Looking at even a single trading group like North America's NAFTA shows a connection between religious or ideological fervor and economic success. Protestant, secular Canada and the almost non-religious United States have had enormous economic success. Meanwhile Mexico, their devoutly Catholic neighbor to the south, limps from one bit of economic chaos to the next with its financial peaks far below the troughs of its northern neighbors. Certainly there are other factors at play (geography, race, culture). However, economists and sociologists have little doubt that the deep Catholicism of Mexico demands that its people concentrate on the afterlife in order to endure the hardships of earthly existence, seen as trials inflicted by the Almighty. The pursuit of economic (or even political) success is difficult if the physical world is to be denied importance by Catholics, or for that matter by evangelical Christians, fundamentalist Muslims, orthodox Jews, ascetic Hindus or abstemious Buddhists.

NOTE: It is not the goal of this section of the book to point out the relative value of one religion/philosophy over another, or reform over orthodoxy. It strives only to show, to some degree, the correlation between the level of belief and economic success. For more on this topic, see the Landes book mentioned above.

Measurements of Wealth

When looking at economic disparities on a global basis, one must consider the fact that the terms "rich" and "poor" are relative to a given society or region. A poor person on the streets of Montreal is in a decidedly different economic condition than a poverty-stricken beggar in Calcutta. In an extreme example of how "poor" is not always a descriptively accurate term, the Heritage Foundation in the United States released a report regarding the families officially designated as "poor" in the United States. Of the "poor" group, 41% owned their own homes, 70% owned an automobile, 97% had color televisions, and 66% had air-conditioning. These same "poor" families are producing male children who eat well enough so that upon reaching adulthood they are, on average, one inch taller and ten pounds heavier than the average American soldier in 1945. This type of "poverty" would be considered upper middle class in most of the rest of the world.

RELATIVE WEALTH

What needs to be considered is whether, in a given nation or region, the population is gaining or losing relative to its recent past. Indonesia serves as a prime example of the vicissitudes of modern economics that affect relative wealth. Up until the late 1960s, Indonesia was just a secular Moslem nation situated on an extensive archipelago that provided raw materials like rubber and wood to the developed world. With a low GDP per person (less than US$100 per year and low single-digit growth) it was a classic post-colonial "third world" economy.

When it was discovered by high-tech and light manufacturing companies, foreign investment flooded in to take advantage of low-wage, highly educated workers. The population flowed in from the countryside to leave the rice paddies for factory and service-sector jobs. By the early 1990s, GDP per capita topped US$1,000 and growth rates were in the double digits. Indonesia was dubbed a "mini-dragon" of Asian economies and its leadership praised for bringing the population out of abject poverty. It was not rich by German, American or Japanese standards, but much better off than China, Vietnam or Cambodia at the time.

A DOWNWARD SPIRAL

After the economic downfall, Indonesia found itself on a new fast-track, this one back to the financial bottom. According to the Population Research Center of the Gadjah Mada University, the number of "poor" people in Indonesia had reached 130 million as a result of the impact of declining job opportunities and a soaring inflation rate. This in a country with a total population of approximately 200 million. Indonesia, whose poor during its best periods have always been decidedly poorer than the poverty-stricken of the developed world, now finds 65% of its population headed back to a type of poverty recognizable anywhere. (Relative to Japan or the United States, 95% of Indonesians are "poor.") The stockbrokers and waiters of Jakarta began returning to their ancestral paddyland in the countryside as GDP growth went negative—but still double-digit (-17.4% in 1998). It has since fought its way back up the economic ladder (per capita GDP nowadays it is around US$4,000 and has a growth rate of 6%) but has not reached pre-1997 levels of prosperity and growth.

What portion of and to what degree the Indonesian population suffers from poverty depends on the yardstick with which it is measured. Relative to Vietnam and Cambodia, it is well off. When juxtaposed to Taiwan or Singapore, Indonesia's failure is stark. What wealth it had flowed back to its original foreign sources or was spirited away by corrupt officials. It is coming back slowly.

Other Relative Forms of Wealth

As discussed several times throughout this book, the matching of GDP per capita from nation to nation does not always reveal a true picture of economic progress. Purchasing Power Parity (PPP) really determines how much each economy's currency units will buy and some nations have a lot more "bang" for the buck, yen, pound or euro than others. But PPP does not give a full or accurate picture. The World Bank's calculation of PPP puts China in second place above Japan and places India at number four just above Germany in reckoning the positions of global economic importance. In actual monetary terms, China and India are far below Germany, but in purchasing power in their domestic markets they are ahead. (Only the Chinese government sought to make anything of this dubious statistic. Given the amount of poverty in China and India, everyone else saw it as the height of "feels good" numbers juggling.)

MONEY ISN'T EVERYTHING

In 1990 the United Nations Development Program (UNDP) formulated a new method for looking at economic and social progress. Calling it the Human Development Index (HDI), they took account not just of raw income data but of life expectancy, adult literacy, and other concerns such as the level of tertiary education. Using this calculation, Canada, France and the United States top the list. Germany and Greece, though vastly different in GDP per person, are very close on the HDI scale. Argentina and the Czech Republic, both with middling but growing incomes, put in respectable levels of HDI ratings. China and India both find themselves far down the list of HDI contenders.

The HDI, along with a variety of other "life-style" indexes, attempts to show that wealth, even relative wealth, only has meaning if the population it serves is advancing socially, not just monetarily. This type of thinking may go a long way to soothe nations like France or Sweden which see themselves as cultural, rather than economic, giants. For them, money does not buy happiness. The truly impoverished nations of the world—some with ancient and deep cultural traditions like China and India—think otherwise. They know that the rich may not necessarily be happy, but they are unhappy in a very nice house.

The Effect of Privatization on National Wealth

Nothing characterizes the economics of the beginning of the 21st century more than the privatization of government functions. In many countries, everything from prisons to banks to road building to military security has been turned over to the private sector for potential profit-making. This change in the "commanding heights" of national economics is seen by many as a worldwide recognition that businesspeople, not governments, are better at providing the goods and services needed by a nation. So desperate are governments to shed themselves of their agencies and state-subsidized companies that they take out full-page ads in business magazines listing branches of their government for sale to the highest bidder. Pakistan has gone so far as to have its Privatization Committee set up a website to sell its assets: <http://www.privatisation.gov.pk>. Point, click, buy a stake in the Habib Bank Limited. Such activity can have both a positive and a deleterious effect upon the relative wealth of a national economy.

RATIONAL NATIONALIZATION

For countries like Ghana, where far too much of the economy had been nationalized, selling off the national cocoa producer and state palm oil refineries (called "parastatals" because they operated for profit with minority private partners) can prove to be a boon. Such actions finally put the means of generating considerable wealth into the hands of the general population. Once there, profits were reinvested in other private projects rather than stashed in state coffers for future "white elephant" projects or siphoned into government-crony offshore accounts. The money brought in from the sales was already spoken for to pay off national debts. Ghana performed this privatization ritual to the tune of US$804 million —a considerable amount for an emerging market in sub-Saharan Africa.

SHORT-TERM DEFECTS, LONG-TERM EFFECTS

Privatization does have its downside. It can cause a sudden rise in unemployment since the private sector needs fewer people to make money than governments need to lose money. In nations like Ghana the rate of joblessness rose 15% during privatization, although it readjusted within a relatively short period of time as new businesses were opened. State subsidies to parastatals also suddenly dry up which causes the price of certain services (transport) or utilities (electricity) to rise for the average citizen. These problems, too, adjust as wages and jobs begin to increase with open competition.

Privatization can also cause a good deal of stock market activity, both domestic and foreign, as the new owners attempt to raise additional capital to expand their recently acquired factories and services. (Keep in mind that some state assets are sold off to foreign interests.) When it goes well, privatization also has the advantage of attracting wealthy foreign investors looking for new territories free of government interference or state competition. Successful private domestic companies send out the right signals to the international capital markets. It is those foreign capital markets that will determine long-term economic success.

CHAPTER 11

Global Investors

MONEY PLAYS THE LARGEST PART IN DETERMINING THE COURSE OF HISTORY. — KARL MARX, 1848

IN MANY OF THE preceding chapters there has been a recurring theme of global capital flow and the pursuit of it by both wealthy and poor economies alike. When a nation (or for that matter a single company) is doing well or is on the upswing, the providers of capital take on the form of great benefactors. However, when things go sour and debts are called due or investment is withdrawn, these benefactors turn into evil and avaricious agents intent on bending everyone to their will. The global investors have not changed—only how they are perceived.

PROPHETS OF PROFIT

National governments in Africa, southeast Asia, South America, and eastern Europe have in the past few decades both hailed foreign investment when it arrived full of promise, and cursed it when it left full of debt. When the IMF appears in the wake of escaping private investors to delineate the tough terms for new loans, these same governments cry oppression and loss of national sovereignty. Everyone, from the average citizen to the prime minister, has lost sight of what the global investors, both public and private, intended to do: make money. There is no intention to oppress or cause the loss of sovereignty and national dignity. Either there is potential for reasonable profit or there is not. Any other concern is extraneous.

Much international capital flow exists outside of government control and in many ways can be seen as having the status of a parallel government. Such a government has armies of money, CFOs as generals, accountants as bureaucrats, and brokers as diplomats. Severely democratic, its elections are held not every few years, but every few seconds as transactions are made. These global investors come in many shapes and sizes, as do their investments. This chapter will look at what they do, how they do it, and the relative importance they have in international economics. Most importantly, it will look at the level of international capital flow, whether it is at its peak in the latter part of the 20th century, and how controlling it can either help or hurt an economy.

International Exchanges

Every day, in New York, Tokyo, London, and Frankfurt, billions of dollars, yen, pounds, and euros of global funding are traded and invested. But these exchanges do not just serve American, Japanese, British, or German companies. In each of these investment arenas, numerous foreign firms have their stocks traded and their future fortunes decided. But it was not always so.

RESTRICTING CAPITAL

Under the Bretton Woods agreement set up after World War II, the flow of global capital was very constricted because sudden capital withdrawals were seen to have been part of the root causes of the war. It was, for example, very difficult in the late 1940s for French investors to buy into the U.S. market (the only real functioning economy for some years) or, for that matter, other European markets. Within twenty years, "euromarkets" had found their way around restrictions and continental banks had branches in many neighboring states. At this time, Asia, in the form Japan and Hong Kong, also began to shift money across borders with growing ease and enthusiasm.

In the 1970s, the fixed exchange rates that had been set up at Bretton Woods caved in and the more developed economies began to cast off their capital controls. The search had begun for foreign investors and investments. The emerging markets soon followed suit in the 1980s. By 1990, the equivalent of US$50 billion of investment had headed towards the developing economies, and soon topped US$336 billion. By 2008 investment inflows to the developing world accounted for 36% of all FDI.

NEITHER FREED NOR FETTERED

The effects of freed capital flows should have been all beneficial. Poor countries with educated populations would no longer be held back by a lack of access to capital (just ask Ireland and Singapore). Savers could spread the risk of their investments around a variety of markets to insulate themselves from downturns in their domestic market. Investors could and would seek the highest rates of return anywhere on the globe at almost anytime, day or night. But capital moves neither as freely nor directedly as people would like.

Theoretically, a poor nation with high capital investment needs like China should have a large current account deficit (capital inflows greater than outflows) while an economy like Germany with high savings rates should have an enormous surplus (capital outflows greater than inflows).

But the opposite has occurred. China regularly runs a current account surplus and Germany has a deficit. The reason for this is that capital is mobile, but not perfectly so. Investment funds do not always find their way across borders to greater profit potential. Even in the capital-hungry economies of the emerging markets, on average only 10% of their domestic investment comes from foreign sources. Though 10% is still a lot, it is smaller than it could—or should—be if capital markets were flowing freely between the developing world and the industrialized / technological economies.

Freedom from Arbitrage

If capital markets did behave freely, then an identical asset (stock, factory) in one market would be the same in real price value as in another. This is because competing investors would, when supplied with the proper amounts of information, push the price of the two assets towards equality through bidding. Between disparate economies like China and Germany this does not happen, but it does happen among the wealthy, information-packed economies in the developed world.

INFORMATION FLOWS

In wealthy economies, like Britain and Canada, competing investors can take advantage of the transparency of a potential deal by utilizing information about forward (a mutually agreed upon future value) and spot (current value) exchange rates, and interest rates. Everything is clear and bound by the rule of contract law. Both the investors and the recipients of the investment are familiar with all aspects of the transaction.

Transparency of information eliminates the possibility of interest arbitrage, which occurs when one investor takes advantage of known price discrepancies for the value of an asset between two different markets. Such an investor will borrow in a market where interest rates are low, and then lend in a market where rates are high, without any risk. Unlike speculation, where risk is assumed, arbitrage relies on some members of a transaction being ill-informed. Arbitrage rarely occurs within or between the developed economies but it can and does happen on a regular basis in emerging markets. The potential for arbitrage-style transactions, made possible by the lack of transparency in developing markets, is one of the reasons that international capital does not flow as its should.

The absence of transparency, combined with the lack of codified commercial law that characterizes the developing economies of Asia, eastern Europe, Africa and South America, makes it difficult for investors from the wealthier economies to put together profitable deals in economies starving for capital. Arbitrage in these regions serves the locals and not the foreign investors. These same investors must ask themselves: Why bother to invest in a shaky, lawless emerging market when money can be made on Wall Street (or in Frankfurt, or London)? The answer in the late 1990s was clear—Wall Street soared and most emerging market stock exchanges went through the floor. Capital flowed not to where it was perhaps most needed, but where it could best generate profit. That was, until the "dot-com" bubble burst in 1999 and every bullish investor "pulled in their horns" and became bearish for a brief period only to be made skittish again by 9/11 in 2001.

International Bond Rates

Even between economies where information is transparent and readily exchanged, there can still be obstacles to free-flowing capital. Interest rates for the bond market (debt) among these nations should be equal because buyers, as is the case with investors in overseas factories, should bid these rates to equality. But this does not occur. Buying an American bond or a Japanese bond is not seen as a choice between equals by investors because there is the very understandable concern about the changes in the value of the two currencies involved. Bonds which may not pay off for 30 years are subject to the most volatile, albeit transparent, market in the world—currency fluctuation and speculation.

STABLE DEBT, UNSTABLE CURRENCY

Theoretically, the difference in interest rates between bonds from different developed economies should be offset by the difference in their respective real exchange rates. These exchange rates should be the indicator of the difference in value between the two economies. And they would be if their value was determined at the time the bonds were purchased. But because bonds, unlike stocks, cannot be cashed in immediately, there is greater fear that future changes in currency value will wipe out the fixed profits hoped for from the bond.

Nations with a currency that remains relatively stable across an array of competitive currencies tend to attract greater bond purchasing than those that fluctuate wildly. For this reason both U.S. government (T-bills) and corporate bonds are some of the most attractive in the world while their Japanese counterparts are among the least attractive. While the dollar and the yen see-saw in comparative value against each other, on the whole the United States is seen as the far more stable, healthier economy of the two. China is "hot" but hard to repatriate profits from when the time comes. Europe's markets are stodgy at best. When compared to all other economies, the United States is the best bet going into the 21st century and still attracts the most FDI even in the worst of times.

CONSERVING VALUE

Bonds, as opposed to stocks, are purchased by conservative investors for their stability. When Russian bond sellers claimed 50% interest on a one-year bond in the mid-1990s they found few takers because the rate was simply not believable given the state of the Russian economy at the time. Lower, but more realistic rates, like a U.S. 30-year bond at 5.09%, find far more takers because, as low as the rate may be when compared with the potential of a stock investment, it is virtually guaranteed. On the other side of the bond market, a comparable Japanese bond (No. 203) might only pay 2.01% and even that may never come to pass (yields from Japanese bonds actually went negative back in the late 1990s).

Bond sales are dictated by long-term belief in a national economy and that belief, correct or incorrect, will help dictate international capital flows. Thus far, the emerging markets that are in dire need of such investment have been unable to convince global investors of their long-term profitability and stability. Usually, the appearance of instability comes from political problems that make the economic forecasts look like self-fulfilling prophecies (look at the success of Ireland versus the failure of Belarus). The supremacy of the U.S. T-bill as a safe haven for bond buyers around the world (including the Japanese and Chinese) just goes to show that, even in international markets, money usually gets loaned to people who don't necessarily need it but who know how to use it.

Emerging Market Xenophobia

When China decided to open its first real stock exchange at Shenzhen in Guangdong province just north of Hong Kong, it became readily apparent that its citizens understood the importance of buying stock. On the first day the exchange ran out of stock certificates and the potential buyers waiting in line rioted. (China had, and still has, a rudimentary banking system so investors must have cash in hand to buy stock.) So chaotic were the next few days that the government moved the exchange to a secret location to avoid more problems.

China, first ever with a secret "public" stock exchange, had also made another characteristic move at Shenzhen—the exchange and its stocks were not open for general use by foreigners. Foreigners can to this day only buy special "B" stocks through special exchanges and are, by law, excluded from ever owning a majority share of any Chinese company. Many investors of Chinese heritage bypass this restriction by purchasing "A" stock through relatives who are Chinese citizens.

ECONOMIC THERMOSTATS

China, like many other developing markets, wanted to grow at a pace that it considers "controllable" and, like most fearful governments, Beijing went too far in its attempt to avoid "overheating" its economy. Chinese investors, all using the domestic renminbi (yuan), could only provide enough capital to get these start-up companies off the ground but not enough to make them competitive in the global marketplace.

Emerging markets elsewhere, like India and Taiwan, have had better success at achieving a balance of foreign and domestic stock investment. Order (certainly more so than in Shenzhen), honesty, and reasonable restrictions on foreign capital have allowed these two economies to attract sufficient funds to compete globally without selling their birthrights. Other markets like Vietnam are unable to get other areas of their financial system (banking) or infrastructure (telecom) organized to the point where foreign investors would feel comfortable transacting large trades.

Some exchanges which have recently returned to the status of "emerging" from "newly developed" (like Indonesia) have lost the trust of foreign capital markets. Meanwhile, fellow economic-casualty Malaysia simply closed its market to foreign investors for a period in a pique of xenophobia. Like Russia, another nation that both fears and needs foreign capital, Indonesia and Malaysia (often called Malaisia) will let their stock markets sputter along, each being too government supported to fall, but too weak to grow.

Government Subservience to Capital Markets

Most economic xenophobia is grounded in a belief that national governments are completely at the mercy of international markets. These markets are, by definition, rife with foreigners. Though not completely powerless, governments have lost considerable ground. They have all retained the instruments traditionally used to affect their countries at the macroeconomic level, such as fiscal and monetary policies, along with the concomitant regulatory bodies. What has changed—and what sends shivers down the spines of government officials around the globe—is the declining level of beneficial impact these traditional methods have in the modern international economy.

EXCHANGING CONTROLS

When a nation greatly limits or stops the flow of international capital across its borders, the results are not helpful to its economy in the long term. Interest rates rise because the government is forced to borrow (selling bonds domestically) to finance domestic programs rather than being able to rely on the spurned equity investment of foreigners. These programs cause a growth in the money supply (though not always on the absurd level of Russian currency printing). In the long term, this monetary expansion causes inflation and the government finds itself faced with a newer, tougher political problem.

Those national economies that have free or freer capital flows are by no means immune to interest rate changes or inflation. However, the effects are lesser and can be more easily corrected. The degree of the ability to make corrections is a function of how much control the government has placed upon that factor which has become increasingly important in the global markets: the exchange rate of the national currency.

LEARNING TO FLOAT

Before capital was re-mobilized in the 1970s, exchange rates were fixed in the non-communist economies (communist economies were working within their own system which depended essentially upon barter). Fixed exchange rates meant that governments could, at least for short periods, expand their money supply and thereby their domestic economy without affecting the value of their currency unit for international trade. That ploy was finished once exchange rates began to "float" as a function of the size and stability of individual economies.

Nowadays, if a nation wishes to fix its exchange rate, or peg its currency to another, stronger currency (as Hong Kong does with the U.S. dollar), it faces a rash of other problems. Should capital suddenly decide to leave, interest rates must be raised enough to stop the outward flow by making domestic market returns more attractive. If the banking system is weak, interest rate increases will cause bank failures (sound familiar in southeast Asia?). When Hong Kong was faced with a choice of either dropping its peg to the dollar (unthinkable under current Chinese rule) or defending it, officials chose to pump money into the local stock market to keep prices high. This kept potential currency speculators from being able to buy low-priced Hong Kong stocks with their profits (otherwise subject to repatriation fees). The "run" on the Hong Kong dollar was thus thwarted, at least for the time being.

The Hong Kong government and its overseers in Beijing have only bought themselves time. Eventually, Hong Kong's banks will weaken, due to the general downturn in Asia, to the point where they cannot fend off speculators. At that point, Hong Kong will have to renege on one of its long-term pledges to the international market community and drop the peg to the U.S. dollar. Governments, and not just those in Asia, are finding that the more they try to exert control, the more instability they create. (Note: They are also losing control over information, with some, notably China and Vietnam, declaring their commercial statistics to be "national secrets." Citizens have been jailed and foreigners fined for releasing even simple agricultural data.)

Reining in a Herd

No market is completely "free" and the same is true for capital flows. Some borders may be more porous than others but every nation has some restriction on the movement of funding into and out of its economy. And that is as it should be. Some economies are more vulnerable than others to the effects of rapid capital flows, especially when the flow is heading out.

Unsophisticated markets like that of Mexico or Thailand found that funding had left their respective economies before their sleepy financial systems had a chance to react. Thailand compounded their problem by suddenly trying to impose capital restrictions, a move which served only to spook what few investors were left.

Another problem which affects the emerging markets is guilt by association. As the Thai economy fell, investment in other regional markets suddenly came under scrutiny and a herd of investors scrambled to get out of Indonesia and Malaysia. This is not to say that those two economies did not have structural problems—only that those problems were exacerbated by a non-existent contagion. When the financial leaders moved, the herd followed.

How Much Control and When?

Market observers and economists all agree that some controls on global capital flow are necessary. Disagreement is confined to the matter of degree. The number of potential controls is vast. Besides just the simple capital-inflow and -outflow controls, there are market-based and quantitative controls, balance-of-payment controls, controls for specific types of capital (infrastructure, high-risk venture capital), and controls for short-term versus long-term capital.

TIMING IS EVERYTHING

The greatest attention has been paid to the problems generated by short-term capital or that type of funding that is only committed for brief periods. Earlier in the book it was discussed how Chile had used "prudential" controls on inflows to help guarantee that investors were committed to the Chilean economy. This is possible if the economy shows potential and patient investors can be found who are willing to let their money sit idle while they prove their commitment. Getting a prudent control of capital outflows is a thornier problem. The IMF reported that much of the outflow damage done to Asian economies occurred not in the 1997 currency collapse, the presumed beginning of the crisis, but three years earlier. The culprits were not foreign investors but domestic corporations and home-grown private investors. Apparently, foreign money was only withdrawn in 1997 when the situation became untenable. If nations cannot convince their own people to keep money in domestic investments, there is little point in trying to woo foreigners.

Paul Krugman, an often contrarian but respected economist, has argued that depressed emerging markets should lower interest rates to discourage capital inflows, his point being that this will allow damaged economies the time to rebuild weak banking systems. Any reinsertion of foreign capital before this renovation is complete will only result in a repetition of recent failures. Malaysia's imposition of capital controls in 1998 was a step in this direction, but it lacked two of Mr. Krugman's key provisos: one, the controls must give every sign of being temporary and two, real banking reform must take place. Malaysia has done little to resolve the problems of its financial system which holds a portfolio of "non-performing" loans equal to 30% of the nation's GDP.

The flip side of the Mr. Krugman's argument about restricting inflows is that the troubled markets in Asia, eastern Europe and South America did not fail because they were too open to the volatility of capital flows, but not open enough.

Believers in the restriction of capital flow couch their arguments in terms of the problems caused by the rapid infusion of capital into unsophisticated markets. What they fail to address, and what proponents of openness do consider, is that these markets permitted only the free flow of money and not the information necessary to use it properly.

FOREIGN MONEY, FOREIGN ADVICE

All of the collapsed or collapsing financial markets of the world suffered because they did not avail their populations or foreign investors of the most up-to-date financial services found in the developed world. Instead, from Bangkok to Rio, Jakarta to Moscow, domestic banks and financial service providers were protected by their respective governments from competing with the heavyweights of international finance. Had foreign firms been permitted to utilize established, well-managed banking services and brokerages instead of the weak and often corrupt financial facilities found in most emerging markets, the "Asian flu" would have most likely been only a sneeze.

By way of example, foreign banks accounted for just 5% of all the loans in hard-hit South Korea, Indonesia and Thailand. Remarkably stable and prudent Chile, on the other hand, does not coddle its domestic bankers and allows free entry and competition by foreign-owned financial service providers. Over 20% of lending in Chile is done by foreign-owned banks, which is roughly the same percentage enjoyed by the U.S. capital market. Japan, deep in the throes of economic depression and finance scandals, still places heavy restrictions on foreign lenders and financial service providers. While U.S. and European banks are hardly perfect, their systems allow for faster recognition and correction of financial deficiencies.

Role of International Aid

The International Monetary Fund (IMF) has joined the growing chorus of observers who claimed that, in retrospect, free capital flows were probably not a good idea. This must have been very difficult for a body which, along with United Nations associate, World Bank, had pumped billions of dollars into the world's capital investment flows. This occurred before, during, and after whichever crisis of the 1980s and 1990s one would like to choose. In the wake of these financial disasters, the question was raised both inside and outside of these agencies of whether or not aid actually helped or hurt the situation.

GOOD MONEY, BAD INVESTMENTS

The World Bank (aka International Bank for Reconstruction and Development), hoping to match the self-deprecating bravado of the IMF, went so far as to publish a book called *Assessing Aid: What Works, What Doesn't, and Why*. The Bank's conclusion was not good: Aid works only if it is spent in "right" countries, and too much money has been spent in "wrong" countries. The "right" countries are those economies that, though poor, have low inflation, minimal budget deficits, open trade policies, the rule of law for both commerce and crime, and competent government bureaucracies with little corruption. The "wrong" countries are missing all or some of these elements.

The book's researchers conclude that aid spent in the right place produces the desired economic growth and that money plowed into the wrong economy actually causes a decline in growth. Specifically, if aid equal to 1% of a poor "right" nation's GDP is offered, that economy will grow by 0.5% of the new enhanced GDP per year. In "wrong" economies the same delivery of aid will cause the GDP to shrink by 0.3% per year. Since most donor-country or World Bank aid is designed to relieve poverty, the question remains as to whether these shifts in GDP affect the poor or only a financial elite in the target economies. Not surprisingly, in "right" countries the poor are helped and in "wrong" economies aid actually diminishes their meager fortunes.

MAXIMIZING AID

Under the methods presently being used to distribute aid, both "right" (India, Ethiopia) and "wrong" (Russia, Mali) countries receive funding. The authors of the book claim that if current standards were used, every additional US$10 billion of aid would lift 7 million people out of poverty. If that same US$10 billion were placed only in poor but "right" economies, 25 million people would see their fortunes change for the better. Nowadays, 30 million people are helped with a global aid budget of US$1,200 per person. Were that same budget applied in the "right" places, 80 million people would be helped at only US$450 per person. Current aid funding, by the World Bank's new measure, is decidedly wasteful both in numbers of people affected and cost per person.

It is little wonder that donor nations, led by the United States, are calling for more stringent guidelines in advance of aid dispersal. Besides wasting money, poorly distributed aid can keep bad governments in power. Aid given without supervision and consequences for misuse can also create *moral hazard*, wherein recipient governments see the aid as a risk-free loan, never to be repaid or profitably invested. When international aid takes on the form of global welfare, the results are usually dependency and economic stagnation. In extreme cases of malfeasance, as in Russia, political implosion is always on the horizon once the aid taps are shut off.

Thirsty Economies and Tax Oases

The most troublesome aspect of the recent emphasis on the freedom of capital flows is the fear it has created among the world's governments that they will no longer be able to engage in their favorite function: tax collection. Even though foreign capital flows as a percentage of global GDP were much higher in the late 19th and early 20th century, governments are growing ever more fearful that they will lose control of their lifeblood. Their fear is not unfounded.

Capital funds can move a lot faster (no more steamships filled with bullion) and to more places (Hong Kong and Singapore were just dingy seaports in 1899) than ever before. Governments are finding that tax evasion and tax incentives offered by rival governments are making it increasingly difficult to collect the taxes they firmly believe are their right. Global business thinks otherwise and has used many means to stay ahead of the taxman.

Transfer Payments

Even in a strictly domestic operation, companies have always transferred assets and expenses between different branches of their business. On an even smaller scale, expenses may be transferred among the chart of accounts in a single store or outlet. This was and is a legitimate form of accounting that accurately matches revenues to proper expenses. However, when a company goes international, it finds that it is now subject to different tax regimens in countries with varying forms of collection, accounting and tax calculation. It didn't take long for business to exploit these differences in a process derogatorily called "tax arbitrage." Using the auto industry as an example, if taxes on profits are lower in one nation than another, profits are "transferred" to that low-tax location by having the other subsidiary outlets or factories pay above-standard prices for the goods (tires) or services (administration) they receive from their subsidiaries in low-tax locations.

Subsidiaries in high-tax locations can generate huge expenses, showing little or no profit and thus pay less or no taxes. The low-tax location in turn buys what it needs (air valves, marketing) from the other subsidiaries at reduced prices, thus improving its bottom line. When and if governments catch on and the tax situation changes, a company can just rearrange its "transfer payments" until the most profitable structure is found. Governments have tried to fight back with franchise taxes whereby they either have flat fees for operating within their borders or, alternatively, they may tax companies based on the overall profitability, not just the subsidiary within the government's borders. Of course, this latter method relies on being able to obtain accurate information from the subject company.

Payroll Taxes

Governments have found that companies that chafe under tough tax regimes could pick up and move elsewhere. This has been especially true (and easy) for service businesses without large, physical factories to move. Harried companies burdened with factories would simply wait until their physical plants fully depreciated in book value and then pull up stakes for less oppressive locales. Once governments saw this trend they began to move their tax schedules away from capital and profits, and on to the much less mobile category of "labor" by creating employee payroll taxes. These taxes can apply either to full-time residents or to visiting workers (even visiting professional sports teams!). Governments will often sign agreements among themselves so that workers from the respective nations are not taxed twice for the same work. While payroll taxes are seen by global businesses as far less oppressive than taxes on capital or profits, such taxes can drive companies overseas when they reach "confiscatory" levels. Germany, where the average worker pays out over 50% of wages to the government, finds it difficult to attract new investment because wages must be high (the highest in the world!) so that workers can take home a decent paycheck.

Tax Havens

Once governments saw that lower taxes attracted new business and capital flows, they were keen to undercut their competing legislatures. The competition among governments to attract "tax bases" at both the international and regional levels is becoming heated and accusatory. The biggest stumbling block in the full integration of the EU economies has not been the euro currency or defense treaties but tax harmonization. Members like France, with high corporate tax rates that are used to bolster its expansive and indulgent social benefits system, want the rest of the EU to raise their taxes to be in harmony. This, they hope, will prevent the capital assets (and jobs) of French corporations and foreign firms operating in France from jumping borders to friendlier (read: lower taxes) parts of the EU like Ireland.

Like Germany, France's industrial base is quite fixed and its labor force resists movement to other parts of Europe (although about 50,000+ have emigrated to the attractive and entrepreneur-friendly US business climate). Ireland, on the opposite side of the tax harmonization issue, is in the midst of a technological and industrial growth spurt. It long ago won approval from the European Commission to lower its corporate taxes to 12.5% (versus France's 33.3%) so as to encourage as much international capital flow as possible. Ireland, along with nations like Portugal and Greece, see tax harmonization as a means to keep them poor and subject to the whims of the more rich and powerful EU members—hardly the grounds for a harmonious relationship. It will be years before it can be resolved and the outcome will hinge on every EU member getting a shot at success but not enough to cause co-members too much discomfort. (Note: In the United States, individual states have differing corporate and income tax regimes. Some have none at all. The states often compete in attracting businesses to their markets, sometimes even openly advertising their benefits.)

Tax Evader Invaders

While the EU bickers, the rest of the globe's national markets strive to protect themselves, not just from competitor economies, but from what many consider criminal tax evasion. The G-7 economies have recommended that the same hard-line approach taken against the laundering of drug money be applied to tax evaders. The Organization for Economic Cooperation and Development (OECD) has called for criminal penalties for those nations and their ancillary territories that promote "harmful" tax competition or actively promote their "tax haven" services to known tax evaders. Switzerland, long a bastion of banking secrecy, has only recently agreed to cooperate in tax evasion investigations, but then only if officials can prove the presence of deliberate fraud. In the tiny Cayman Islands, which holds about half as much investment funding as the entire United States, the government is more defiant. It will arrest and imprison any of its bankers who cooperate with international investigations. For the Caymans, as well as for the Bahamas or the Canary Islands, being a secretive tax haven is a vitally important national industry, much like France's wine or Vietnam's rice.

Of course, as governments scratch and kick to keep what companies and taxes they have from leaving, corporations expand and dictate terms to nations thirsting for new capital flows. Governments resigned themselves some time ago to the fact that they were always a few steps behind the world of commerce. Government officials may now have to accept the reality of dancing to a tune written and played by the corporations in the international economy of the 21st century.

CHAPTER 12

Global Projections

EXPERIENCE IS THE COMB THAT NATURE GIVES US WHEN WE ARE BALD. — BELGIAN PROVERB

It is very dangerous to project the future of anything so given to unscheduled changes as the world economy. It was only less than a decade ago that respected economists and politicians from a wide spectrum of nations were predicting (or bemoaning) the rise of the "Pacific Century." This epoch was to be presumably dominated by an Asia modeled on Japan. China was supposed to overtake the United States early in the 21st century while India and Europe would cling to the periphery. Russia would shed its brutal communist past to become a technological growth market. South American and African nations would develop a mysterious "third way" of blending socialist ideals with capitalist realities to thumb their noses at (and perhaps outshine) former colonial masters. Reality has been far different.

The United States, having nimbly changed its methods, still dominates the world economy while Japan struggles to maintain itself in Asia and the EU threatens to overwhelm the yen and the dollar as "the" reserve currency. China, the land of the dubious statistic, has finally come to grips with its duplicitous banking system. (China demanded to be admitted to the WTO as a "developing nation" even while crowing about its "Number 2" slot in global GDP levels—PPP, of course.). Southeast Asia is stable but still recovering from the economic slump at the end of the last century. Meanwhile, India has taken advantage of its educated English-speaking population to create a multi-billion dollar software industry well in advance of its Chinese neighbor (and rival). Russia has regained its economic footing although it is totally dependent on the volatility of the oil markets. South America is resilient with Brazil leading the way, while a few holdouts like Venezuela talk socialism while scooping up oil profits. Africa is still stuck on the first rung as bloody wars or political infighting continue to block progress.

Two Sides, One Outcome

The optimism (or pessimism, depending on your viewpoint) of the mainstream predictions for the 21st century has been shattered by the reality of the outcomes. That said, it should also be noted that many of these outcomes were predicted by a minority of economists who had taken what were considered very contrarian views on world affairs. Throughout the 1980s and 1990s, anyone who did not predict the demise of the West and the rise of Asia and the Third World was dismissed as either racist, unobservant, uneducated, or all three. The contrarians were, of course, none of these. They had merely looked at the same statistics and trends as everyone else but had done so without the burden of a political agenda or an emotional wish list. In retrospect, the results of all of the economic reshuffling that went on after WWII and through the 1990s were really quite obvious if not always pleasing. In light of this fact, the following projections regarding the economic future of the globe will attempt to take a view more akin to that of the modern contrarians than the now-refuted mainstream.

Projection One: Emerging Markets Pay the Piper

In the legend of the Pied Piper of Hamelin, the citizens refused to pay the piper who had helped them rid the town of rats. So he exacted vengeance upon them—he took their children. The emerging markets of Asia are facing a similar fate for not holding up their end of the bargain in international funding. Money poured into emerging Asia and everything—but profits—came back out. Private and international agency money alike was squandered on corrupt officials and pointless projects with political backing. A region once thought to be the future of capitalism is now mired in debt with little hope of attracting major investment in the near future. While the former funders of Asia will not actually seize the region's children, they will certainly hold the future hostage.

The only hope for emerging Asia is to alter the politically driven economic landscape. The former pattern of joint ventures, unjustifiably lopsided in favor of local partners, will cease as foreign investors demand total control and majority ownership for any venture financing. Although certain sectors such as military manufacturing and broadcast media may be exempted, there will be a wholesale move towards liberalized foreign-direct-investment packages. The most difficult part of this process will be the development of independent judiciaries and codified commercial laws that guarantee contracts. Because this will require not so much a revamping of cultural attitudes as a loosening of political control, major upheavals in the political realm will take place. Within ten years, the die-hard communist governments of China, Vietnam, Laos and North Korea will be either out of power or liberalized beyond recognition. The same will be true for the political machines that run Indonesia and Malaysia. The penalty for not changing will be abject poverty for tomorrow's children. Put bluntly, there will be just too many other regions of the world in which to make a profit for foreign investors to put up with any shenanigans in developing Asia. Even "wealthy" China is looking outside of Asia for the bulk of its foreign investment. Asia will have to accept hard bargains or none at all. Much "face" will have to be relinquished to pay for past hubris.

Projection Two: The Dawn of Global Labor Flexibility

One of the reasons that is given for the continued success of the U.S. economy is the flexibility of the American labor force. Workers freely move and are moved to those geographical regions and industry sectors where they are needed. Unionism is low in the United States and jobs follow capital, not the reverse. If a high-tech manufacturer moves from California to New Mexico to avoid high local taxes, a good portion of the workforce moves with it. Those left behind receive minimal severance packages. For rich EU countries like France or Germany with expensive social systems and strong unions, this appears unthinkable. For example, would a Parisian move to Madrid or a Berliner to Athens just for a job? If he or she chose to stay put, would either one accept a few weeks' severance pay (or no pay at all)? In the past, No; in the future, Yes!

In a joint study completed by Harvard University and the University of Bonn it was shown that the more flexible a nation's labor force the lower the unemployment rate and the greater the overall employment (number of jobs). For example, if France had had the same labor flexibility as the United States, its overall employment would be 4.4 percentage points higher and its unemployment rate 1.7% lower. In a country like France, where "real" unemployment can hover above 10% for decades and governments change dramatically because of it, these numbers are significant. If the EU wants to compete with the United States—and that is, after all, why the EU was formed—it must get all of its workforce (not just the poor) prepared to move to those sectors or regions where they are most needed. The same holds true for all of the developed economies. As long as capital remains mobile, workers will have to either obtain specialist skills that allow them to stay put or keep their suitcases packed.

Projection Three: Services Eclipse Manufacturing and Agriculture

In the G-7 economies, the service sector is already the dominant force (United States 75%, Japan 57%, Germany 64%, United Kingdom 67%, France 71%, Italy 64%, Canada 66%). For the larger emerging economies, the service industry (China 31%, Indonesia 41%, Brazil 49%, India 42%) is still overshadowed by manufacturing and agriculture. It is increasingly apparent that the "real money" in the global economy (where total services account for 32%) is in knowledge-based services, not physical labor. (The G7 have an average GDP-per-capita 10 times that of the four emerging markets mentioned above and five times the world average.) Some of the increase in the service-sector percentage is due to an actual expansion of the number of new services over previous decades (software, movies, wireless telecom). But a good deal is the result of an increase in the monetary value now placed on services that have been in existence for centuries, (e.g., accounting, design, engineering, and legal services). These services, once thought to be only handmaidens to the dominant industrial manufacturing, are now full-blown industries themselves. In the United States they have overwhelmed their former masters. The developed world, where services reign supreme, has decided, it seems, that intellectual pursuits will be more highly valued than physical ones. The reader might agree, but the ramifications for both individual domestic economies and the global economy in general are potentially dangerous.

Most people are willing to accept that individuals as well as nations can have differing physical attributes (physical strength, geography) that may permit one person or society to do better than another economically. However, when the deciding factor between wealth and poverty is couched in terms of intellectual attributes, emotions run high and hot. For decades, emerging markets have been demanding that technological investors from the developed world supply not only money but "technology transfers" (a euphemism for "know-how"). These demands were to keep the developing populations from becoming the worker bees for a wealthy drone elite primarily in the West. It has not worked—at least from the perspective of the emerging markets. While there has been some rapid increases of wealth in limited pockets (urban China, entrepreneurial Poland), most of the world is still poor but, according to the United Nations, less poor than it used to be. The G7 nations are getting wealthier and their service (primarily intellectual) sectors are doing the best. Demands by the developed world for "intellectual property rights" underline the economic disparity ("We are on top, and we plan to remain so"). As the service sector continues to increase its global domination, we can expect the impoverished societies of the world to demand either greater compensation for physical work or greater access to intellectual tools.

Projection Four: Human Longevity Demands Economic Restructuring

The hallmark of a developed economy is not just a rise in GDP per capita. Such wealth is also accompanied by a decline in birth rate and an increase in life span. Many of the economies of the EU have low population growth rates (France 0.31%, Germany 0.02%) while the United States maintains its meager growth (0.87%) primarily through immigration. Emerging economies like Nigeria (2.96%), Ethiopia (2.21%) and Bosnia (3.63%) dwarf the global average of 1.3%. More importantly, life spans in the developed world tend to be 10-15 years longer than the global average of 63 just as they are 10-15 years shorter in the underdeveloped regions. All of this is occurring as the developed world moves decidedly towards wealthier knowledge-based service economies, and physical labor is shifted to the impoverished emerging markets. The world is experiencing not just greater demarcation between the traditional "haves and have-nots" but between those societies that live longer and those that die sooner. The former economies are increasingly supported in their physical needs (consumer goods, food, pharmaceuticals, chemicals) by the latter. The over-55s, once thought to be a potential burden to their own families and society in general, are now set to be the economic backbone and, in some wealthy nations (e.g., Japan), a majority subset of the main population by 2020. Fifty may not be the new forty, but twenty will be seriously outnumbered.

This new demographic will not only change the way the elderly are treated in the technological service economies (feared, not just revered), but it will also affect the way the developing world sees its role in the global economic family. Not only is there the potential for emerging markets to see themselves as being just subservient colonies of the powerful developed world but also as supporters of "grandparents" they did not know they had. These hardworking grandchildren will undoubtedly see that they are being significantly cut out of an "inheritance" to which they are, at least in their own minds, entitled. A Word to the Wise: These same emerging markets (e.g., Russia, China, Kenya, India) that are chock-full of young men looking at declining lifespans are also in the midst of enormous military expenditure growth. The potential for elder abuse at the macro-level is very real.

Projection Five: Academia Takes Control of the Workforce

One of the consequences of the rise of knowledge-based service economies has been the growing respect paid to academic training. This is a major change since the days of industrial dominance when, at least in the West, academia was derided by business moguls with phrases like "those who can, do—those who can't, teach." Times have changed. In 2007, an MBA degree (Master of Business Administration) was no longer just a ticket to an executive position as it was in 1987, but a prerequisite for many entry-level management jobs. Management, once thought to be something that could only be learned "on the job," is now considered best learned under the tutelage of business school professors. Not uncharacteristically, the United States has led the world in this "certification" of management and the desire to quantify managerial skills. A two-year MBA program from a top US academic institution can cost a student well in excess of US$200,000, and competing universities regularly boast in advertisements about the "return on investment" their graduates receive for the education. The European schools, having come late to the MBA movement, are struggling to catch up with the Americans, while universities from both markets are opening "satellite campuses" in Asia and South America. This level of academic influence is just the beginning.

Business schools will increase their dominance of managerial training and extend it further into the non-managerial workforce on a global scale. This will occur for two main reasons. The first is that, after many decades of denial, companies have come to the conclusion that on-the-job training is not terribly efficient for post-industrial, knowledge-based societies. The majority of work skills (e.g., accounting, computers, office organization)—for both managers and staff—are common to most businesses. These can be taught, primarily at the student's expense, prior to actual hire. The savings to companies are enormous and the "certification" places the onus of competence upon the training institution. The student/employee arrives as a warranted, paid-for commodity.

The second reason academia will dominate the workforce is that business schools have taken great pains to make sure their professors can function (and profit) in the "real" world. Many of these professors actually run thriving companies and the balance regularly consult to major corporations. Much to the delight of the companies that will eventually derive the benefit from the training, students get their instruction directly from "the horse's mouth." (Even multi-millionaire TV host Oprah Winfrey has taught business courses at Northwestern University.)

One of the most recent trends in business schools is for corporations to open their own schools or endow MBA programs to ensure that the "right" training is being dispensed. The early 21st century will see two new trends: one, the professionalization of non-managerial personnel (thereby saving companies even more training costs) and two, demands by emerging markets for access to the same academic training as the advanced economies as another form of technology transfer.

Projection Six: Micro-Lending Becomes a Major Financial System

Central banks from every type of economy on the globe have long pondered how to disperse the trillions of funding dollars controlled by the governments and commercial institutions in their purview. Major infrastructure projects, technology development and military expenditures were all discussed, planned and financed. All this was done in the name of maintaining or enhancing the lives of each society's members. For all of the billions of francs and millions of rupees budgeted, few if any from these institutions gave any consideration to the investment needs of the lowest strata of their respective economies. At these lower levels, entrepreneurs think in terms of a few hundred or a couple of thousand dollars worth of funding. That level of investment is far below the consideration of the average bank. This is precisely where micro-lending institutions, however, have found their niche. From Africa to the Indian subcontinent, micro-lenders have loaned small amounts at reasonable rates to thousands of would-be entrepreneurs. Much of the lending has been to women who would otherwise be excluded from consideration when starting small businesses. Micro-loan defaults have been minimal (some would say minuscule when compared to some of the defaults from major banks in Asia and Africa) and most systems have been profitable. In Kenya and Bangladesh these micro-lenders have been so successful as to cause their mainstream competitors great concern. In South Africa, the micro-lenders have recently stepped in to service a population angered by the major banks who have adopted a policy (as in Kenya) of "we are not a charity." The micro-borrowers, of course, do not see themselves as charity cases, but rather as potential small business owners.

The global implications of micro-lending are becoming apparent as this field grows. Large international aid projects, as discussed earlier in the book, have not been particularly successful at doing more than just feeding poor populations. As can be seen by the constant reappearance of economic problems in Africa and south Asia, little has been done by large agencies to advance the lives of the truly impoverished. Some of the disconnect between large lenders and the needs of small borrowers comes from the attitudes of the political leaders of emerging economies, not just the international lenders. Leaders from India to Indonesia, Mali to Malaysia, and Kazakhstan to Kenya have a common characteristic of wanting to move their populations directly into the 21st century while skipping what in some cases may be 300 years of economic development. Major petroleum pipelines, high-tech design centers, cellular phone systems and automobile plants, financed in the name of economic advancement and national honor, end up just serving as monuments to these leaders and cash cows for their political cronies. The beneficial effect on the billions of poor people who populate the emerging markets has been almost negligible.

The IMF and the many development banks are already beginning to see the error of their lending ways. By the next century we will witness micro-lending as a mandatory part of international aid programs. Micro-lending will also see a surge in the developed world as the poor in these economies start demanding access to entrepreneurial funding and control of their own financial futures. The old adage of "give a poor man a fish and he can feed himself, teach him to fish and he can feed his family" will soon have the addendum of "finance a fishing boat and he can start a business, make a profit and pay taxes." In 2006, Muhammad Yunus of the microlender Grameen Bank won the Nobel Peace Prize for his efforts in this burgeoning field of finance.

Projection Seven: Governments Battle Over Internet Taxation and Costs

Governments as politically diverse as the democratic United States, interventionist France and communist China have all expressed concern about content on the freewheeling Internet. The United States fears pornography and violence, France fears the steady advance of the English language, and China fears its people may find out the truth. But there is another area in which all governments share the very same fear: loss of national tax revenues. Their common fear is a reasonable one because the Internet is shattering the concept of national borders for trade. If a buyer in Japan purchases a jacket after viewing the on-line catalog of a Canadian company that posts its site on a server in Ireland, where was the sale made and which country (if any) is entitled to tax the transaction? Customs in Canada and Japan will certainly receive some duties and the Irish service provider will pay taxes on its profits, but sales taxes may be uncollectible on any of the three. The problem is exacerbated when the transfer of the product takes place electronically and the product is digital, as is happening in the world of entertainment (music, movies, books) and technology (software). Even education has gotten into the act with major universities offering very expensive courses on-line that are available 24-hours a day anywhere on the globe.

Governments have already accepted that there may be little they can do about recouping lost sales tax revenues from each step of a complex Internet transaction. They will have to be content instead with taxing the incomes of the Internet providers and product distributors within their respective borders. However, if they cannot focus on sales, then governments will turn to looking at costs. The governments of China and the ASEAN nations have made a play to get the United States to help pick up the cost of their Internet telecom infrastructure based on the fact that most Internet traffic and content involves U.S. service providers. So far the United States has ignored the request as just another attempt to shake down a Western economy. The Asian governments' concept is not without precedent, however. If indeed the Internet is an "information superhighway," then tolls can be demanded just as in any normal road system where the highways are used to transport products. The same usage-toll concept for cargo shipping was applied to seaports centuries ago and to airports just within living memory. The collected fees were used to maintain the roads, harbors and air traffic controls. Doesn't the telecom infrastructure needed for the Internet require similar maintenance? If so, where will the funding come from?

Right now, the wrangling is between the United States and a few struggling economies in Asia but we can expect other governments to jump into the fray as Internet commerce increases. There is little doubt that the lion's share of Internet commerce has an American component either in product distribution or in service provision. Consequently, Washington DC collects the most taxes (corporate and personal income, if not the sales variety) related to the Internet. Internet users will see a major revision of "e-commerce" as governments (especially the EU) start to whittle away at the benefits the United States enjoys of having the most "trucks" on the "superhighway." We can also expect that the high-tech companies will stay a few car lengths ahead of the bureaucrats when it comes to collecting taxes.

Projection Eight: Economies Say "No" to the Globalization of Culture

When Deng Xiao Peng wanted to move the Chinese economy away from central planning to market economics he pronounced that, contrary to communist theory, "to become rich is glorious." Sincere he may have been, but most likely he was unaware that only a small percentage of his people would become glorious any time soon. As in all market economies, wealth in China is not distributed evenly and the social system, by virtue of market forces, has little impetus to make remedies. As market economics has swept around the world so has the culture of personal gain ("I've got mine, you're on your own"), once thought to be only an American disease.

Other cultural elements like the breakdown of family structure, sexual promiscuity, teenage pregnancies, violent criminal behavior, drug use, and even disrespect for elders have all been attributed to the competitive nature of a market economy. The message to nations that want to participate in the modern global economy is that they must be prepared to accept the realities of these cultural problems if they want the glories of wealth. The next few decades will see a movement by many nations to simply say "no" to this economic-social quid pro quo. Interestingly, the movement to cure the bad effects of capitalism will not find its earliest proponents in Deng's China or in any of the other hierarchy-based societies of the emerging economies. Those nations (e.g., Malaysia) are more likely to throw away market economics itself rather than its benefits. The real attempt at sanitizing capitalism will be in the West and most likely in the expanding EU. Having already grumbled for years about the deleterious effects of McDonald's hamburgers and Sylvester Stallone movies, it has finally come into its own. Europe has a culture that is ancient (unlike North America) and social systems that are admired worldwide (unlike Asia). European culture is seen as worth saving. Many of its nations also have entrenched social systems (France, Germany, Netherlands) that can be defended on moral, if not completely economic, grounds. Unlike the United States where personal freedom is directly linked to the ability to economically succeed (or fail), Europe is unwilling to see its cultural traditions and less successful citizens sacrificed on the free-market altar. More importantly, they are big enough (combined Europe has a greater population than the United States) and already wealthy enough (more so than a combined Asia) to do something about it. The EU, especially as it expands eastward, will try to show the rest of the world that market economics can succeed globally without destroying local cultures. This concept, in and of itself, may constitute a new global culture.

CHAPTER 13

Glossary

ABSOLUTE ADVANTAGE An economic pattern wherein a nation or a company uses fewer resources-per-unit of production than its competition.

AGGREGATES The study of markets taken as a whole in relation to their individual components.

ANARCHISM An economic theory promoted most notably by Mikhail Bakunin in the 19th century that calls for very small autonomous groups who work collectively in an economy with no central authority.

ARBITRAGE A form of risk-free trading wherein the trader (arbitrageur) buys in one market and sells in another to take advantage of price differentials between the two markets.

AUSTERITY MEASURES Extreme fiscal policies imposed upon a country by its government in hopes of protecting the nation from economic decay.

BALANCE OF PAYMENTS An overall statement of one nation's economic transactions compared with that of other nations, including current and capital accounts.

BARRIER TO ENTRY The various formal (e.g., taxes) and informal (e.g., cultural bias) obstacles that prevent potential participants from entering an economy or marketplace.

BILATERAL TRADE The commerce between two countries.

BLACK MARKET Buying or selling of products and commodities, or engaging in exchange of foreign currencies in violation of government restrictions.

BOND MARKET That sector of an economy that buys and sells securities in the form of private and governmental debt with set redemption dates. See also EQUITY MARKET.

BOOM PHASE A period of great economic growth accompanied by large gains in per capita income.

BULLION Gold or silver in bulk form regarded as a raw material for use in industry, coinage, or as a nation's reserve.

BUSINESS CYCLES The regularly occurring periods of growth (peaks) and contraction (troughs) in an economy that dictate overall stability. The relative severity of the cycles can be affected by domestic business, politics, natural phenomena, and external trade.

BUYER OF LAST RESORT An economy whose stability, strength, and regular levels of consumption permit it to assist smaller, troubled economies through the purchase of goods and services during periods of economic crisis.

CAPITAL Financial, physical, and intellectual assets that are used to produce goods and services.

CAPITAL ACCOUNT The total of one nation's exchanges of assets and liabilities with other nations.

CAPITAL FLIGHT The transfer of money or other financial resources from one country to another as a hedge against inflation or poor economic or political conditions.

CAPITAL GOODS Manufactured goods that are for productive industrial use. For example: machine tools.

CAPITAL GAINS The profits derived from the sale of an asset, or the increased value of an asset from time of purchase until the present.

CAPITALISM An economic theory wherein the owners and managers of assets (capital) derive the greatest portion of profit from the use of those assets.

CAPITAL MOVEMENTS The flow of assets from one economic sector to another on both a domestic and international basis.

CENTRAL BANK The bank (public or private) designated by a government to have overall control of the money supply, interest rates and other subordinate banks within a national economy.

COMMAND ECONOMY An economic system where resources and decisions about production are controlled by a central government authority.

COMMUNISM (scientific socialism) An economic theory wherein all members of a society have equal rights to all of that society's assets and each member "gives according to his means while taking according to his needs."

COMPARATIVE ADVANTAGE An economic theory that purports that even when an economy (or company) can produce a wide variety of goods and services, it should only concentrate on those areas where it is more cost efficient than its competing economies (or companies).

COMPETITION An economic situation in which willing participants can buy or sell at freely determined prices. See MONOPOLY and MONOPSONY.

COMPETITIVE MARKET A market system that permits and encourages competition among its domestic companies as well as with international rivals.

COMPONENT COST The cost of the individual items that go into the manufacture of a final product (e.g., labor, materials, component parts).

CONSUMER PRICE INDEX (CPI) A series of quantifiable indicators based on the price of various consumer goods that seeks to monitor growth or contraction in a national economy. See also GDP DEFLATOR.

CONSUMER SURPLUS The excess of benefits that consumers derive over the price paid for the purchase of goods.

CONTRABAND Illegal goods or services brought across international borders or distributed internally.

CONVERTIBILITY The ability of one currency to be exchanged for another currency on the open international market.

COPYRIGHT The legal right recognized in varying degrees by different nations for individuals or companies to claim profits from the reproduction of artistic, literary, dramatic, musical, or scientific materials such as books, CDs, live performances, or software.

COST The value of an (all) input(s) required to produce a product or service.

CRONYISM The granting of contracts for government and private projects, or commercial loans with favorable interest rates to the friends and family of government officials.

CURRENCY BOARD The group of government officials that oversees the direct matching of domestic currency exchange rates to a predetermined foreign currency or group of currencies. See also PEGGING.

CURRENT ACCOUNT The difference between national revenue inflows and outflows which, when viewed with other factors, is an indicator of an economy's overall health. Usually denoted as a current account surplus or deficit.

DEADWEIGHT LOSS A loss of surplus by both consumers and producers in an economy brought about by government-enforced price controls.

DEBT SERVICE The amount of money needed by an individual, company or a national treasury to make interest and principal payments on outstanding debt.

DEBT/EQUITY RATIO The ratio of a company's outstanding liabilities to its equity. A high debt/equity ratio (in comparison to other firms in the same industry) indicate greater debt and therefore greater investment risk. (Also used in general terms to describe the relationship between the bond and the stock markets in a national economy.)

DEBT The sum total of all monies owed by an individual, company or national government to both private and public creditors.

DEFICIT (national budget) The annual total of the debt accumulated by a national government through spending in excess of revenues (differs from a current account deficits generated by a nation's businesses).

DEFLATION An economic condition during which prices either steadily decrease or there is a progressive reduction in market activity due to a drop in effective demand.

DEMAND Pressure place upon an economy by consumers to produce or import certain types, qualities and numbers of goods and services. See also SUPPLY.

DEVALUATION The lowering of the value of a national currency in terms of the currency of another nation.

DIAGRAMMATIC ECONOMICS A form of economics education invented by Alfred Marshall in which charts and diagrams replace mathematical formulas for the purpose of explaining principles.

DIMINISHING RETURNS, LAW OF (aka Diminishing Marginal Product) The theory that successive increases in the units of input will, over time, lead to a decreased yield of outputs per unit of input (e.g., increasing the units of labor applied to an acre of farmland will eventually decrease outputs per labor unit).

DIRECT (FOREIGN) INVESTMENT Investment that is made to acquire a lasting interest in an enterprise operating in an economy other than that of the investor.

DISPOSABLE INCOME Personal income minus income and other taxes that can be used for consumption or savings. It is used as a general indicator of an economy's wealth and development.

DOMESTICATION The process by which a government forces a foreign company to accept a local partner with majority ownership rights.

DUE DILIGENCE The procedure of thorough investigation that precedes a major transaction wherein all pertinent information is exchanged among participants.

ECONOMICS From the Greek for "home management," this term denotes the study of all human production and how limited resources could or should be distributed along with the various consequences. Economics is often called the "dismal science" by those who do not understand its principles.

EMERGING MARKETS A blanket term that replaced "third world" as the designation for poor nations pursuing investment.

EMINENT DOMAIN The right claimed by all governments to act as the ultimate arbiter for the use of all assets within its borders and to take private property for public use, usually for compensation. See also EXPROPRIATION.

EQUITY MARKET That sector of the economy devoted to the trading of stocks as investments in companies. See also BOND MARKET.

ERM (Exchange Rate Mechanism) A process used with minimal success by the European Union (EU) to control the exchange rates of its member economies by forcing each to be valued within a set band of fluctuation regardless of market activity or true value.

EURO The name for the common currency of the members of the European Union set to be issued in physical form in the year 2002.

EUROCURRENCY A blanket term for any currency held outside of the issuing nation's borders (e.g., eurodollar, euroyen). There is no indication at this time that "euroeuro" will be an accepted term.

EXCHANGE RATE(S) (nominal & real) The international exchange value of a currency as determined by an issuing government (nominal rate), or the value of a currency as determined by the relative prices of similar goods (real rate) among different economies (e.g., the price of a Big Mac).

EXPORTS Those goods and services sold to foreign nations in exchange for other products or for money.

EXPORT PROCESSING ZONE (EPZ) A designated area (usually near a major port) where both foreign and domestic firms are encouraged to set up manufacturing specifically for export at reduced or zero tariffs in an effort to garner foreign hard currency or offset excessive importation.

EXPORT PROMOTION A government policy that uses subsidies and tax incentives to encourage domestic businesses and foreign-owned local companies to export goods in an attempt to offset importation or to garner hard currency.

EXPROPRIATION The process by which a government seizes the assets of a foreign firm working within its borders without compensation or due process. See also EMINENT DOMAIN.

FEEDBACK EFFECT An economic reaction in which price and quantity adjustments in one market cause similar adjustments in another market. (e.g., a drop in the price of fuel will cause a drop in the price of airline tickets).

FEUDALISM An economic system characterized by the voluntary or involuntary attachment of groups of people to powerful elites that own all local means of production (capital) and secure rents and fees from subordinates (vassals, serfs) using that capital.

FIAT MONEY Currency whose value is determined by a government's ability to assure the international markets of the stated value of the currency, as opposed to backing the currency with precious metals such as gold or silver.

FINANCIAL INSTRUMENT A document which has monetary value or is evidence of a financial transaction. Examples include checks, bonds, stock certificates, bills of exchange, promissory notes, and bills of lading.

FIXED COSTS Those costs that do not rise or fall based on the amount of production.

FOREIGN DIRECT INVESTMENT (FDI) Capital entering an economy from foreign lands, on either a short- or long-term basis, for use in acquiring assets, as opposed to international lending.

FRANCHISE TAX A levy placed upon a company operating in many locations or nations by local authorities so as to tax those parts of the operation that derive profits within the borders controlled by the government.

FREE MARKET Describes the unrestricted movement of items in and out from the market, unhampered by the existence of tariffs or other trade barriers.

FULL DISCLOSURE That information required for proper DUE DILIGENCE (see above) prior to a major transaction. A term not recognized or practice performed in many emerging economies.

G7 (aka: The Group of Seven) the seven largest economies of the world that act as a group to help steer international development (United States, Japan, United Kingdom, France, Germany, Italy, Canada). Russia was added in 1997 as an "observer," forming the G8.

GDP DEFLATOR A broad-based economic indicator that includes investment prices, government purchases, and consumer activity used to determine a rise or fall in GDP. See also CONSUMER PRICE INDEX.

GENERAL EQUILIBRIUM An economic state wherein all sectors of an economy are considered simultaneously.

GOLD STANDARD The use of gold to back a nation's currency as opposed to floatation of the currency on the open market. See also FIAT MONEY.

GREEN ECONOMICS A form of economics based in the belief that all aspects of growth and development must proceed only with regard to how they impact environmental issues.

GREY MARKET That part of an economy that is a mixture of both legal and illegal commercial activities such as parallel importing. See also BLACK MARKET.

GROSS DOMESTIC PRODUCT (GDP) The sum total of outputs produced within a nation over a set period (usually a fiscal year) but excluding that output produced by domestic companies operating overseas.

GROSS NATIONAL PRODUCT (GNP) Total output produced domestically (during a fiscal year) but excluding that generated domestically by foreign-owned firms but including that produced by domestic companies operating overseas.

GUILD SOCIALISM An economic concept formulated by G.D.H. Cole in which a national economy is organized around trade guilds and consumer associations.

HARD CURRENCY A national currency of high value that is freely convertible on world markets. Examples include the US dollar, the Japanese yen, the German deutschemark, the French franc and the Dutch guilder.

HEDGE FUND An investment that uses private money to finance a wide variety of projects so as to lower risk by betting against both upturns and downturns in market activity simultaneously

HYPERINFLATION An extremely high level of inflation (over 50% per month) that exceeds the ability of the affected national economy to control it.

IMPORTS Those goods and services purchased from foreign nations in exchange for other products or for money.

IMPORT COLLAPSE A phase of economic disruption, usually caused by currency devaluation, during which a nation is incapable of buying foreign products which it considers necessary, or for which there is high domestic demand.

INFLATION An economic condition in which prices and wages rise disproportional to other factors in the economy. See also DEFLATION.

INFRASTRUCTURE Those capital investments used to produce publicly accessible goods and services such as telecom, power, transportation, or water resources.

INPUTS Components of the production process such as labor, materials, energy, land, or finance.

INSTITUTIONAL ECONOMICS A school of economics devoted to demonstrating the impact of institutions upon a national or regional economy.

INTELLECTUAL PROPERTY Personal property rights to creations of the intellect (as opposed to real property or physical goods) such as books, music, film, software, and manufacturing processes and designs. Such rights are often, but not always, protected by copyrights, trademarks, patents, and licenses.

INTEREST ELASTICITY The measure of how an economy responds to the demand for money as interest rates change.

INTEREST The cost for borrowing money, or the profit that is derived by lenders for extending credit.

INTEREST RATES The additional costs added per unit to the principal amount that are charged to a borrower by a lender.

IPO (initial public offering) The process by which private shares of a company are first presented for sale to the general public.

JOB MOBILITY The tendency of a population to move from areas of high unemployment to other locations in search of work.

JOINT VENTURE A business in which the providing of capital, profits, and potential risks are shared by two or more partners (usually applied to businesses with foreign partners).

KIERETSU The system of corporate linkages that characterizes the Japanese economic system (formerly Zaibatsu or "financial cliques").

LABOR MARKET The sum total of those available and qualified to work in a business sector, a regional market or a national economy.

LABOR THEORY OF VALUE An economic theory that claims that the "true" value of goods and services is really determined by direct and indirect inputs of labor with little or no regard to other costs.

LAISSEZ ALLER ("let go") An economic policy proposed by Adam Smith that would allow entrepreneurs to grow until their interests conflicted with public good, at which point government restraints would be applied.

LAISSEZ FAIRE ("let alone") An economic policy under which government would in no way restrain the activity of business and markets.

LEGAL TENDER Any form of money which a creditor, business, or government is legally obliged to accept as payment or settlement of debt.

LENDER OF LAST RESORT A term used to describe an international organization (such as the IMF) or a central bank from a large, stable economy which can act as a supplier of finance to troubled economies.

LIABILITY The legal obligation to pay a debt incurred by either private citizens, businesses, or governments.

LIQUIDITY The relative ability of assets to be turned into cash in the short term.

MACROECONOMICS The study of the larger aspects of economics including the determination of aggregates and averages for entire markets or national economies. See also MICROECONOMICS.

MALTHUSIAN A theory of potential economic downfall brought about when growing populations exceed market output and drive per capita incomes down to the subsistence level.

MANDATORY BENEFITS Those employment benefits which a government requires a business to provide their employees. The relative level of such benefits can affect the level of investment in the locale by business.

MARGIN BUYING The purchase of securities (or options) by placing a deposit in lieu of the full price in hopes that payment will not be demanded until profits are realized.

MARGINAL COST The additional cost generated by an increase in production of one unit.

MARGINAL RATE OF SUBSTITUTION The additional amount of one product needed to compensate consumers for a decrease in quantity of another product, per unit of the decrease.

MARGINAL REVENUE The increase in total revenue realized when one additional unit of production is sold.

MARGINAL UTILITY The increase to an individual's benefit (utility) derived as goods or services are consumed (such utility tends to decrease as more is consumed).

MARKET CLEARING The setting of prices for products or securities so that the forecasted supply will exactly match demand.

MARKET ECONOMY A form of national economy which allows most economic decisions to be dictated by market forces such as supply and demand. See PLANNED ECONOMY.

MARKET GLUT An economic pattern in which a particular market sector is oversupplied thereby driving down prices.

MARKET MECHANISM A blanket term describing the processes by which a market economy allows its various markets to make decisions (e.g., supply, demand, incentives, pricing).

MARKET PRICE Those prices dictated by supply and demand; or, the method of measuring an economy's income by the total prices (including taxes) that consumers actually pay.

MARKET SHARE That portion of an entire market sector which an individual business or corporation serves.

MARXIAN SOCIALISM An economic theory based on the writings of Karl Marx that maintains that the value of labor (and its exploitation) is at the root of all economic measurement. See also LABOR THEORY OF VALUE.

MATURITY The date at which a security can be redeemed; or, when applied to markets, a designation of advanced economic organization and sophistication.

MEDIUM OF EXCHANGE The use of currency to facilitate the exchange of goods and services.

MERCANTILISM An economic policy by which governments use protectionism to assure that the nation runs continual balance-of-payments surpluses in an effort to stimulate the economy.

MERGERS AND ACQUISITIONS (M&A) The combination of two or more firms (voluntarily or involuntarily) into a new, single business entity.

MICROECONOMICS The section of economics devoted to the study of choices by individuals or smaller sectors of the economy. See also MACROECONOMICS.

MIXED ECONOMY A national economy with both government-run and private enterprises, usually applied to economies with a prevalence of government-run industries.

MONETARY POLICY The tendency of governments to use interest rates and money supply controls to influence economic growth or contraction.

MONEY LAUNDERING The use of complex transactions to cover the original (usually criminal) source of cash holdings.

MONEY SUPPLY The total amount of money (foreign and domestic) or monetary instruments (checks, postal orders, stamps) permitted in an economy.

MONOPOLY A market condition in which there is only one seller of a particular product. Monopolies are illegal in some economies while promoted in others.

MONOPSONY A market condition in which there is only one buyer of a particular product.

MORAL HAZARD A condition in which a contract influences participants to make immoral decisions by allowing participants to gain (or at least not lose) by such decisions (e.g., full insurance for uncollateralized loans encourages reckless lending).

NATIONAL DEBT See DEBT.

NATIONALIZATION A process by which a national government seizes the assets of a private company (foreign or domestic) without compensation.

NOMINAL PRICE The stated price in currency of goods and services (not including additional costs such as tax and warranties). See also REAL PRICE.

NONCOMPETITIVE MARKET An entire economy or sector of an economy that is not open to competition. Noncompetitive markets are brought on by government intervention or monopolistic practices.

NORMATIVE ECONOMICS The study of how economics should work if all principles were in effect. See also POSITIVE ECONOMICS.

OLIGOPOLY A market condition in which there are only a few sellers of a particular product.

OLIGOPSONY A market condition in which there are only a few buyers of a particular product.

OUTPUT That which is produced by the combination of inputs in production processes.

PARALLEL IMPORTS A system of imports in which goods are exported to developing countries at low prices and then returned to the country of origin at prices that undercut the domestic market.

PARASTATAL A business organization that, though privately owned, operates under government auspices or directives.

PARTIAL EQUILIBRIUM An economic state wherein only certain sectors rather than the entire scope of an economy are studied.

PATENT A government-granted right to inventors to derive exclusive economic benefit from their inventions and which bars unlicensed duplication (not recognized by all governments).

PEGGING The process by which a national currency is directly linked to the value of a more stable national currency.

PHILLIPS CURVE A now largely discredited economic charting system and formula that sought to show an inverse relationship between inflation and unemployment.

PHYSIOCRATIC ECONOMICS A school of economics devoted to dismantling guild structures while promoting laissez-faire policies.

POSITIVE ECONOMICS The study of how economics actually works. See also NORMATIVE ECONOMICS.

PRICE CONTROLS A government policy that sets maximum prices for key items such as food, and fuel during times of economic or political crisis.

PRICE FIXING An anti-competitive practice wherein two or more companies conspire (collude) to set prices at an artificial level.

PRIME RATE The favorable interest rate that commercial banks offer to their best customers (often used as the base rate for other lending policies).

PRIVATE SECTOR Those businesses and activities not undertaken by government agencies or personnel.

PRIVATIZATION A general term used to describe the sale of government assets and agencies for use and application by private citizens or businesses. See also NATIONALIZATION.

PRODUCER SURPLUS The amount of profit that a seller or producer retains above the lowest possible price at which a product could be sold in the marketplace.

PRODUCTIVITY A measure of efficiency that studies the amount of output as a function of each unit of input.

PROFIT The amount of revenue taken in by a business minus expenses paid out over the same period.

PROFIT MAXIMIZATION The pursuit of the greatest amount of profit over a projected time period with allowances for suitable risk.

PROLETARIAT A general term used primarily by socialists and communists to describe the working class as distinct from the capitalist class.

PROTECTIONISM The belief that the practice of restricting the importation of foreign goods and the outflow of capital is a healthy economic policy.

PUBLIC DOMAIN Intellectual property that is no longer bound by patents, copyrights, trademarks, or licensing agreements, and are open to free use by the public.

PUBLIC SECTOR All activities undertaken by government agencies or personnel.

PURCHASING POWER PARITY An economic theory that states that the exchange rates between two national currencies is determined over the long term by the amount of similar goods and services each currency can buy within their respective societies.

RATE OF RETURN The annual return on a loan stated as a percentage of the principal amount borrowed.

REAL ASSETS Assets with physical substance such as land, machinery, or buildings.

REAL PRICE The purchase price of a product relative to other goods and services in an economy measured over time.

RECESSION A phase (usually two successive fiscal quarters) in an economy during which demand is sluggish, output is stagnant, and unemployment rises.

REGULATORY CAPITALISM A type of capitalism, exhibited most notably by the United States, wherein businesses are not owned by government but subject only to regulations nominally designed to protect consumers and general public welfare.

RETURN ON INVESTMENT (roi) A general term used to measure the earning power of assets, but when applied to a national economy it designates the sum total of a nation's ability to efficiently use its resources.

REVENUE For private business this term denotes the amount of receipts derived from sales; for a government, the amount of taxes collected (e.g., internal revenue, inland revenue)

RISK The degree of uncertainty in outcome caused by random occurrences; the success of Western economies is largely attributed to the ability of its populations to calculate and manage risk.

SAVINGS That portion of income not used for consumption or debt service.

SECURITIES A general term for financial instruments that show ownership, such as debt (bonds), equity (stocks), or rights (options); also denotes collateral used to support a loan.

SEIGNORAGE The profits a government derives from issuing money; such profits may come from direct fees charged to banks (foreign or domestic) for currency, or from goods and services given in return for creating new currency.

SHAREHOLDER A person or company holding equity shares in a company.

SMUGGLING The act of bringing illegal products (contraband) across national borders for sale; or, the willful avoidance of tariff payments on legal products distributed internationally.

SOCIALISM The school of economics that promotes the idea that resources must be used in the interest of the group while eschewing the private ownership of land and capital; a concept considered to be a precursor to communism.

SOFT CURRENCY A national currency that is considered unstable and of lesser value than hard currencies; some soft currencies have no convertibility in the international market. See also HARD CURRENCY.

SOVEREIGN DEBT The sum total of debt generated by an independent nation; such debt can be subject to repudiation or unilateral rescheduling by the debtor nation.

SPECIE A term used to describe coin currency as opposed to paper money.

SPECULATION The willful taking of risk for the sole purpose of extracting profits from the buying and selling of goods, services, currencies or stocks; at one time considered an economic crime punishable by imprisonment and/or death.

STANDARD THEORY An economic theory first promulgated in the late 1960s (Friedman & Phelps) that implied that every national economy has an inherent level of unemployment below which inflation will rise.

STATE SOCIALISM A form of socialism carried out on a national basis wherein all property is held communally by all of the population; such economies are given to central planning by the ruling government.

STOCK EXCHANGE The institution through which a company or government trades stock shares; not all governments permit the existence of stock exchanges within national borders, nor do all permit their populations to trade internationally.

STOCK MARKET A general term used to describe the work of stock exchanges on either a local (London), national (Japan), regional (southeast Asia), or global level.

STRATEGIC TRADE POLICY (STP) A set of national policies designed to affect the economy, trade policies, or politics of another nation or trading bloc.

SUBSISTENCE LEVEL The absolute minimum level at which an economy can operate and still allow its population to physically survive.

SUPPLY The total amount of particular goods or services offered for sale. See also DEMAND.

SYNDICALISM A form of centrally planned economy wherein strong unions design and regulate production nationwide.

TAX HARMONIZATION An agreement among separate governments acting as a single economic entity (e.g., the EU) stating that taxation will be standardized among the participating members. Tax harmonization is designed to prevent disparities of capital or labor flow.

T-BILLS A nickname for U.S. Treasury bonds.

THIRD WORLD A term now in limited use once denoting the poor nations of the globe that were not associated with the West (First World) or communist countries (Second World). See also EMERGING MARKETS.

THOMISTIC ECONOMICS Another name for the medieval European form of feudal economics; so derived from the influence exerted by Thomas Aquinas.

TRADE DEFICIT A term that describes the situation in which a nation imports more goods and services than it exports. Populist politicians often fail to include services when calculating trade deficit or surplus figures. See also TRADE SURPLUS.

TRADE SURPLUS A situation in which a nation exports more goods and services than it imports. See also TRADE DEFICIT.

TRADE UNION An organization of workers (employees) in a particular industry or possessing a particular skill, formed for the purposes of collective bargaining with employers (managers) in regards to wages and working conditions. Trade unions are not recognized by all governments.

TRADING BAND (aka exchange rate bands) The maximum and minimum levels between which a national government will permit its currency to be traded; designed to be a temporary means of stabilizing a currency against speculation.

TRADEMARK A publicly registered and legally protected symbol, name, or logo used by the public to readily identify the seller or maker of products. Not all governments recognize trademark status.

TRANSFER PAYMENTS The internal accounting process used by international companies to move revenue and expenses among global subsidiaries in an attempt to place profits within the national economy with the most advantageous tax structure.

TREASURY BONDS (aka treasury bills) The debt instruments offered by national governments for open sale.

UMBRELLA INDUSTRY A term used to describe the overall business type under which a variety of other business types operate (e.g., tourism, transportation).

USURY A term originally meaning the taking of any interest payments on loans; current Western usage describes only "excessive" interest on lending. Nations with Islamic governments use the term in its original sense and forbid its practice.

UTILITY An economic term used to describe the welfare of the individual (utility rises with consumption and decreases by work).

UTOPIANISM (aka utopian socialism) An ideal form of socialism in which all members of society willingly work for the benefit of the group with no concern for personal gain.

VALUE ADDED TAX (vat) A levy upon goods and services at all levels of transaction (production, wholesale, retail) based upon value added by each member of the distribution chain up to and including the end-user.

VALUE ADDED The total sales of a company minus the purchases of inputs from other companies; or, the concept of increasing the worth of raw products, components, or intangibles by application of manufacturing processes or supplemental services.

VARIABLE COSTS Those costs that increase or decrease depending upon the level of output. See also FIXED COSTS.

VARIABLE COST PER UNIT The additional cost of producing one additional unit of production.

VENTURE CAPITAL Capital invested in high-risk projects by private companies or individuals in search of a higher-than-average return on investment.

ZAIBATSU The pre-WWII name for the Japanese system of domestic conglomerates. See also KIERETSU.

CHAPTER 14

Resources

Bloch, Marc *Feudal Society*
Univ. of Chicago Press, Chicago, IL USA 1961

Coopers & Lybrand *International Tax Summaries 1997*
John Wiley & Sons, New York, NY USA 1997

Diamond, Jared *Guns, Germs, and Steel*
W.W. Norton, New York, NY USA 1997

Hazlitt, Henry *Economics in One Lesson*
Three Rivers Press, New York, NY USA 1946

Henderson, David *The Fortune Encyclopedia of Economics*
Warner Books, New York, NY USA 1993

Hinkelman, Edward *Dictionary of International Trade, 3rd Edition*
World Trade Press, Novato, CA 1999

Hourani, Albert *A History of the Arab Peoples*
MJF Books, New York, NY USA 1991

Hutchison, T.W. *The Politics and Philosophy of Economics*
New York University Press, New York, NY USA 1981

Kindelberg, Charles & Lindert, Peter *International Economics*
Richard D. Irwin, Inc. Homewood, IL USA 1978

Landes, David *The Wealth and Poverty of Nations: Why Some Are Rich and Some Are Poor*
W.W. Norton, New York, NY USA 1998

James, Lawrence *The Rise and Fall of the British Empire*
Little, Brown & Company, London, UK 1994

Oser, Jacob *The Evolution of Economic Thought*
Harcourt, Brace & World, Inc. New York, NY USA 1970

Pindyck, Robert & Rubinfeld, Daniel *Microeconomics*
Macmillan Publishing, New York, NY USA 1989

Pribram, Karl *A History of Economic Reasoning*
Johns Hopkins University Press, Baltimore, MD USA 1983

Reischauer, Edwin & Fairbank, John *East Asia: The Great Tradition*
Houghton Mifflin Company, Boston, MA USA 1960

Rodinson, Maxime *Islam and Capitalism*
Pantheon Books, New York, NY USA 1973

Warsh, David *Economic Principals: Masters & Mavericks of Modern Economics*
The Free Press, New York, NY USA 1993

The Economist
The Economist Newspaper Limited, London, UK

BIOGRAPHY

Jeffrey Edmund Curry, MBA, Ph.D., is an international businessman and educator. He is a visiting professor at numerous universities in Europe and Asia as well as a member of the International Affiliate Faculty at the Audencia Ecole de Management in Nantes, France. He is the author of books about business practices in Vietnam and Taiwan (*Passport Vietnam* and *Passport Taiwan*) as well as books on marketing and economics (*A Short Course in International Marketing* and *A Short Course in International Negotiating*). He resides with his wife and son in San Francisco.